Deborah Snow is an award-winning senior reporter for Fairfax Media. A journalist of four decades' standing she has previously worked in the Canberra Press Gallery, been as a reporter on *Four Corners* and the ABC's London and Moscow correspondent. *Siege* is her first book.

INSIDE THE LINDT CAFÉ

SIEGE

The powerful and uncompromising story of what happened and why the police response went so tragically wrong

DEBORAH SNOW

ALLEN&UNWIN
SYDNEY • MELBOURNE • AUCKLAND • LONDON

First published in 2018
This edition published in 2019

Allen & Unwin
83 Alexander Street
Crows Nest NSW 2065
Australia
Phone: (61 2) 8425 0100
Email: info@allenandunwin.com
Web: www.allenandunwin.com

NATIONAL LIBRARY OF AUSTRALIA
A catalogue record for this book is available from the National Library of Australia

ISBN 978 1 76087 625 8

Set in Minion Pro by Midland Typesetters, Australia
Printed and bound in Australia by Pegasus Media & Logistics

10 9 8 7 6 5 4

FSC www.fsc.org MIX Paper from responsible sources FSC® C008194

The paper in this book is FSC® certified. FSC® promotes environmentally responsible, socially beneficial and economically viable management of the world's forests.

CONTENTS

AUTHOR'S NOTE

Writing a book about the Lindt Café siege was always going to present some unique challenges.

The first was the sheer scale of the event, which entangled hundreds of people over the seventeen hours of the siege itself and then hundreds more during the long tail of the aftermath. The saga swept up not just police officers, but paramedics, fire crews, defence personnel, intelligence agencies, politicians, their staffers, lawyers, the media, and of course the hostages themselves and their families and friends.

In piecing together a narrative from these multiple perspectives, I have relied extensively on evidence given to the inquest, police statements, exhibits and transcripts where these became part of the public record, the coroner's report itself, more than fifty interviews I conducted with key players (some on the record, some off) and media reports.

I could not have written this book without the extraordinary help given to me by two of the hostages, Louisa Hope and Jarrod Morton-Hoffman. Theirs are the main voices in the narrative sections set inside the café. Of the other surviving hostages, some gave me assistance of a background nature, others I was unable to reach in the time available, or else I received word they did not wish to re-visit the event. In those instances, I have relied on police statements, the extensive evidence they gave, and interviews they did in the months after the siege.

The experience of each of the sixteen survivors was traumatic for all of them. On some details, memories vary. I have done my best to reconcile any disparities by seeking out those descriptions and recollections where the weight of consensus among them is greatest.

A second challenge was the need to make extensive use of pseudonyms in order to comply with non-publication orders issued by the Coroner's Court during the inquest. Where a police officer has been given a particular pseudonym by the coroner, I have adopted the same name as the inquest. Where the coroner relied on a job description only to shield identity, I have coined pseudonyms of my own for ease of reading. Thus, to the two senior police officers who were in charge at different times at the Forward Command Post—perhaps the most critical roles on the night—I have given the code-names 'Lima' and 'Victor'. Some officers *are* able to be named because their identities were not shielded.

Monis' murdered former wife was given the pseudonym Helen Lee by the courts for the protection of her children, and I have adopted that as well. Again, in line with court requirements, some people are referred to by initials only.

PROLOGUE

15 December 2014, ten days out from Christmas

A tall, thick-set man with a light beard and baseball cap, wearing a large black backpack, walks steadily through Martin Place, a broad pedestrian plaza that slices through the heart of Sydney's business district. The plaza is thronged with people on this bright Monday morning. Shoppers mingle with office workers spilling out of the twin entrances to the nearby underground railway station. There is a crackle of anticipation and urgency in the air as the city bustles to get its business done before the long summer break.

The man betrays no sign of nervousness. Nothing about him signals malign intent. A large Christmas tree softens the civic space. Long, shimmering banners, designed to reflect light and to add to the festive air, are strung at intervals along the plaza. Nothing could appear less threatening. Yet they too will come to play a role in the drama that is to come.

It's not long after 8.15 a.m. now. The man maintains his unhurried pace. He crosses several intersecting streets following the slope of Martin Place up towards the colonial-era State Parliament building which sits near the top of the rise. But that is not his destination.

One block short of the end of the plaza he reaches the Lindt Chocolate Café, sited on the ground floor of a handsome thirteen-storey building clad in red granite and terracotta masonry. The distinctive crest of the famous Swiss chocolate-maker sits over the main entrance, its double doors set at a pleasing diagonal across the corner of Martin Place and Phillip Street. On the floors above, a warren of barristers' chambers hosts some of the biggest legal names in the city.

At 8.33 a.m. the man pushes through the doors into the café. No one gives him a second glance. Only the silent sentinel of the CCTV camera posted at the Reserve Bank across the road notes the precise moment of his entry.

He takes a seat near the front, among the early-bird lawyers and finance workers who frequent the café at this hour, and orders tea. Then he waits.

Eight floors above, thirty-three-year-old barrister Michael Klooster has been toiling away in his office since shortly after 5 a.m. and decides he needs a caffeine hit before his first court appearance of the day. He rides the lift down to the ground floor and enters the café via its rear entrance, a set of glass doors from the barristers' foyer accessed off Martin Place.

At 9.20 a.m. he is placing his order when a heavily accented voice calls his name. Turning around, Klooster sees a tall, thick-set figure who he can't momentarily place. Then the penny drops. It's a former client, Iranian-born Man Haron Monis, looking very different to the last time Klooster saw him, when Monis had been decked out in the flowing robes and cap of an Islamic cleric.

Now the man is sporting camouflage pants, a baseball cap and a long-sleeved shirt and his once-long beard has been trimmed much closer to his chin. The chance encounter catches both by surprise.

'Hi Michael, how are you going?' Monis asks. 'I didn't know you worked here.'

They discuss the family law matter Klooster handled for him some months previously, an application that Monis lost and is now appealing. It's a brief conversation. Monis invites the lawyer to join him for coffee, but Klooster begs off, saying he has to be in court in ten minutes.

The exchange is friendly enough. Nothing about his one-time

client's demeanour rings any alarm bells. Klooster bids him farewell and Monis returns to the table he is now occupying, close to the lobby doors.

The decision to leave the café and prepare for court may just have saved the barrister's life.

Shortly before 9.40 a.m. Monis pushes aside the tea and chocolate cheesecake he'd ordered and asks the young waitress to call over the manager.

They don't know it yet, but the eighteen staff and customers in the café with him are caught tight in his trap. The ordeal they are about to face will test them in ways very few of us will ever have to experience. Two of them will never walk out of the café alive.

CHAPTER 1

IN THE BEGINNING

Tori Johnson arrived early at work that day, as he did most weekday mornings, entering the café shortly after 6 a.m.

The fair-haired thirty-four-year-old had been in charge of the team at the café for just over two years and was preparing for his third Christmas at the Lindt Café. At this time of year it wasn't unusual for him to have up to a dozen staff under his charge.

At 6.30 a.m. he was joined by Harriette Denny, thirty, whose shift normally started at 7 a.m. but whose habit was to come in early and share a coffee with Tori. The petite, experienced Philippines-born barista and her boss swapped stories about their weekend—whom they had seen, and what they had cooked (Tori and his partner Thomas were keen foodies). Tori was particularly excited about the fact that he and Thomas would be hosting his family's Christmas for the first time at the couple's Surry Hills apartment.

Soon afterwards the third permanent staff member, food supervisor Paolo Vassallo, joined them briefly before disappearing into the kitchen to check over supplies and start preparing for the week ahead.

Paolo and Tori were the two longest-serving staff members at the café and had become good friends. But Paolo sometimes felt the strain of understaffing in the kitchen. He didn't blame Tori for this; he was sure the fault lay with someone higher up the chain. Grumbling inwardly, he resigned himself to the fact that today was going to be another one of those days where he would be run off his feet.

The Lindt Café was a well-known landmark in this prosperous part of town, tucked into the ground floor of a fine art deco edifice that dated back to 1936 and was widely known as the Overseas Union Bank Building, or sometimes the APA Building.

With its tall ceilings, generous interior, beautifully proportioned windows and marble columns, the Lindt Café had more in common with the grand old cafés of Paris or Vienna than with the stark minimalist vibe favoured by many of Sydney's newer establishments. It was a room to relax in, a room that whispered of a more leisurely past.

That European atmosphere had been deliberately fostered by the man who'd initiated the concept of the café a dozen years earlier, Michael Magnus, a wildly successful advertising guru who had gone on to become one of Sydney's leading patrons of the arts.

Magnus' father Walter had been a dentist, a refugee from Nazism who fled to Sydney to start a new life. Unable to practise here, Walter had successfully reinvented himself as a restaurateur and bon vivant who was determined to educate Australian palates about serious European food. Among his ventures was an elegant restaurant called Savarin, which he set up on George Street near the bottom end of Martin Place in the late 1940s.

Son Michael wanted to build on that legacy. By 2003 he'd retired from advertising and persuaded Lindt and Sprungli—a former client to whom he was by then consulting—that the city was ready for a chocolate retailer and café in the finest European tradition; he began working with Lindt's Swiss headquarters on a special range for the Australian market. When the ground floor premises of 53 Martin Place—a former restaurant—became free, Magnus persuaded the company that it would be the perfect place for the project. Sydney's Lindt Chocolate Café was born, launched with a glamorous party in late 2004 after a $1.1 million fitout. It was a pioneering move, among the first enterprises of this type that the Swiss company had opened anywhere the world. Michael Magnus died in 2007, but he lived long enough to see his pet project take root and flourish.

While the building itself carried echoes of a bygone Sydney, the café staff who trickled in for work that morning were the multicultural face of the city's future. They were of mixed ethnicity, and overwhelmingly young. Apart from the three full-timers, Tori, Paolo and Harriette, the other five who turned up for work that morning were part-time wait staff and university students, none of them over the age of twenty-three. Two of them, Communications student Jarrod Morton-Hoffman and Dentistry student Fiona Ma, were just nineteen years of age. Although barely embarked on adult life, the pair would play pivotal and remarkable roles in the dark hours that lay ahead.

Jarrod, tall and dark-haired with an unusual confidence for his years, had not originally been rostered to work that morning. But a fellow worker had taken a family reunion trip abroad at short notice, and Jarrod agreed to fill in.

As the clock ticked towards opening time at 7.30 a.m., he busied himself stocking up napkins, arranging cutlery and dishes and refilling the shelves.

The first customers arrived promptly when Jarrod opened the doors, and by around 8 a.m. the café was swinging into the busy rhythm of a Monday morning. Those who were not coming in for coffee or tea were browsing the chocolate displays, picking up small Christmas gifts for colleagues or friends leaving early for the holidays.

Jarrod paid only fleeting attention to the heavy-set bearded fellow with the baseball cap who'd come in just after 8.30 and was now occupying a table on his own, close to the front door.

Fiona Ma arrived on the shop floor at around 9 a.m. She was new to the café, and had been on staff for only a week. Based in Queensland, she'd got the job for the Christmas break through her sister, Helen, who also worked there.

Fiona was a calm, steady presence, already proving herself a valued member of the Lindt team.

The first customer she served was the man with a beard and a cap at Table 36. Approaching him, she saw he already had a menu in front of him and a cup of tea.

She asked him if she could get him anything else. He was scanning the cakes, so she took him through the different choices and noted his order, a velour chocolate cheesecake.

He asked if he could smoke. Only if you go outside, she told him, indicating the café tables and umbrellas set up on the concourse outside. He declined.

A short time later the man asked Harriette to watch his large backpack while he slipped off to the toilet at the back of the café. She agreed, although something about his smile made her feel oddly uneasy.

When he returned to the table he caught Fiona's eye again and asked if he could move. He wanted to sit at the back of the café, at the unoccupied L-shaped booth table tucked into an alcove near the art deco rear doors, which led out into the building lobby. The staff knew it as Table 40. Fiona told him that would be fine, and offered to help. He said he could manage on his own.

Twenty minutes later he summoned Fiona yet again, this time with an even more unusual request—he asked the manager's name and then said he wanted to speak with him. Fiona went to fetch Tori, but she was puzzled. If the man was gearing up to complain, why did he seem so calm?

When Jarrod emerged from the kitchen a few minutes later, he noticed Tori sitting at the back table locked in intense conversation with the customer. Tori beckoned the young waiter over. Like Fiona,

Jarrod wondered if the food or service was the problem (the man's cheesecake was almost untouched).

Then he caught sight of Tori's face. The manager was reddening, and blinking furiously. The longer-serving staff members knew Tori well enough to understand these were sure-fire signs he was under intense stress.

Whatever the issue, Jarrod reckoned it was clearly more than just the food.

A few tables away, Louisa Hope settled down to tea and toast with her elderly mother, seventy-three-year-old Robin. The pair lived a good distance from the CBD, in Sydney's outer western suburbs, and had stayed in town the previous night at a nearby hotel so as to be on time for an appointment at ten that morning in the legal chambers above the café.

An engaging woman with large, expressive eyes, fifty-two-year-old Louisa had been living with multiple sclerosis for the last twelve years. The disease caused her frequent discomfort, but you would be hard pressed to guess this from her customarily cheerful manner, which was underpinned by a strong Christian faith. She was the kind of person who naturally reached out to strangers, and she and her mother found it easy to strike up a conversation with the three young barristers—two women and a man—sitting at an adjoining table: Katrina Dawson, Julie Taylor and Stefan Balafoutis.

Louisa was struck by the elegance of the two women, particularly Katrina, who looked the height of professional chic in a black tailored pants suit combined with a designer zigzag-patterned blouse. She had teamed the outfit with silver gingham-patterned high heels that caught the eye of Louisa, who was a keen shoe fancier herself.

'Katrina gave the impression of being a happy, sophisticated, smart young woman,' Louisa recalls. 'As she was walking in, Katrina hit her foot on a chair leg or table leg, and my mum made a comment about her beautiful shoes. Katrina laughed and said, "Oh, I don't want to scuff them!" We had a little laugh and a quick conversation, as you would, just exchanging pleasantries. I remember, as the day went on and into the night, how she had to abandon those beautiful shoes and go barefoot.'

Soon the time was edging towards 9.40 a.m. and Louisa headed for the counter to pay the bill. The three barristers were wrapping up as well, ready to head back to the small mountain of clients' demands that undoubtedly awaited them before the Christmas break.

But the intense discussion taking place between Tori Johnson and Monis at Table 40 was about to blow all those plans to dust.

When Jarrod arrived at the table where his agitated manager sat with the bearded customer, Tori said to him in a low tone: 'I need you to go get my keys from the office and lock the doors. We're closed. Everything is okay. Tell all the staff to be calm.'

Struggling to make sense of this, Jarrod walked into the office, a small room situated next to the kitchen that was screened from the main café by a floor-to-ceiling partition.

After asking Paolo which was Tori's bag, he rummaged around, found the café keys and was on his way back into the kitchen corridor when he bumped into another young member of the wait staff, twenty-two-year-old Joel Herat.

'Something's wrong, Tori just told me to lock the doors. I think the Reserve Bank is being robbed across the road,' Jarrod told Joel, although more sinister possibilities were already preying on his mind.

Jarrod had a Stanley knife stashed in his apron pocket from cutting up boxes earlier that morning. He made a snap decision to hang on to it, and handed another blade to Joel along with a pair of scissors: 'Dude, have these just in case. Something doesn't feel right.'

The young men walked back into the main room of the café. Jarrod headed first for the automatically opening main doors on the Martin Place/Phillip Street corner, which he secured by turning a key in the control mechanism to disable the sensor. Then he walked to the art deco doors at the rear of the café, which opened onto the Martin Place lift lobby, and shot the bolts at the top.

Fiona, as yet unaware of what was happening, saw customers trying to enter. She walked towards the front entrance to let them in, but someone shouted at her to stop.

Regular customer Rosemary Birt had turned up outside the main doors and was pushing against them, wondering why they wouldn't open. After a few more shoves, she gave up and walked around to the building's foyer entrance off Martin Place. She went inside and tried the lobby doors into the café, only to find they wouldn't budge either. Peering into the café, Rosemary noticed the two men at the table just inside the double doors. One, she noted, was heavy-set and wearing a baseball cap. The other, younger and fair-haired, was in suit trousers and a dark shirt. She was struck by the serious looks on their faces.

Oddly, a young waitress suddenly approached the door where she was standing with a hand-written sign bearing the single word 'Closed'. Rosemary, frustrated and curious, kept peering in. Other customers were impatiently lining up behind her, including a man with two young children in tow.

Inside the café the man with the cap was reaching into a large bright blue shopping bag. Now Rosemary could see what he was pulling out of it: a long-barrelled firearm about a half metre in length. Frantically she backed away. She reached for her phone and dialled the emergency number, triple zero.

Louisa was still standing, facing the counter, when she began hearing muttered complaints about the doors being jammed or locked. No big deal, she thought. They'll get the building manager and it will be sorted pretty swiftly.

Then she caught the expression on the face of the young woman behind the counter, who was staring past Louisa with her mouth agape. Following the woman's gaze, Louisa swivelled and saw Monis brandishing a sawn-off shotgun. At first she thought this might be some kind of outlandish prank. Then the realisation hit her: 'My God! This is real!'

Monis had now significantly altered his appearance, having donned something like battledress. Over his shirt he'd pulled a black vest with ammunition pockets. The backpack was on his back. His baseball cap had been replaced by a black headband emblazoned with white Arabic script, and he'd put on a matching wrist-band. Much later they would learn what the letters read: 'We are your soldiers Muhammad . . . May Allah honour him and grant him peace.'

At first, there was stunned silence as Monis herded the terrified and confused customers and staff towards the northern wall of the café, where a long, lounge-like padded bench—a banquette—ran almost the entire length of the room under the windows that faced Martin Place.

Jarrod was heading towards the main doors on the Martin Place/ Phillip Street corner holding another hand-made 'Closed' sign to stop customers knocking on the glass. Monis pulled him up short.

'Where are you going?' Monis demanded.

'I am putting up the sign,' Jarrod replied.

'No, you're not,' Monis shouted. 'Sit the fuck down.'

Jarrod did what people always did in the movies—he raised his hands and sat down. It felt simultaneously shocking and unreal.

Now the gunman was speaking with deliberation, making sure they could all understand him despite his strong accent. Harriette sat shaking and crying, with Fiona holding her hand.

'He was saying that we would be safe if we listened to him and did what we were told,' Jarrod recalls. 'He was saying that this was an Islamic State attack on Australia, and that he had a bomb and that people he called his brothers had bombs as well, and it was because of our military involvement in Syria and Iraq against ISIS.'

The gunman's manner was harsh, but controlled. He did not speak his name or give them any other clue to his identity. Jarrod felt he was relishing the moment, playing God with their lives.

In a childlike hand, Monis had written his garbled demands on a sheet of paper, before entering the café. 'Australia is under attack by the Islamic State,' the note read. 'There are 3 bombs in three different locations. Martin Place, Circular Q [*sic*] and George Street. I want to contact other brothers and ask them NOT to explode the other two bombs but I cant contact because they don't carry phone with them. They have radio with them, I can say that throug [*sic*] ABC radio. The plan is to request Tony Abbott to call them or me, and to have a debate while it is broadcast live on ABC national radio. So that's why they have radio, and the best way to contact them is by my voice message to announce that they should not explode the bombs. They listen to me anything I tell them. The device placed inside the Radios is another way of exploding the bombs.'

Monis had already put this note in front of Tori and ordered him to begin relaying its contents to the triple zero emergency line as the pair were still seated at Table 40.

Tori did as he was told and at 9.41 a.m. was connected through to the emergency operator. The call seemed to progress at an agonisingly slow pace.

At one point Tori apologised: 'Sorry, I have a gun in front of me.'

The operator was unfamiliar with Martin Place, and struggled with the information Tori was giving her. Martin Place—was it actually a street, she asked?

'Yes,' he assured her, 'a pedestrian street.'

'But it's not actually a road? I need a road,' the operator said.

'We're above Martin Place train station,' Tori went on patiently.

Throughout the call, the manager remained almost preternaturally calm. Towards the end, he indicated that customers and staff were being ordered to raise their hands. He hung up at 9.53 a.m. A long time later, Tori's family would have to endure the almost unendurable agony of hearing that twelve-minute call played back in court.

Monis told his eighteen captives to put phones and ID cards on the table. He seemed especially keen to make sure that none of them was a police officer.

Jarrod's phone began ringing incessantly, putting the young waiter's nerves further on edge. He wished it would stop. No one, at that moment, wanted to draw attention to themselves.

Monis started interrogating Tori about the entrances to the café. Apart from the automatically opening doors set on the Martin Place/Phillip Street corner and the double swing doors that led to the barristers' lobby off Martin Place, there was a third exit—a fire door, the entrance to which was not visible from the main room. It was accessible off the kitchen and led out onto Phillip Street, facing the Reserve Bank. It couldn't be locked but could only be opened from inside, not from the street, Tori explained.

Monis was suspicious, and hostile. 'If you are lying to me I will shoot you,' he shouted. Some of the younger women had begun quietly sobbing.

The gunman started ordering the hostages where to stand, arranging them at intervals around the café. The room had eight tall, narrow windows: four along Martin Place and four along Phillip Street. Some hostages were to face out towards Martin Place; they were told to mount the banquette with their hands raised and splayed against the glass.

This would place them in full view of the Channel 7 TV newsroom directly across from the café, as Monis well knew.

A final prop remained to be added to his macabre tableau. From his bag Monis drew a banner, a *shahada* flag bearing the words in Arabic of the universal Muslim declaration of faith: 'There is no God but Allah; Muhammad is his messenger.'

For a brief moment it seemed as though the female barristers, Katrina Dawson and Julie Taylor, might get a reprieve. Monis had motioned the pair towards the entrance. Stefan, standing near the two women, would later insist he heard the gunman saying they could go. Julie would also remember Monis saying, 'You two, go to the door . . . Yes, these two are nice, they can go.'

Katrina hesitated. Could Stefan come as well, she asked?

'Are you all together?' Monis asked.

'Yes, he's our friend,' she replied.

Katrina picked up her bag and the trio had only just reached the door when Monis abruptly ordered them to stop. He told them to stand with their hands up in the windows, like the others. Katrina's bag would remain by the door for the duration of the siege.

Had Monis genuinely flirted with the idea of letting them go? Many were later unsure. But Louisa is convinced he had a snap change of heart: 'He definitely said they could go, they could leave,' she says. 'They were standing up and Katrina said, "What about him [Stefan]?" I don't know what happened then, but suddenly it was no longer happening. If she had only turned and walked out that door, then she would have been free, she and Julie.'

The chance—if it had ever been a chance—was snatched away as quickly as it had suddenly appeared.

Holding up the banner was hard work. The hostages' muscles ached, and it was difficult remembering to keep their eyes closed. Every so often Monis would order a change of shifts, but time dragged by relentlessly for those on window duty.

Each was locked in his or her own thoughts, ordered to remain mute by the gunman. The anguish on their faces was all too plain as Channel 7's news cameras homed in on them from the other side of Martin Place. From where he stood, Jarrod could see reporters holding up smart phones to take pictures. He was conscious that he and the other hostages were being made to look like hunting trophies, strung up for display. It struck him that these images were now speeding around the globe, a thought that was both surreal and appalling.

The distance from the Channel 7 cameras to where they were standing would have been no more than forty-five paces. But it felt more like half a universe away.

Monis ordered Louisa to join the others standing on the banquette with her hands in the air. He is relishing this, she thought. He wants the world to watch.

Louisa told Monis she would not be able to climb onto the banquette because she had difficulty balancing. 'I might fall,' she said, indicating her walking stick. He ordered her to drop it to the ground, and then kicked it away. 'Sorry,' he told her. 'You understand?'

The idea that someone might try to use the stick as a weapon against him was preposterous, Louisa thought. Monis was heavy-set, six feet or more in height and, although veering towards pudginess, more powerfully built than any of the hostages.

Without her stick, Louisa soon faced a dilemma. She needed to use the bathroom. The female toilets were located up a set of very steep narrow stairs at the rear of the café and thus impossible for her without support. Even the male toilets, which were down a smaller set of stairs, would be a challenge without assistance.

She signalled she needed help and Monis suddenly called out to Fiona: 'You, the Chinese girl standing with the two men.' He instructed the nineteen-year-old to help Louisa to the bathroom, giving the pair a few precious minutes out of the gunman's earshot.

'Fiona, do you pray?' Louisa gently inquired.

'Not really', Fiona said.

'Don't worry,' Louisa replied. 'I'll pray enough for both of us. We will get out of this.'

Word was now spreading throughout neighbouring office blocks that something distinctly odd was going on at the Lindt Café. People gathered in the windows of nearby buildings, staring down at the concourse as the first police arrived to clear pedestrians away.

At Channel 7, an announcement came booming through the internal speakers: 'Emergency—evacuate now, this building is going into lockdown.' While others headed for the exits, veteran Channel 7 cameraman Greg Parker was heading determinedly in the other direction, towards where he could set up his cameras.

Parker had picked up word of the siege while on the Eastern Distributor, driving back to the office from another assignment. He'd pulled up on Macquarie Street, one block above the station, and sprinted in through the Channel 7 building's rear garage door. 'As I arrived the building was under police protection,' he recalls. 'I argued with our security and head of operations that I wanted to stay, and was going to do so.'

He set up one camera in the very exposed newsroom on level 3 with direct line of sight into the Lindt Café, and then started a second production camera rolling as well. He went to retrieve the big powerful zoom lenses from a storage facility to use with yet another camera that he set up on the level above. 'I was alone in the building for some time, rolling on what I knew was incredible footage. I was shocked at what I was filming.'

Thinking he'd successfully evaded the evacuation order, Parker settled in next to the level 4 camera, but a general duties police officer came through and ordered him outside. After a few minutes on the street, he and the station's head of security, a former Special Forces officer, managed to get themselves back into the building.

Parker was busy changing camera batteries when specialist police from the elite Tactical Operations Unit (TOU) suddenly appeared. The black-clad and helmeted figures were police snipers, searching for vantage points. They asked him where the best positions were. 'Come with me,' Parker told them. 'I'm just checking on my cameras now.'

The spots he'd chosen gave a clear view in through the café's Martin Place windows. Monis was plainly visible, gesticulating and barking orders at his captives. Parker's powerful zoom lens was picking up incredible images of the hostages, with Monis intermittently darting into shot as he passed the windows. 'We really need the surveillance this camera is providing. Are you prepared to stay?' the TOU officers asked him.

'Of course,' he replied, thinking what a bizarre twist the day had taken. He'd gone to work expecting a day like any other. Instead he was now pulling on a bullet-proof vest and bearing witness to a terrorist attack in full view of his own newsroom. Remembering that bullet-resistant glass had recently been installed on the TV station's street-facing windows, he placed an urgent call to help locate its specifications.

Parker's powerful lens brought the hostages disconcertingly close. Their faces were masks of distress. Long years of training had taught him to keep his nerves steady and his emotions at a distance when he was filming, but this was getting to him. Through his viewfinder, he could see the grim expression on Katrina Dawson's face, a shocked-looking Julie Taylor, a desperately worried Jarrod, and Fiona Ma, a study in stoicism. This is a form of torture, he thought, as he watched Monis bullying the captives, ordering them around with his gun at their backs. He desperately wanted to see those trapped men and women receive some reassurance. He hoped they could glimpse the police presence inside Channel 7 and hold on to that for some slight comfort.

Outside, police radios were pumping out the first emergency calls, summoning all available vehicles in the city to the café at 53 Martin Place.

Elsewhere, senior officers began scrambling. Down at the police station in Sydney's historic Rocks district, Inspector Tony Bell rang the café several times to see if anyone would pick up the phone. No one did.

At Walsh Bay, on the edge of the CBD, motorcycle cop Senior Constable Paul Withers heard the call-out on police radio, activated his siren and sped towards Martin Place. He arrived within minutes, parked his bike near the concourse just below the café and approached the building warily, endeavouring to stay out of sight. A visibly upset Rosemary Birt greeted him and told him what she had seen through the glass doors of the internal lobby—the bearded man pulling a firearm from a bag.

Courageously, Withers mounted the outer steps, which led up from Martin Place to the lobby entrance, and then up five more into the lobby itself. From there he edged over to the café's glass doors, each guarded by a tall green marble pillar. Peering cautiously around the column, he was confronted with the sight of senior Westpac IT manager Marcia Mikhael weeping, her hands high in the air on the other side of the doors.

'How many?' he mouthed silently.

She lowered all her fingers except the index finger on one hand.

'Where?' Withers mouthed again.

Marcia almost imperceptibly inclined her head in Monis' direction.

Suddenly the lift doors in the foyer whooshed open, disgorging unsuspecting tenants from the floors above. Withers turned and frantically waved them out.

He craned further around the pillar. Monis loomed into view, issuing orders and brandishing the shotgun.

Withers activated his radio: 'The shooter is male Caucasian with a beard, early fifties. He's wearing a black backpack, a black vest, a white T-shirt underneath. He has a sawn-off shotgun. He also has what appears to be wire running from his backpack out to his person.' The observation about the wire would prove to be mistaken. It amplified police fears about the bomb threat from the earliest stages of the siege.

Other officers were now starting to arrive in Martin Place, among them Detective Senior Constable Brendan Rawling, who pulled up in his police vehicle on Elizabeth Street, a block below the café. Grabbing a ballistic vest from the car boot, he ran up Martin Place towards the café, along with Detective Senior Constable Jeroen Huisman.

Crossing cautiously to the Lindt side of Martin Place, they could just make out the figure of Withers still exchanging signals with Marcia. The two armed cops drew their weapons and mounted the steps to the foyer.

'Male with a shotgun,' Withers told them. Rawling motioned the other two back, as he was the only one wearing body armour. Edging forward, he too could see Marcia framed by the art deco double doors, visibly shaking.

Now these three officers were ordered to withdraw as senior commanders took control. Withers signalled to Marcia that she should try to remain calm; he mimed how to take deep breaths. Then he vanished from her sight.

Marcia, forlorn, could see no one else there to replace him.

Sergeant James Asimacopoulos was dressed in grey shorts, sunglasses and a black polo shirt, working undercover along the seedy Kings Cross nightclub strip two and a half kilometres away, when he heard the police radio call-out at 9.45 a.m. For his undercover role he had also shaven his head, making him look every inch the street tough.

Now he and three other officers leapt into a police car and sped towards Martin Place. They reached the top of the plaza, drew their weapons and sprinted down towards the corner where the café was situated.

They stopped outside the Reserve Bank across the road. Here Asimacopoulos sought cover behind a large metal sculpture while he assessed the safest way to try to see inside.

Along the café's eastern (Phillip Street) side, Christmas advertising decals were plastered across most of the windows. The least obscured was the window closest to the fire exit, adjacent to a large and empty vehicle loading bay. Asimacopoulos crossed the street, took cover inside the loading bay and then inched along the wall towards the window. Peering in, he could see the hostages lined up and looking terrified.

Then the gunman loomed into view. Middle Eastern looking, the officer noted: thinning hair, fleshy face, close-cropped beard, black vest and bandana, and armed with a pump-action shotgun held at chest height, right hand on the trigger and left on the barrel. He appeared to be yelling and pacing agitatedly. It was almost impossible to carry out an accurate head count, because of the limited view through the window and the display cases.

The officer glanced up towards the Westpac Bank building on the diagonally opposite corner to the café. The façade was almost entirely of glass. He could see people gathering at the windows peering down below. Asimacopoulos had been to the scene of a bombing before and knew the extraordinarily destructive effects of a shockwave, with the potential for multiple casualties from flying glass. He'd heard a broadcast repeating the gunman's claims of several bombs having been planted around the city. He radioed in, suggesting that the Westpac office workers should be moved away from the windows as soon as possible.

Thousands more workers occupied offices around the café, within a potential blast zone. Some buildings were already going into lockdown. Others were being ordered to evacuate. It was not always clear why some were being told to stay, and others to leave.

At 170 Phillip Street the sole exit was dangerously exposed to the café; police formed a human shield as they shepherded the workers out of the building ten at a time.

Above the café, in the barristers' chambers, many of the lawyers remained unaware of the drama unfolding on the ground floor until texts and emails started arriving from friends and family.

The building manager came through and told them they were in lockdown, that there were hostages and quite possibly a bomb. The only way out of the building was via the fire stairs, which passed close to the lobby at ground level—too close for comfort if a bomb went off, the police judged.

Initially some of the more nervous staff members took shelter under tables. Others began speculating about how strong the floors were, given the collective belief that the building had once been a bank. Most tried to make the best of it and kept on working.

The first hour ticked by, and then a second. But on a floor high above the café, one executive was growing increasingly concerned. He'd already asked the building manager to find plans and give them to police. Why the hell were they being told to stay put, he and the scores of others still in the building? There was a duty of care issue here. He'd had friends who'd been in the New York Twin Towers attack of 9/11 and he knew what fate had befallen those who obeyed orders to stay. He told his secretary to get on to the police and urge them to evacuate the building.

Things started to move. Black-clad tactical operations police came through floor by floor to escort the lawyers and their staff down the fire stairs, one small group at a time. 'Take your high heels off,' the women were told. 'You need to exit in total silence.' The fire stairs led to a basement and a warren of below-ground corridors from where they would be able to exit onto the city block below the café.

There were lighter moments, despite the tension. One formidable-looking officer lined up his evacuees ready to tackle the stairs, but promptly took a wrong turn into the men's toilets.

Eventually the upper floors were emptied—progress not helped by the fact that police were having difficulty with the keys to the fire doors on upper levels. The building had mostly been cleared by the early afternoon. But one group, caught inside the ground floor library of Frederick Jordan Chambers directly across the lobby from the café, were about to undergo an ordeal of their own. With them was a ten-week-old baby.

Frederick Jordan Chambers occupied the first six floors of the Lindt building. At ground level, its glass entrance doors allowed a partial view through to the café. Behind the chamber's airy reception desk was a well-stocked legal library, partitioned off from the main room by wooden panelling, with tall windows looking out over Elizabeth Street. The windows were well above street level because of the downward slope of Martin Place.

As the siege began, thirteen people found themselves thrown together here: four lawyers, five legal staff, and four members of the public, including the baby boy who had been left in the care of his grandmother. The group included barrister Paresh Khandhar, and barristers' clerk, Elleanor Gillard.

Paresh had come down in the lift and seen two women at the café's lobby doors with their hands up, but at first he thought they were putting up Christmas decorations. His first inkling that this was a crisis was when a policeman ordered him into the chambers' office opposite, and told everyone inside to stay there. They had no access to the fire stairs unless they came back out into the lobby, which would expose them to possible attack.

The group thought they were in for a short wait, but an hour passed with no word from police. From friends outside, they were hearing of possible multiple attackers inside the café. Paresh called his family: 'I tried to keep it calm but I was worried this might be it—that was horrible.' Elleanor rang The Rocks Police Station asking for help. You're okay, she was told; officers already on site would take care of the situation. Yet those gathered outside seemed to be doing nothing more than waiting. In desperation, the group scrawled their mobile numbers on A4 paper and held them up to the windows. When that drew no response, they put up another sign: 'CAN WE BREAK OUT WINDOW?'

Police shook their heads in reply. Incredulous, Paresh and another lawyer climbed up to a suspended interior walkway—built to give access to the higher bookshelves—to prise open a hinged panel near the top of one of the windows. He'd managed to get halfway out the window when police began telling him to go back inside. 'They told me we were safer inside the building,' he recalls indignantly. 'I said, "No way, there are only two glass doors between us and what is going on at Lindt."' He continued climbing out onto a metal awning.

For the next twenty minutes, he was left squatting there. 'It was bizarre,' he says. 'No one [from the police] would communicate with me.' It was only when those left inside hauled a table to the window and held up the baby that the Fire and Rescue Squad turned up with ladders and released the entire group. By that stage nearly two hours had elapsed.

'It should have happened hours before,' Elleanor told me. 'They had every opportunity; there was no reason, as far as I could see then, or now, why they didn't.'

Inside the café, Marcia was still stuck at the lobby doors, thinking despairingly of her three children and how much she wanted to get home to them. Should she try to run? All she had to do was see if she could slide down the lock at the top of the doors and she might be able to escape. But fear kept her frozen.

Stefan, one of the three barristers, was having similar thoughts. He was sneaking glances towards a green button set low in the wall beside the entrance. It was only a metre and a half away. Was it worth a try? 'I think we should run,' he whispered to Julie. This might be their only chance.

Julie worried about what might happen. What if the door didn't open? Or worse, what if they got out and then the others got hurt. 'No,' she said softly. 'I don't think we should go.'

They looked down the street. It seemed utterly deserted, and eerily quiet.

CHAPTER 2

THE FIRST HOURS

Monis' choice of the Lindt Café as a terrorist target was a twisted stroke of evil genius. The café lay at the very heart of the city's intersecting political, legal, financial and media worlds.

The New South Wales Parliament was a stroll away, near the top of Martin Place. The old Supreme Court building lay at the end of Phillip Street, a two-minute walk from the café, while closer still was the Law Courts Building that housed the Federal Court and the modern Supreme Court complex.

In the tower above Channel 7 at 52 Martin Place, a stone's throw from the café, were the offices of the New South Wales government's key ministers and their staffers. The Department of Premier and Cabinet and the Treasury had recently taken up office space there as well, with the last of the premier's departmental staff only moving in that morning. As Monis launched his attack eight ministers were working inside the tower, including Deputy Premier Troy Grant.

The state's leading financial institutions all had flagship buildings in the immediate vicinity. These included a multi-storey Westpac building on the corner diagonally opposite the café (since redeveloped), the Reserve Bank directly opposite, and other national and international banks and insurance companies planted around the prime real estate in surrounding blocks.

Nearly all the floors above the café were taken up by legal chambers, including two of the most distinguished in Sydney: Frederick Jordan

Chambers and Sir Garfield Barwick Chambers. Between them, they accommodated dozens of Sydney's most sought-after and highly paid legal minds.

But the primary drawcard for Monis was almost certainly the proximity of Channel 7, home to many top-rating TV programs.

Channel 7's city premises dominated the block that faced the café across the pedestrian precinct of Martin Place. Prominent LED news ticker displays sent headlines chasing around the façade of the building in brightly lit red and white. The ground level newsroom at the higher end of the slope was encased in floor-to-ceiling glass, a sort of giant human fishbowl for the amusement of the passing public. The view from those windows into the café, Monis knew, would guarantee his attack a prime-time audience on national television.

Monis had history with the station, and a particular fixation with its top-rating breakfast program *Sunrise.* He'd taken umbrage with its coverage of terrorism in the past, lodging a series of complaints with the media regulator ACMA. In June 2008 Monis and his girlfriend, Amirah Droudis, clad in a black burqa, had travelled to Martin Place to mount a protest against the station, and had been observed there by federal agents handing out pamphlets to passers-by.

Later that month, Monis again turned up at the station. He waited until *Sunrise*'s stars came out onto the Martin Place concourse to sign autographs and then rushed at them shouting, bizarrely, 'You are killers and terrorists.' Channel 7's security chief swiftly intervened and called the police.

In 2012 Monis had portentously declared on his website that *Sunrise* had woken him from a 'deep sleep', further proclaiming: 'God can awaken a person by many different means, even by a terrorist broadcast from the program *Sunrise* on Channel Seven from the Australian TV.'

Following the siege, there was speculation as to whether Monis' original plan had been to seize hostages live on the Channel 7 breakfast show. Several months before the siege, the station had increased its security measures. And authorities had raised the general terrorism threat level in Australia to 'high' following a call in September 2014 from Islamic State leaders to their supporters to randomly target western civilians. On 18 September 2014, Prime Minister Tony Abbott publicly referred to 'intelligence' that IS sympathisers in Australia were being exhorted to 'conduct demonstration killings here in this country', and some media reporting had pointed to Martin Place as the setting for just such an attack. But no evidence ever emerged to support a theory that the station itself was Monis' original target.

What is clear is that the café's prime position opposite a major TV network presented Monis with the near-perfect means of holding national and global attention for as long as he could maintain the siege. Several Lindt staff would later tell police they recollected someone very like Monis visiting the café in the two weeks leading up to the attack.

From their offices on the twentieth floor of 52 Martin Place, high above the Channel 7 newsroom, Premier Mike Baird's personal staff commanded a bird's eye view of the Lindt Café. They crowded to the windows trying to make sense of what was happening below. At first someone suggested it looked like an attempt to rob the small armoured van parked near the Westpac building on the opposite corner. Someone else thought the café was the target. But why would anyone hold it up on a Monday morning, rather than on a Friday afternoon when it would have been flush with cash?

Then Monis' *shahada* flag appeared in the café's windows and the hard-heads could see this was something different—and potentially a lot more serious than a holdup. Down below, police were closing off the surrounding streets as well as Martin Place Station, with its entrances near the café.

At around 10 a.m. an emergency siren woop-wooped through the government offices, accompanied by a nervous-sounding announcement from building security to stay calm while the building went into lockdown. The effect of the announcement was precisely opposite to the one intended, recalls John Redman, then a staffer to Police Minister Stuart Ayres. 'The voice on the intercom had so much tension in it, everyone was looking around panicked,' he told me.

Redman and a small handful of Ayres' trusted staff had more reason than most to feel jumpy. They had been quietly informed that there was possibly an explosive device in their building as well. 'So, we were sitting there thinking, "Holy shit, we've just been told there is a bomb in the building, but we can't leave because of the lockdown". We're wondering if we were about to explode at any minute; no one knew what was about to go down.'

In the opening minutes of the siege, Premier Mike Baird remained blissfully unaware of what was unfolding back at Martin Place. Accompanied by a junior press aide, he was about to hold a press conference on mental health at Kings Cross. Abruptly, he was pulled aside by a member of his security detail, who briefed him on the first reports coming out of the café.

It was agreed the premier would have time to quickly sweep by Parliament House before meeting his director of strategy Nigel Blunden and senior officers at the Sydney Police Centre, located less than two kilometres away. From there they would rendezvous with Baird's chief of staff Bay Warburton, press secretary Imre Salusinszky, and key ministers and bureaucrats at the State Crisis Centre, a purpose-built facility that was then located just outside the CBD in Redfern. Designed as a safe retreat for the nerve centre of government in times of crisis, this was the first time it had ever been activated. It was rapidly becoming clear that what was unfolding inside the Lindt Café was the first full-blown terrorist attack on Australian soil.

There had been a harbinger of trouble three months earlier when Ahmad Numan Haider, a self-radicalised eighteen-year-old, attacked two officers with a knife outside a suburban police station in Melbourne and was instantly shot dead. Lindt, however, was on a vastly more threatening scale.

As arrangements were being made for Mike Baird to get to the Sydney Police Centre, Police Minister Stuart Ayres was proving harder to reach. At 9.45 that morning, he had been sitting in the front row of the hall at Kingswood High in the outer western Sydney suburb of Penrith as guest of honour at the school's annual presentation day. He had his phone switched to silent, but was conscious of it vibrating persistently in his pocket.

As the event wound up, Ayres left the hall with the school's headmaster and rang his office to find out what was so urgent. In the same instant he was met with the unlikely sight of his driver, not the most athletic of men, sprinting towards him across the playground. A member of Ayres' staff had phoned the driver and told him to get the minister into town—now. Ayres piled into his official car and sped to the city fifty-five minutes away, conferring en route with Mike Baird and Police Commissioner Andrew Scipione.

Inside the government offices above Channel 7, officials and advisers were still pinned down in the complex waiting for clearance to leave. They were told to gather in the ministerial boardrooms, away from the windows. TVs were being switched on and now they could see the first news images of stricken hostages in the café.

A palpable sense of shock took hold. It was beginning to sink in that any one of them could have been in there, even the premier. Baird was a regular customer, and his two-man security detail often spent time in the café if the boss was held up in the office. 'The gravity was pretty immense straight up, because Lindt was less than one hundred metres from the government offices, and plenty of our people went there,' a senior staffer said later. 'There was every chance someone we knew could be in there. Despite everything you see globally, no one expected that to happen in our backyard.'

Redman messaged one of his mates, a producer at Channel 7 'You guys might want to go on some sort of delay.' 'With all this live footage of people with their hands up, we had a real concern that someone was about to be executed. Live. And on TV,' Redman recalls.

Soon after 11 a.m. the all-clear was given to evacuate the government offices and there was a minor stampede towards the lifts. Even some ministers, confronted with the crush, were forced to wait their turn.

On the ground floor, the masked officers of the Tactical Operations Unit (TOU) stood on guard with high-powered weapons at the ready. The flood of government workers was herded out through the rear exit, onto Elizabeth Street, a block below the café.

Chris Hall, the police minister's chief of staff, had been on the phone almost constantly with Adam White, key aide to Andrew Scipione. Now Hall raced up to Parliament House to collect his car for the drive to Redfern. Accompanying him were the minister's two press secretaries and a senior counter–terrorism official, Feargus O'Connor. Senior ministers and their aides were now converging on the crisis committee headquarters from all directions.

On paper at least, New South Wales Police were well prepared for the siege. Fourteen years earlier Sydney had proudly hosted the 2000 Olympic Games, and the federal government had poured money into the states to boost their defences against terrorism. Politicians spruiked the message that the country was fully prepared. New equipment had been bought, training had been stepped up. Elaborate manuals existed dictating the command structures that would be set up in the event of a terror attack. There was a National Counter-Terrorism Plan, a New South Wales Counter Terrorism Plan and any number of standing committees and protocols locking all the administrative machinery into place.

In theory, it looked impressive. But the system had never been tested in a real-life scenario—the kind of scenario that was now unfolding at speed.

———

The first senior officer to hear breaking news about the café was Superintendent Allan Sicard, then the relieving commander for the Sydney city area.

At 9.45 a.m. Sicard was on his way to a meeting in the city's north when the first police radio alerts came through. He immediately made a U-turn and headed for Martin Place, phoning in along the way to his immediate superior, Assistant Commissioner Mick Fuller, who had overarching responsibility for the Sydney metropolitan region.

Fuller told Sicard to mobilise the elite and heavily armed TOU immediately. Fuller's next step was to activate the special command facility known as the Police Operations Centre (POC), located at a metropolitan police centre several kilometres from the café. (Police insisted on keeping its exact location secret at the inquest.)

The POC had been purpose-built by the New South Wales Police for managing what they termed 'state significant events'. It was activated up to fifty or sixty times a year for fixtures such as New Year's Eve, the city's famous annual gay pride Mardi Gras, the mid-winter Vivid Sydney and Australia Day. The POC was also 'stood up' for events like World Youth Day, or the visits of international leaders. It was designed as a unified command post, allowing other key agencies to come and sit alongside senior police throughout a major event. Rarely, however, had it been utilised for a crisis such as this. Equivalent to a battle commander's headquarters, it would be where all the strategic decisions governing the police response to the siege would be made.

The POC, a self-contained command unit set apart from the rest of the complex where it was situated, had been state of the art when first set up at the time of the Sydney Olympic Games, but by the time of the siege it was showing its age. Its communications systems had been outstripped by the rapid advances of recent years, its analogue platforms were incompatible with digital CCTV video feeds and it was no longer large enough to accommodate all the specialist teams that a critical incident brought together. Its deficiencies would become more exposed as the day wore on.

Fuller now stepped into the first command shift at the POC, tasking Sicard with finding somewhere to set up a field operations post close to the café from where a possible rescue attempt could be launched. In the meantime, Sicard deployed the force's special mobile command bus, which was driven to Elizabeth Street a block below the café to serve as the temporary field headquarters.

Sicard got to Martin Place shortly after 10 a.m. and was briefed on what the first officers at the scene had managed to learn from their glimpses inside the café. The TOU officers began taking up positions nearby, but out of sight of the windows.

No one knew how many hostages were inside. At this stage, Sicard had an unknown number of lives hanging in the balance.

The highest-ranking police officer in New South Wales, Police Commissioner Andrew Scipione, had started work early that morning, arriving at the police executive offices opposite Hyde Park on Elizabeth Street at 7 a.m. Three hours into his working day, at around 10.30, his second in command, Deputy Police Commissioner Catherine Burn, formally notified him of the Martin Place crisis.

Scipione was to discover his own family had escaped the siege by a whisker. His wife Joy and their daughter had gone into town that morning as part of their annual pre-Christmas visit to the big stores, and had called into the café less than an hour before Monis launched his attack. Tori Johnson had given the two women a personal tour.

As the crisis unfolded on live television, Scipione's wife and daughter followed the saga with horror, knowing they could have been standing in the hostages' shoes.

The craggy-faced Scipione inhabited the police chief's role as if he'd been born for the part—the top cop from central casting. His British migrant parents had brought him to Australia as an infant on an assisted passage to Sydney. His father's early death, when Scipione was in his mid-teens, had propelled him into the workforce early. He'd been an electrical apprentice before joining Customs, and then moving on to join the police in 1980. By his mid-teens Scipione had become a devout Christian, drawn to the teachings of the church through neighbours who had invited him along to the local church-run youth group. It was here that he met Joy, whom he married aged twenty.

Faith became a driving force in his life, something he and Premier Mike Baird deeply held in common. Scipione had a 'million' leadership books at home, he told a Christian magazine in a rare interview in 2017. But the one that had been most important to him as police commissioner, he revealed, was 'the one that sits next to my bed every day and it's my Bible'.

Over the years the commissioner had evolved into a polished public performer and canny master of backroom politics. He was acutely conscious—to a fault, some said—of the force's image and reputation, and would sometimes commission focus groups to find out what the community wanted from its police. In an interview he gave just before stepping down as police commissioner in April 2017, he told crime writer Dan Box he would sometimes observe these groups' deliberations himself from behind the opaque glass.

By the time of the siege, he had been in the commissioner's job for eight years. This was far longer than any of the ministers gathered with him in the State Crisis Centre that day had occupied their jobs. It would be the police chief's judgment and advice that would largely drive the state government's overarching response to the crisis.

Of Scipione's three deputies, the one who had the highest profile during the siege was Catherine (Cath) Burn, who held responsibility for police specialist operations, including counter terrorism. She was seen as his strong ally and it was an open secret that she hoped to succeed him when he retired, thereby becoming the first female police commissioner in New South Wales history.

As the siege unfolded, Scipione largely confined himself to the State Crisis Centre while Burn spent much of her time at the POC. The pair provided regular updates to ministers while liaising with other agencies, checking in with the senior police commanders and giving media briefings.

At 10.30 that morning the most urgent decision Scipione faced was whether to officially declare the siege a terrorist incident. Doing so would profoundly influence how it was managed. Should it be formally designated a terror attack, this would trigger the 'Task Force Pioneer' protocols that mandated only senior officers who'd undergone counter-terrorism training could take direct command roles during the siege.

By 11 a.m. Scipione had conferred with advisers and made the call: the Lindt siege would be designated a terror attack. Pioneer-trained commanders would thus take charge of the response. This would also trigger a special investigative response, dubbed Strike Force Eagle, that would bring in Commonwealth agencies such as the Australian Federal Police and the country's top spy agency, ASIO.

In the inquest that came after the siege, Scipione and Burn would repeatedly point out that the Pioneer protocols constrained them from providing any advice, orders or guidance to their subordinates throughout the attack. Thus, in the midst of one of the greatest challenges New South Wales Police had ever encountered, the two would largely hold themselves aloof from the operational response.

By late morning the State Crisis Centre was swinging into action in earnest. At the time of the siege, its location in Redfern was a closely held secret (it has since moved). Dozens of people had crammed into a space where a conference room ran down one side, separated from the rest of the area by a soundproof glass partition. Banks of TV monitors crowded the walls and the floor space was eaten up by rows of desks and computers set up for officials and advisers.

At the centre of all this activity was the state's Crisis Policy Committee, comprising Premier Mike Baird, Deputy Premier Troy Grant (himself a former police officer), Police Minister Stuart Ayres and the state's attorney-general, Brad Hazzard. Other ministers would be pulled in throughout the day, in particular the Health and Transport ministers, the latter tasked with handling the bomb threats to transport hubs around the city.

The shockwaves from the siege had already reached Canberra, 300 kilometres away, where Prime Minister Tony Abbott had been on the point of winding up a meeting of federal cabinet's National Security Committee. Not long before midday, he received a snap personal briefing from Scipione and Baird.

At 12.15 p.m., a secure video link was organised between the New South Wales Crisis Policy Committee and Canberra. Abbott offered to mobilise any federal resources, including military assistance, that the New South Wales Police might need. But, given the assurances he received from the police leadership, Baird thanked the prime minister and told him that the state police had the situation well in hand.

Soon afterwards Abbott's office released a statement confirming he had spoken to Baird and 'offered him all possible Commonwealth support and assistance'. 'This is obviously a deeply concerning incident but all Australians should be reassured that our law enforcement and security agencies are well trained and equipped and are responding in a thorough and professional manner,' the prime minister added.

In fact, every element of the police response—training, equipment and professionalism—would come under the heaviest scrutiny after the siege, and much would be found wanting.

The city was now in a state of shock. 'DEATH CULT CBD ATTACK' shrieked a special afternoon edition of the *Daily Telegraph*. 'TERROR HITS HOME' warned Fairfax websites.

Many people were flooding out of the central parts of the city by whatever means they could. One government staffer who'd been in Washington when the 9/11 attacks happened recalled that the mood felt eerily similar. 'People were just trying to get out because no one knew how severe this was going to be. The word had got out that there was a bomb at Wynyard and possibly down at the Opera House. The general feeling was "Let's just get out of here".'

Police set up an exclusion zone bounded by Elizabeth Street, Hunter Street, Macquarie Street and St James Road, an area normally populated during business hours by nearly 15,000 workers. Many remained locked down in nearby office blocks, some for several hours.

From his vantage point at the law firm Allens, which took up six floors of the Deutsche Bank building at 126 Phillip Street, senior managing partner Michael Rose could look down the street towards the Lindt Café where all was deserted. In the other direction, across the top of the New South Wales Parliament towards the Domain parklands, life seemed undisturbed. It was as if Sydney was two different cities, Rose recalls. 'Over in the Domain people were still playing soccer like they do every day at lunchtime, people were having picnics in the gardens, people were taking photos outside the State Library—it was kind of weird. We were in lockdown, but over there it was like an ordinary sunny Sydney day.'

Rose's firm was meant to be hosting important clients for lunch and top-notch catering had been delivered to the boardroom. However, given the lockdown, none of its several hundred workers had been able to leave. The boardroom feast became lunch for all, a modern day 'loaves and fishes'.

Meanwhile police teams and sniffer dogs were combing the city's main transport hubs for the bombs Monis claimed his 'brothers' had planted. Police focused their search on railway stations at Wynyard, Town Hall and Circular Quay, where the city's ferry network hooked up with key bus and train interchanges.

Nearby at the city's famous Opera House school groups were having a day out with teachers. It too was evacuated and Education Minister Adrian Piccoli was urgently summoned to help coordinate communication with the schools and parents whose children had inadvertently been swept up at the fringes of the crisis.

At shortly after 6 p.m., police were surprised to get a call about a woman still inside the Lindt building on an uppermost floor. A team was sent to extract her, and a renewed search of buildings within the perimeter took place to ensure no one else had been left behind.

At the State Crisis Centre, the premier was feeling the pressure. Mike Baird had only been in the state's top job for eight months, the role of leader having fallen into his lap abruptly in April when his predecessor Barry O'Farrell found himself in the sights of the state's Independent Commission Against Corruption because of a lapse of memory over an expensive gift of a bottle of Grange Hermitage.

The telegenic Baird, forty-six, boasted a distinguished political pedigree. His father, Bruce, had once aspired to be premier himself before moving to Canberra to become the Liberal member for Cook. But no one expected Baird junior, who'd entered politics from a highly successful banking career, to hang around as premier for too long. Most of those in his inner circle thought he'd use his time as leader to bring some entrepreneurial oomph to the government and then engineer an exit back into the private sector by the time he'd turned fifty or so. Baird's comfort zone was the state's economy and the Treasury portfolio, where he'd been the shadow Treasurer and then Treasurer for nearly six years before entering the top job. Now he was in deeply unfamiliar territory, facing the first serious terror attack on Australian soil right on the state government's doorstep.

'You don't go into politics expecting that,' said an aide. 'Mike went into politics to sort out the budget and build some infrastructure. He didn't go in there to be premier during a terrorist siege. It's not what anyone would expect going in to work on a Monday morning.'

The machinery for managing the siege was now in place. Identifying the hostages and the gunman was the next most urgent task, but Monis was doing everything he could to remain anonymous. By now he was mostly staying well out of sight of the café windows. Beyond declaring himself the perpetrator of an attack in the name of Islamic State, he'd given no clue as to his identity. And he was refusing direct dialogue with police, instead using the hostages to repeat various iterations of his original demands.

At first police suspected Monis' actions might be linked to a series of raids they'd launched earlier that day as part of Operation Appleby, an ongoing counter-terrorism investigation focused on suspected radicalised networks in western Sydney. But each of the Appleby targets was tracked down and accounted for; none could be linked to the crisis in Martin Place. Thus, it was late morning before two eagle-eyed homicide detectives based in the city's outer western suburbs came up with the first lead as to the gunman's identity.

Detective Senior Constable Adam Thompson and Detective Senior Constable Melanie Staples were all too familiar with Man Haron Monis.

They knew him to be someone with a very dark recent past. They'd teamed up the previous year on Strike Force Crocker, an investigation into the particularly brutal murder of Monis' ex-wife, 'Helen Lee' (whose real name remains suppressed by the courts).

Strike Force Crocker led to charges being laid against Monis and his new partner, Amirah Droudis, over Lee's murder. Staples, Thompson and other investigating police were horrified when the charged pair had been allowed to walk free on bail; neither of them had yet been brought to trial for the vicious crime.

At 11.30 a.m., Thompson was watching live TV coverage of the siege when he became certain that the gunman—who in earlier replayed footage could be glimpsed fleetingly through the café windows—was Monis. He phoned Staples, who checked her screen and agreed. She passed this information on to the intelligence branch, and she and Thompson began scrambling to prepare a brief distilled from the extensive files they already held on Monis. Despite their early tip, it took a while for this vital information to reach the ears of senior commanders and the negotiating team at the forward command post (considerably longer than it should have, the coroner would find later).

By 2 p.m., Thompson had submitted a more formal report stating there was 'strong consensus from detectives with personal knowledge that the person is Monis'. But the Joint Intelligence Group (JIG), the supposed central clearing-house for all intelligence related to the siege, still had six to seven suspects on its list, of whom Monis was only one.

The Australian Federal Police, which had a seat on the JIG, began combing through its own files. Federal agents discovered they too held an extensive dossier on Monis. Of particular significance was a series of abusive letters he had written between 2007 and 2009 addressed to the families of Australian servicemen who'd died while fighting in Afghanistan. After a long journey through the courts those letters had earned Monis a conviction on postal offences, but the sentence had been lenient: just 300 hours of community service.

It wasn't until just after 2.30 p.m. that the POC and forward commanders were told all fingers were pointing towards Monis as the hostage taker. This was confirmed in a formal briefing at 3.30 p.m.

Now the police commissioner was going to have to break the distinctly unwelcome news to his political masters that the gunman had launched the attack while on bail for serious offences, including being an accessory to murder.

As the investigative teams were getting to grips with the attacker's identity and history, police on the ground were assessing the café for possible vulnerabilities and entry points. The building posed serious challenges: its position on a corner was highly exposed; the fortress-like façade and the tall narrow windows made it more difficult to see into than the wide glass frontages of modern buildings; the Christmas decals on the Phillip Street windows obscured vision even further on that side; and the building's solid construction was going to make drilling into walls or floors for surveillance, or any other purpose, difficult.

On the other hand, it did have three exits, which was a distinct drawback for a single hostage-taker trying to monitor all three simultaneously. By 10.30 that morning, the police had liaised with building manager Vince Mirenzi, who talked them through possible ways to get into the café, including the rabbit warren of fire corridors that snaked below ground level from Elizabeth Street through to Phillip Street.

Superintendent Sicard was still searching for somewhere to set up a forward command post but, as he was not Pioneer trained, he would soon have to hand over command to someone who was.

Close to noon, police planners decided that the NSW Leagues' Club, a few doors down Phillip Street from the café, would have to serve as both hostage reception centre and forward command post. Its key advantage was its proximity to the café, less than eighty paces away. The hundred-year-old club was a legendary institution that had served as watering hole, spiritual home and sanctum for rugby league in New South Wales for decades. Now its public bar was about to be transformed into the unlikely nerve centre for a response to a terrorist attack.

———

The frantic task of identifying the hostages was also proving tougher than anticipated.

Tori Johnson, the café manager, was the easiest and first to be identified, as the initiator of the triple zero call at 9.41 a.m. Louisa Hope, who had been ordered by Monis to make another call to triple zero just after 10 a.m., was also identified early on.

At 10.15 Alistair Keep, the retail manager for Lindt Australia, provided police with details of the staff roster for that day along with contact details. This gave police the names of Paolo Vassallo, barista Harriette Denny and the waiters Jarrod Morton-Hoffman, Joel Herat, Fiona Ma, Elly Chen and April (Jieun) Bae.

But confusion still reigned over total numbers trapped in the café. At midday Mick Fuller handed command of the POC to a fellow officer, the counter-terrorism trained assistant commissioner Mark Murdoch. Fuller had not been given the details of Tori's first phone call and so mistakenly briefed Murdoch that there were only half a dozen to a dozen people inside the café.

As the afternoon wore on, the estimate of hostage numbers fluctuated wildly.

A police negotiator, 'Sasha', started transferring all the names onto a white board in the leagues' club set up outside the gaming manager's office. At one stage the board had twenty-four names on it; by 4 p.m. the police had a list that included all the names of those actually being held captive, plus several others who were not. Indeed, a completely accurate list of hostages was never arrived at by police until after the siege had ended. One internal intelligence bulletin still had a photo of a woman against Tori Johnson's name until the middle of the afternoon, despite Alistair Keep giving police a correct photo of Tori hours earlier.

For the purpose of identifying the non-staff hostages, police were dependent on phone intercepts out of the café and worried inquiries from family, friends and work colleagues.

At Westpac a head count had established that two members of the IT team, Viswakanth (Viswa) Ankireddi and Puspendu Ghosh, could not be accounted for. Soon afterwards, Viswa's wife Shilpa opened her front door to see a worried looking manager from her husband's office on the doorstep. He produced a photo of Viswa standing hostage in the window of the café. The shock felled her where she stood.

John O'Brien had disobeyed Monis' instruction to surrender his phone, so when his wife rang, he was able to tell her quickly where he was. Monis saw him on the phone and immediately ordered him to drop it on the floor.

A cold sense of dread was taking hold among members of Katrina Dawson's family. Knowing her habit of dropping into the café with Julie of a morning, Katrina's husband Paul Smith tried to ring her but her phone was switched off; her office confirmed she had gone out. Using the smart phone 'Find My Phone' function, the Dawsons established well before midday that Julie and Stefan were almost certainly inside the café, which most likely placed Katrina there as well.

Both Katrina's brother Angus and her mother Jane, rang an emergency hotline set up by police. They were told their calls would be returned within minutes, but the calls never came. For the family, this would be the start of a pattern of frustration and mounting apprehension—fuelled by little or incorrect information from the police—that would continue over the next seventeen hours.

Harriette's image was seen by a member of her extended family on a TV set in the Myer department store, which was streaming live coverage of the siege. The shocked girl, a niece of Harriette's partner Jorge, rang her mother to pass on the news.

On the Central Coast, an hour and a half north of Sydney, Tori Johnson's mother Rosie Connellan was helping her partner Daniel construct a new stone wall for a neighbour. Seeking a few minutes out of the sun, she ducked home for water and walked in to see a light flashing on her home phone. It was a message from her ninety-four-year-old mother about trouble at the Lindt Café. Rosie called her mother back straightaway. Then, Rosie recalls, 'I just went to the deck of our house, and screamed like a banshee.' She and Daniel hastily showered and piled into their car, heading straight for the city.

Marcia Mikhael's husband of twenty-five years, George, was driving across Sydney's Anzac Bridge when his phone pinged. A three-word message had come in from Marcia. 'At Lindt,' it read. 'Hostage.'

CHAPTER 3

SHAPE-SHIFTER

The man at the centre of all this heartache, Man Haron Monis, was a shape-shifter, someone who'd experimented with so many guises and told so many lies over the years that it's possible he'd lost track of the truth himself. He'd adopted and discarded identities as easily as others might change a suit of clothes: religious scholar, travel agent, businessman, refugee, carpet seller, security guard, poet, faith healer, would-be Islamic cleric, spy and self-proclaimed 'peace activist'. Now posterity would add the word 'terrorist' to that list.

During his eighteen years in Australia he had used up to twenty different aliases—a daunting maze for investigators to enter when later they tried to piece together his life story. But common themes came through in the accounts of anyone who'd had extensive dealings with him.

Monis had an extraordinary talent for manipulating the trust of others. He was a serial abuser of women, exploiting and using with utter callousness those who had the misfortune to enter his orbit. He had a persistent fascination with the world of intelligence and espionage. And he was quick to seize on grievances and nurture them to the point of obsession. At times he could adopt a veneer of sincerity and charm, but his overweening ego and sociopathic lack of empathy was never far from the surface.

In his personal life Monis was often secretive, to the point of paranoia. Yet periodically he would thrust himself into the spotlight with bizarre one-man protests, chaining himself to courthouses and parliament railings, wearing billboards and clamouring for media attention. Tragically, that pattern seemed to have bred something veering dangerously close to complacency on the part of Australian authorities by the time he walked into the Lindt Café on 15 December 2014.

Monis' story began in the western Iranian city of Boroujerd, a small but ancient city of some 200,000 people that sits in a natural bowl rimmed by the Zagros mountains. His family was reputedly of modest means.

His mother Zahra had already brought five daughters into the world when Monis was born on 19 May 1964. As the youngest child and only son, it is likely that his later and often remarked-upon sense of 'being special' stemmed from the unique position he had in his family. He grew up in the Shia religious tradition, the dominant form of Islam in Iran, and was originally known as Mohammad Hassan Manteghi, which was his father's full name. It appears his father died when Monis was in his teens, at a time when Iran was undergoing a profound religious and political upheaval.

For centuries there had been a monarch sitting on the Iranian throne. The most recent had been Shah Mohammad Reza Pahlavi, who'd ruled for nearly four decades, but in 1979 all that was swept away and replaced by a revolutionary Islamic theocracy with a supreme religious leader, the Ayatollah Khomeini, at its head. From that point on, power and influence in Iran would flow from religious connections. And, through luck or design or most probably both, Monis found a key to open the door to this new world.

His stroke of good fortune took the form of a young woman, Zahra Mobasheri, whom he met on the campus of the freshly established Imam Sadiq University on the outskirts of Tehran. Zahra's father, Habibollah Mobasheri, was a highly placed official at the university and right-hand man to its founder Ayatollah Kani, who in turn had close links to the ruling regime.

When Zahra and Monis married (most likely in 1985), it was a significant step up for him socially and gave him entry to networks of privilege and influence he would almost certainly never have accessed otherwise. The following year, the first of the couple's two daughters was born.

After graduation, Monis attended the Abdol Azim College of Hadith Sciences, a theological academy in southern Tehran, apparently with aspirations of rising further up the hierarchy of Shiite clerics. By the early 1990s he and Zahra were reportedly living in a large, well-appointed apartment in a gated quarter frequented by other university staff and government officials. He appeared to enjoy a degree of insider privilege.

A friend at this time who one day dislocated his shoulder marvelled at Monis' ability to whisk him away from the run-down local hospital and into an expensive private facility on the strength of a single phone call, breezing past a 'scared-looking' security guard with a flourish of an ID card. Others suspected Monis had links to the intelligence services in Iran, but it was a dangerous topic to broach.

By 1994 Monis had gained the rank of *hojatoleslam*, or 'authority on Islam', which bestowed on him the rank of teacher; but he was still well below the status of ayatollah, which he would later falsely claim for himself. He'd picked up a working knowledge of English, and had apparently mastered classical Arabic on top of his native Farsi (Persian).

With his and Zahra's second daughter on the way, Monis now embarked on a business career. He threw himself into a series of enterprises of doubtful legitimacy, of the kind that only those with government connections could hope to operate—buying and selling government-owned tyres and textiles. A year or so later he moved into a new field, this time becoming manager of the Rahelenoor Tour and Travel Agency. The agency specialised in organising visas, itineraries and tickets for wealthy Iranians looking to study, work or in some cases move permanently abroad. Large sums of money washed through the books.

But trouble was brewing for Monis on both the home and work fronts, and by July 1996 the failed cleric was secretly checking out visa options to travel to Australia.

On 1 October 1996, Monis turned up at the Australian Embassy in Tehran seeking a business visa. He claimed to be a legal consultant to the head of an Iranian marine engineering company who needed to meet with mining giant BHP Billiton. It was an elaborate fiction, sucking in the Australian government's overseas trading arm, Austrade, which backed his application. On 10 October Australian security agencies cleared Monis for entry, and he arrived in Sydney on 28 October 1996.

No sooner had he landed than his story changed. The mining consultant was now an entrepreneur in the carpet trading business, or so his incoming passenger card declared. Three weeks later Monis sought political asylum in Australia. He had turned his back on his country of birth, and would never see his Iranian wife and daughters again.

Monis polished up his bid for protection. He struck the pose of heroic dissident, saying he'd been secretly working for a banned sect, the Ahmadi. That line was swallowed by Amnesty International, which supported his asylum claim. Monis also said he was in danger because of a book of dissident poetry he'd published in Iran, *Daroon va Boroon* (*Inside and Out*), which he later republished in Sydney to decidedly lukewarm reviews.

But the murkiest element of Monis' refugee story was his claim that he'd been secretly working—under the noses of Iranian intelligence—with the CIA. He claimed to have met US agents in Romania, in Cyprus and later in Washington DC itself, travelling to the US from Iran via Malaysia and Singapore.

The CIA refused to either confirm or deny these claims when I contacted the agency in 2017. However, the coronial inquest into the siege did turn up one man who in January 1996 travelled as far as Malaysia with Monis. The man, codenamed FG by the inquest, said Monis had given him German currency worth close to US$7000 to carry from Iran to Kuala Lumpur. Monis had insisted they sit separately on the plane and stay in different hotels. He then vanished without explanation on the second day of the trip.

In April 1997, Monis had to submit further details to Australian authorities to back his claim for asylum. He amped up his story, saying he was a dissident Shia cleric who had engaged in intelligence gathering for foreign governments, and was thus at risk of being tracked down and assassinated. He claimed his wife and daughters were being detained in Iran because of his fugitive status (although it later emerged his wife was rising steadily through the ranks of university officialdom after his departure).

Immigration officials were beginning to develop grave doubts about Monis' story. They referred him to the domestic spy agency, ASIO, for review. In January 1999 ASIO issued an adverse security assessment and Immigration officials considered cancelling Monis' bridging visa, but instead they sent his case back to the spy agency for a second look. This time around ASIO dropped its objections. In August 2000, Monis won his protection visa. He was now able to apply for welfare assistance and a Medicare card. But there would be one more hurdle to clear before he gained much-coveted Australian citizenship.

In 2001 Iranian authorities put out an Interpol alert for Monis' arrest and extradition, accusing him of absconding with several hundred thousand dollars from the travel agency in Tehran. But they did not follow up with supporting documentation, and no extradition treaty existed between Australia and Iran in any case.

Monis of course had a competing story to explain his hasty departure from Tehran. He said he'd been blackmailed by the Iranian Ministry of Intelligence and Security (known by the acronyms MOIS or VAVAK) into spying on the regime's political rivals. The inquest would later hear a different version of this story: that VAVAK had planted Monis inside the travel agency as a mole with the express aim of discrediting the reformist politicians who had a stake in it. Perhaps all of these elements contained a modicum of truth. The only certainty is that the real history of his relationship with Iranian intelligence lies buried somewhere at VAVAK headquarters.

One man did make it his business to try and unearth more of Monis' past. His name was Dr Nazir Daawar, and he was one of the many lawyers Monis would have dealings with as he embarked on years of sparring with Australian authorities.

Nazir Daawar, resplendent in dark suit and purple tie, sits behind a dark wooden desk in a small legal office set in a strip of shops near the Auburn Station, in Sydney's west. It's the same office he once threw Monis out of.

Daawar, who holds degrees in law and medicine and comes from a prominent military family in Afghanistan, arrived in Sydney after some years working with the United Nations in Kabul. Fluent in several languages, including Farsi, the urbane criminal lawyer was a well-known figure among a number of Sydney's émigré communities.

It was close to closing time in mid-January 2010 when Daawar heard someone talking in Farsi at the top of the stairs outside his first-floor office. In walked Monis, dressed in the garb of an Iranian cleric, with long flowing robes and a turban. The stranger, who had come in off the street, seemed polite, intelligent and well spoken at first. But that impression quickly soured when Monis started claiming to be a figure of some note telling Daawar, 'You will of course have heard of me,' which the lawyer hadn't.

Monis then explained that he needed urgent legal representation for a case that was coming up for a first mention at the Downing Street court complex in central Sydney the next morning. He'd been accused of sending abusive letters to the families of Australian servicemen who had died in Afghanistan. But the charges were a mistake, he insisted. It was a conspiracy against him. Really, he was a 'peacemaker' and the letters were his 'bouquets' of consolation.

Daawar agreed to meet Monis at court early the next day, but from the outset he proved a handful. Monis refused to bow to the magistrate or remove his headwear in court, claiming it was against his religion. He ignored Daawar's warnings against speaking to the media and made a beeline for a TV camera directly after his court appearance, pulling a pre-written statement from his inside pocket. The lawyer was already having serious misgivings about this new client.

It wasn't until the matter came before the court again a fortnight later that Daawar was finally able to examine the brief of evidence. He was shocked at the contents. Between them, Monis and his partner Amirah Droudis had contacted the families of six servicemen, describing them, among other things, as murderers, pigs and criminals. In one case Droudis had tricked a sergeant's widow into revealing the time and place of her husband's funeral. Droudis turned up wearing a flowing niqab, the black all-body covering, carrying a package she said was from 'Sheikh Haron'. Inside was a copy of a letter authored by Monis accusing the dead man of being a murderer.

Daawar summoned Monis to his office. He pulled one of the letters from the file and asked him to read it. In the letter, Monis told the bereaved family that their son would be burning in hell. 'Did you write this?' Daawar asked him.

'Yes,' Monis replied.

'How well do you speak and understand English?' the lawyer inquired.

'Perfectly,' came the answer.

Then, said Daawar, he had no option other than to advise him to plead guilty as charged. If Monis expressed contrition, the lawyer might just be able to secure him a reduced penalty.

This was advice the Iranian did not want to hear. 'I will make you famous,' he wheedled, to which Daawar responded, 'I don't want that fame.' The debate became increasingly heated, with Monis insisting that Australian troops had no right to be in Afghanistan and Daawar pointing out that they were there under UN mandate.

With his eyes bulging and hands shaking, Monis rose abruptly, his chair crashing onto the floor behind him. 'Do you know who I am? I am Hassan Manteghi! I pay money to you and what I say, you do.'

As the Iranian 'peacemaker' towered threateningly over the lawyer, Daawar ordered him out of his office. 'You will regret that decision,' Monis shot back.

Some weeks later one of the Daawar's former clients, a member of an outlaw motorcycle gang, rang the lawyer to warn him that Monis was offering $20,000 to have him killed. 'Take the money,' Daawar replied in jest. But for a while he took the precaution of being more vigilant than usual.

After the siege, Daawar made extensive inquiries about Monis among members of Sydney's Iranian community. Those contacts led him to a man, now living abroad, who had worked alongside Monis in the Tehran travel agency. The source told him that not only had Monis swindled money from the agency but that he had been facing investigation for sexual assault. This had been another factor, the source believed, in Monis' decision to flee.

'For me he was a person who needed attention, a person who suffered from being nothing,' Daawar says.

Despite claims from Monis' Iranian wife that he had abused her during their marriage, the inquest would later find that Monis stayed in intermittent email contact with at least one of his daughters in Iran until mid-2014.

Monis' first few months in Sydney were typical of those of a migrant settling here without family support. He found a flat in Auburn, in the heart of the Middle Eastern émigré community. He secured a driver's licence and trained as a security guard, gaining a certificate for the use of a revolver and semi-automatic pistol.

He found security work at the Greenfield shopping village in western Sydney, and made a generally good impression on his employer. But in private his oddities puzzled acquaintances. Fellow immigrant Amin Khademi, who moved into the spare room in Monis' apartment in late 1999, recalled his obsessive secrecy: no visitors, no opening the door to anyone, and no entry to Monis' room at any time. The room was kept locked, even when Monis was inside.

In early 2000 Monis moved across the continent to Perth, where he picked up work in a Persian carpet gallery. He appeared to live well, taking a furnished two-bedroom flat with an ocean view and driving a late-model black Jeep. (Monis' liking for a good automobile would be another of the few constants in his life. At one time, in 2003, he had three expensive cars on rotation: a Mercedes, a Jeep and a Peugeot.)

But life in Perth soon unravelled. In November 2000 he staged the first of his public provocations, chaining himself to a pole outside Parliament House and announcing he was on a hunger strike against the Iranian regime. The 'hunger strike' collapsed after a few hours when someone called an ambulance. In December he was demoted at work, and not long afterwards forcibly evicted from his workplace by police.

Back in Sydney Monis staged another public protest, this time chaining himself briefly to the fence outside the New South Wales Parliament and demanding that Prime Minister John Howard pressure Tehran over the supposed detention of his family. This pattern would become tediously familiar to the police and security agencies.

By now he had adopted the name Michael Hayson Mavros. Needing money, he began advertising his services as a 'spiritual consultant' in July 2001, placing notices in ethnic community newspapers in western Sydney. The ads clearly targeted lonely and insecure women from sheltered migrant backgrounds, and promised to help them find love, predict fortunes, ward off evil spirits and lift curses using astrology, numerology, meditation and 'spiritual healing'. The business was soon generating a tidy income. Over the next five years, tax records would show it produced revenue of nearly $450,000.

But if the money was good, even better was the steady stream of gullible young women it delivered into his hands. Monis would persuade them to come for 'treatment' weekly or fortnightly, sometimes for months on end. The most vulnerable of them he preyed on for sexual gratification. His sickening modus operandi would only be fully exposed when forty charges of historical sexual assault were laid against him in 2014, the bulk of those charges being brought just two months before the siege.

Monis always began his 'consultations' by playing the role of a solicitous health professional taking a patient's history, but the questions would soon become highly intrusive. He would exit the room while the women he marked out as targets undressed, and come back wearing a white long-sleeved robe and white cap. He would 'paint' them with liquid from a bowl, before instructing them to lie on a massage table so he could heal them with 'sexual energy'. On a number of occasions intimate touching proceeded to full intercourse, with the victims too terrified or submissive to resist and too ashamed to tell anyone.

Typical of the women he assaulted was Ms F, who visited Monis fortnightly for four months in 2003 after separating from an abusive and controlling husband. Following their sixth session, Monis told her she was suffering from a 'relationship' curse, which could only be lifted if she had sex with someone. According to a later police facts sheet, she was raped on his massage table.

Another victim, Ms M, gave a similar account. At first she felt reassured by Monis' room appearing to be set up like a doctor's office—with two yellow sofas, a desk and a computer. But she was uneasily aware of a digital camera on top of the TV.

Monis introduced himself as 'Marcos', explained his background was Greek-Egyptian and interrogated her about her sexual history. After hearing of problems in her marriage he diagnosed her as having been struck with a curse, and told her, 'The evil inside you is flickering like a flame and has to be extinguished.' He advised her to abstain from sex and return the following week.

On the next visit, Monis told her she was suffering from cervical cancer caused by black magic and that she needed his 'sexual energy' to cure it. After painting liquid inscriptions on her body, he pulled out a sofa bed, undressed, touched her insistently and then penetrated her while she lay there confused, frozen and terrified. Afterwards Monis threatened that if she told a soul, he would curse her with black magic.

She drove home so traumatised that, after taking a shower, she threw everything she had been wearing, including her shoes, into a bin. In late 2004 she went to police and filed a statement against 'Marcos'. 'I did not want this man to do what he did to me,' she said. 'I was very frightened and believed he could harm me and my family.' The police files record, simply, that 'the investigation did not progress'.

When police raided Monis' flat nearly ten years later, they found a black case stuffed with photos and computer discs. On them were recorded highly personal details relating to more than five hundred clients. Among the items were photos of those who had become his victims, including Ms F and Ms M.

In 2004, Monis (as he had now named himself) finally obtained Australian citizenship. The then Department of Immigration and Multicultural Affairs even granted him a private citizenship ceremony, for reasons it refused to divulge except to say it was 'at the request from this individual's legal representatives'. He had again passed muster with ASIO, despite the 2001 Interpol query from Tehran. He got an Australian passport the next day and made a number of overseas trips over the following four years, to Thailand, the US, Hong Kong, Canada, Fiji and New Zealand. Their purpose was never discovered.

By now he was well into a relationship with the woman who would pay the highest price for crossing his path: his de facto Australian wife, who became known to the court system as 'Helen Lee'.

They'd met in late 2002, when she was just twenty and studying Biological Science at the University of Western Sydney. He introduced himself as Michael Hayson Mavros and spun the well-worn story about his mixed Egyptian and Greek parentage. He displayed no religious fervour; indeed, he drank, smoked and sometimes accompanied Lee to nightclubs.

She took him home to meet her parents in early 2003 and they threw an 'engagement' party for the couple. Some kind of marriage ceremony appears to have been held a few months later, but the union was never formally registered. Lee remained blissfully unaware that Monis was seriously involved with two other women during this period. They were Amanda Morsy whom he dated from January to July 2003 and to whom he unsuccessfully proposed, and Irene Mishra, whom he would continue to see for the next nine years.

By September of 2003, Lee was pregnant. Monis continued to live a largely separate life, showing little interest in the pregnancy. He provided no financial support after his son was born, and avoided the child's first birthday party. On one occasion Lee described how he dumped her and the child by the roadside at night in pelting rain. Yet, despite his abusive behaviour towards her, their relationship continued off and on for several years. In early 2007 Lee discovered she was again pregnant.

It was from around this time onwards that Lee noted a marked change in Monis. During dinner one night, he revealed his true origins: that he had been born in Iran and worked there (he claimed) as a spy. He announced he was going to set up an Islamic website to teach the faith. Over the following months Monis grew a beard, stopped listening to music, abandoned western clothes and gave up alcohol. He started to pray five times a day. On his increasingly infrequent visits to Lee, he barricaded himself inside the house, pulling down the blinds and spending hours hunched over his laptop. He barred his sons from playing outside. He tried to force Lee to wear Islamic clothing and prevented the boys from seeing non-Islamic friends. At times he used physical force against the oldest boy, and over the next two years the children grew increasingly fearful of him.

In October 2009 Lee's fears reached new heights when counter-terrorism officers turned up on her doorstep to investigate the activities of 'Sheikh Haron'. She had not heard this name before; she also learnt for the first time of Monis' wife and two daughters in Iran. The federal agents took away a fax machine, videocassettes and Islamic books. With chilling foresight, a female officer took Lee aside to warn that she should keep Monis well away—from herself and from the boys.

Meanwhile Monis was becoming ever more consumed with an online campaign against the west's military adventures in the Middle East. He plastered his newly founded website, *sheikharon.com*, with hectoring videos and vitriolic condemnations of western governments. He vowed to counter US President George Bush's 'War on Terrorism' with his own 'War on Oppression'. He launched a volley of letters, addressed to figures as diverse as Australian politicians, the Pope, British prime minister Gordon Brown and Queen Elizabeth.

On Australia Day 2008 Monis authored an open letter describing his adopted country as being 'chained by evil' and denouncing 'lesbians and gays [as] the cancer on society's body'. He called for multiculturalism to be replaced by so-called 'muslimculturalism'.

In March 2009 he wrote to Prime Minister Kevin Rudd and Victorian Premier John Brumby asserting that Victoria's devastating Black Saturday bushfires—which took 173 lives—were divine punishment for Australia's participation in the Afghanistan and Iran wars. Australians 'deserved to be burned in the fire of hell', he said.

On 17 August 2009 Monis became the target of an investigation by the Joint Counter Terrorism Team (JCTT) based in Sydney. He was assessed collectively by the Australian Federal Police's Protection Intelligence, the New South Wales Police's Terrorism Investigations Squad and its Terrorism Intelligence Unit, ASIO, the Defence Department and the JCTT. None tagged him a threat to national security. Ironically, it was soon after that Monis enrolled in an online university course that promised to deliver a Bachelor of Criminology and Open Justice. Of ten required modules, he managed to pass three, including a unit titled 'Introduction to Forensic Psychology', but with an average grade of only thirty per cent he failed to complete the course.

Monis had some personal experience of the mental health system. Between May 2009 and September 2011, he visited ten different doctors complaining of a variety of symptoms, many of which were deemed psychosomatic. One doctor made a provisional diagnosis of chronic schizophrenia; however, Monis stopped seeing her after seven sessions and stopped taking the drugs she had prescribed. A forensic psychiatrist would later conclude that Monis had a severe personality disorder with some paranoid features, but that he did not suffer from impaired judgment and was capable of choice and deliberate action.

Despite his holier-than-thou moralising, Monis kept chasing women. By 2006 he'd found a new partner and devotee, a Greek Orthodox woman named Anastasia Droudis whose mother Soula had come to Monis for 'treatment'.

Anastasia was a single mother and former hairdresser, 'not

particularly well educated' according to one of her cousins. Droudis fell so completely under Monis' spell that by 2008 she'd converted to Islam and adopted the name 'Amirah'. On Christmas Day 2008, Monis surprised her family by pulling out a ring and announcing that the couple were engaged. The following Easter, Droudis and her daughter wore Islamic-style head coverings to the traditional family gathering. It was deeply unsettling for her extended family.

As he'd done before, Monis presented himself as Egyptian-born and made a good first impression. But some in the family circle were harbouring doubts about the newcomer. Droudis' cousin was discomfited by the man's strange disinclination to answering everyday questions, such as where he worked. She noticed his utter aversion to the camera at family gatherings.

She told Droudis' mother, Soula, of her concerns: 'There's something wrong here. Is he hiding something?' Soula replied: 'No. That's just probably his religion, they don't take photos.' But the younger woman knew something was amiss. When news broke of Monis and Droudis' appalling letters, the worst fears of the more sceptical members of the family were confirmed.

Droudis was pulled further into the dark vortex of Monis' growing extremism. In 2008 she featured in eleven videos of an increasingly confronting nature, all scripted by him. In each she would wear the niqab with just her eyes visible. The content was extreme. Droudis praised the mastermind of the Twin Towers attacks, Osama bin Laden. She expressed happiness about the Bali bombings, in which eighty-eight Australians perished. She issued a warning to Prime Minister Rudd that Australians would die at the hands of Muslims.

In one video, Droudis railed against US presidential candidate Barack Obama for being an 'apostate' and concluded her message with the words 'finish it', miming stabbing motions with her hands. In January 2009 she declared herself happy about the 'punishment' inflicted on the Jews through the Holocaust.

All this time Monis was playing his habitual game of tease with Australia's intelligence agencies. Previously he had offered information about threats to the Olympics and then about the 9/11 attacks. He was assessed as having nothing credible to offer. In 2005, and again in 2007, he volunteered to become an ASIO source, posing as an intermediary with Islamic youth. The offer was declined.

ASIO reviewed Monis again in late 2008 and early 2009, concluding that he still didn't pose a threat: 'At this time there is no indication Sheikh Haron or his associates are likely to personally engage in violence.'

New South Wales Police reached a similar conclusion. A confidential dossier prepared by the Terrorism Intelligence Unit dismissed Monis' rhetoric as 'ambiguous'. He had next to no following that they could detect, and remained outside the communities fostered by Sydney's mosques.

In their last assessment of him before the siege, in November 2013, New South Wales Police refined their judgment to warn that Monis had some potential to become a terrorist in future. But at that juncture, they said, nothing pointed to him having any involvement in terrorism-related activities.

He seemed then to drift away from the active gaze of the intelligence agencies.

By 2011 Monis' relationship with Lee was deteriorating rapidly. She ended it in June, and the following month complained to police that he had threatened her in the car park of McDonald's at Hinchinbrook in Sydney's south-west. Monis told her: 'If I don't get to see more of the kids than I am now, I'll make sure you pay for it, even if I have to shoot you.'

The confrontation led to a charge against him of domestic violence and a provisional apprehended domestic violence order was issued to protect Lee. However, the charge was dismissed in May the following year.

By the end of 2011 Monis and Lee were locked in a legal battle over the custody of their sons. In court affidavits, Lee reported Monis making repeated threats. He warned that he would do 'everything he could' to make sure the kids were taken away from her and her parents. Lee also claimed he told her, 'One day I will do something that will make me a martyr'. She told police: 'I feel that his main purpose of wanting sole custody of the boys is to turn them into extremists.'

In August 2012 Lee succeeded in her custody battle; Monis was allowed access visits every second Sunday. The exchanges would take place at Monis' residence at Parkes Avenue, Werrington, although he was rarely there and mostly living with Droudis closer to the city at Croydon. During these access visits Monis encouraged his boys to address Droudis as *mumi* (pronounced 'Mummy'). He told them this was her name, which upset Lee and prompted angry messages between her and Monis.

Things took an even nastier turn in January 2013 when Monis and his two sons, accompanied by Droudis and her thirteen-year-old daughter, dropped in to the home of Lee's parents. They claimed they were on their way to a public swimming pool and had turned up to collect some clothes. But Monis had brought along a bizarre escort: two members of the Mt Druitt chapter of the Rebels outlaw motorcycle gang. Lee's parents protested as did her boyfriend, Jayesh Goundar. There was a confrontation during which Goundar was warned not to accompany Lee to Monis' unit when she picked up the children. As subsequent events were to prove, this would leave her dangerously exposed.

Monis' fleeting association with the Rebels was another example of his many failed attempts at achieving acceptance, standing and prestige. For a while he turned up at the gang's clubhouse for Friday evening social gatherings, often sporting a bandana and a chain on his jeans 'like he'd watched too many American movies', according to one clubhouse member. He tried to curry favour by buying drinks, but no one warmed to him. He needed a bike to impress his new acquaintances and a female friend lent him $25,000 to purchase a Harley Davidson.

In late 2012 and again in early 2013, Monis approached members of the gang seeking help to have his ex-partner killed. They laughed him off, saying they 'didn't do that sort of thing'. Ultimately, Monis was rejected as being too weird. 'People were jack of him asking for knives and guns,' a gang member recalls.

On 7 April 2013, Monis and Droudis took the boys skateboarding and for rides on the mini train at Darling Harbour in the city. Three days later, having never previously insured his apartment, Monis took out a policy worth $150,000. Police would later argue this pointed to foreknowledge of a fire that would break out at his unit in the wake of Lee's murder.

On 13 April Monis began the construction of an elaborate alibi. He contacted friends he had not seen for three years and asked them to come and meet his children on the Sunday of the following week, one of his access days. What followed was a series of events that Justice Johnson of the New South Wales Supreme Court would later describe as 'seemingly farcical if they were not so serious'.

On Sunday 21 April, Lee dropped the boys off and Monis took them to meet his friends and their kids at a nearby park. The group then headed for the Penrith swimming pool. Monis had brought a video camera along and enthusiastically documented the outing, often turning the lens on himself. It was a way of carefully creating a record of his location at key points throughout the afternoon.

Towards 4 p.m., when Lee would normally be preparing to come and collect the boys, Monis and his friends started packing up at the pool. He filmed the time on the pool clock—3.52 p.m.—and filmed his sons as they were strapped into his friend's car at 3.56 p.m. They planned to drive home in convoy, with Monis alone in his black Jeep Cherokee.

But Monis hit a parked car outside Penrith Police Station. He blamed this on a sudden onset of severe chest pain, although police would later describe the accident as 'driver commanded divergence'. Monis was taken by ambulance to Nepean Hospital, where he got the all-clear but remained under observation. It did not escape the attention of investigators later that Monis did not ring Droudis all day.

Ignorant of Monis' supposed accident, Lee and her boyfriend pulled up around the corner from his apartment block at the appointed time so she could collect the children. She had felt sick that day so was running a few minutes late. She reached the stairwell alone and began the ascent to his flat.

Seconds later, the stairwell filled with the sound of piercing screams and neighbours rushed to their doors to see Lee cowering under a frenzied attack from a knife-wielding woman cloaked in a veil and tunic. Lee was screaming 'I have children'. Eighteen times the attacker plunged the blade into Lee's upper body and torso. Then the veiled figure set the dying woman alight with petrol and matches, turned and fled.

When police arrived at the hospital at 8.45 p.m. to tell Monis of his wife's death, he feigned shock, but by the next evening he and Droudis were back in her unit playing at happy families. Droudis cooked while Monis blithely filmed her in the kitchen and recorded himself reading to the boys in their pyjamas.

Monis did his best to convince police that Lee's father was to blame for the murder, but he and Droudis had been under surveillance since Lee's death and were secretly recorded discussing ways to direct suspicion away from themselves. In November 2013 police swooped and the pair were arrested. Droudis was charged with murder and Monis with being an accessory. Lee's parents won custody of the boys.

This was the beginning of a torrent of legal troubles that was now to begin pouring down on Monis. In April 2014 he was charged with the first of the sexual assaults the police had now begun to thoroughly investigate from earlier years. More would follow in October, bringing to forty the number of sexual assault charges against him.

Astonishingly, despite a brief period in jail, Monis walked free on bail after a hearing before a magistrate. Many factors combined to bring that about: a relatively benign bail regime at the time (since toughened up), and errors and omissions by the Office of the Director of Public Prosecutions and some also by the police, despite the passionate efforts of investigating detectives to keep him behind bars.

Unfortunately, New South Wales Police also remained ignorant of the fact that Monis had committed some of the sex assaults while he was on bail for the federal postal offences. He had pleaded guilty to those offences in September 2013, after a long legal tussle saw the matter go before the courts no less than twenty-six times, all funded by legal aid. Had the Commonwealth and New South Wales legal jurisdictions more thoroughly compared notes, it is almost certain he would never have been at large at the time of the siege.

Monis might have been free on bail, but by now he had no money. He was reliant on student grants, enrolling in and dropping out of a number of courses. Soon Centrelink would cut off those payments too. His life was spiralling downwards.

On 19 September 2014, Monis attended a protest in Lakemba against a counter-terrorism operation. Covert observers noted that he stood out as the 'only visible Shia in a crowd of Sunni Muslims'. Three weeks later he wrote to Attorney-General George Brandis asking if it was legally permitted to write to the leader of Islamic State.

Anyone closely monitoring Monis at this time, would have noticed his social media activity going into overdrive. On 6 November he set up a Twitter account and tweeted 157 times over the following eight days, with posts linking to graphic depictions of dead children in Middle Eastern war zones.

On 17 November, Monis took another step that should have rung a loud warning bell. In a highly unusual move, he publicly abandoned his Shia identity and pledged allegiance instead to the Sunni-aligned Islamic State 'Caliphate'. On his website, he wrote in Arabic: 'I pledge allegiance to Allah and His Messenger . . . and the pledge of allegiance is with Allah, His Messenger and the Commander of the Faithful. The Caliph of Muslims.'

In early December 2014, less than a fortnight before the siege, ASIO took another look at Monis. The agency decided he fell 'well outside the threshold' for inclusion in its 400 highest priority counter-terrorism investigations. But out in the wider community others were seeing reasons to be concerned. In the week before the siege, eighteen calls came in to the National Security Hotline about Monis' Facebook page. The authorities, again, decided on a preliminary assessment that nothing pointed to an imminent threat, or a 'desire or intent' to engage in terrorism.

On 12 December, just three days out from the siege, the High Court (in a highly unusual tied judgment) dismissed the constitutional challenge Monis was trying to mount against his conviction on the letter-writing offences. Shame and frustration—and the prospect of years in prison—were all that lay ahead.

For how long had he planned the siege? No one—apart, possibly, from Droudis—knows. What is known is that on the afternoon of Saturday 13 December, Monis visited two automatic teller machines and drained his remaining funds: $850 in total. He travelled to the Twin Shoes and Accessories store in Campsie and acquired a Camel Mountain backpack (the store was one of only two in Sydney to sell that brand).

Where he spent the night before the siege remains another mystery. At 5.02 p.m. on Sunday 14 December, he reported for bail at the Campsie Police Station. CCTV footage from inside the station shows Monis dressed in a white T-shirt and long camouflage trousers talking casually to someone at the front counter.

At around 6.30 p.m. that night, Soula Droudis saw Monis parking her daughter's black Jeep outside the family home. He clambered out of the vehicle wearing a dark-coloured backpack, and walked down the street until he was out of view. Nearly an hour or so later, she glanced out the window. The vehicle was gone.

Man Haron Monis would not be heard of again until he walked through the doors of the Lindt Café the next morning.

CHAPTER 4

THE HOSTAGES

As the first hour of the siege crawled by, Monis periodically shuffled the hostages around, permitting some to step down from the windows for a break and ordering others to take their place. Unless he asked them to perform a task, they were under instructions to keep their eyes shut and not to talk without permission. This made it almost impossible for the hostages to plan any kind of collective resistance—no doubt exactly what Monis was trying to guard against.

Even so, the thought did cross the minds of the two young waiters, Jarrod and Joel, who early on found themselves doing a 'shift' together standing on the banquette holding up the gunman's banner. Monis was sitting on a chair below them, slightly distracted. Joel and Jarrod exchanged glances. Each could sense what the other was thinking: they had box knives stashed in their aprons—could they jump him? Both were young and fit, but neither had the gunman's heavy build. Overpowering him would be difficult.

It was a conversation that Jarrod later recalled happened almost subliminally. 'I just knew that's what Joel was thinking because of the way he looked at me and then kind of looked down,' Jarrod says. 'We both thought it was potentially doable. I sneaked a look downwards and could see that Monis' gun was leaning over his leg, but that he had a whole bunch of hostages in front of him. Maybe we could wound him, or potentially disarm him. But I was worried that, even if we did manage to jump him, he might discharge the gun on some kind of reflex. And Julie was sitting right in front of him, so I'm thinking: "I'm not willing to risk the life of a pregnant woman so I can live".'

Towards Monis himself, Jarrod held no compunction. If it had been possible to eliminate the gunman, he felt he could have done it. 'He wasn't like a human being to me. He was just a threat, a primal threat.'

Others were also quietly calculating the odds of escape and whether they could live with the possible consequences for those left behind. Stefan and Julie had already had a whispered conversation as Stefan eyed what seemed to be an emergency exit button set low in the wall next to the front door. Paolo was calculating the odds as well, knowing (unlike the customers) that the kitchen door led to a small passage, beyond which lay a fire door and freedom.

For those hostages weighing up the risks of an escape attempt, churning over these painful dilemmas was a dark and lonely process. There was next to no chance to compare notes, to talk things over. Except for the staff, they were by and large strangers to one another. Yet now they were all bound by the most visceral of struggles: the desperate desire to stay alive.

Every life in that café hung on the split-second decisions others might make. Somehow they had to find a way to work together.

The eighteen hostages inside the Lindt Café that morning were an extraordinarily diverse collection of individuals swept together by the sheer randomness of the event. Millions of the city's inhabitants felt it could just as easily have been them, or someone just like them, caught up in the drama. What more routine start to a day could there be than dropping into a café for a caffeine boost?

The oldest of the hostages, John O'Brien, was eighty-two but unusually fit for his age. He had been a champion tennis player in the 1950s and skilful enough to have played at both Wimbledon and the

French Open. After leaving the tennis circuit, he'd spent many years in Europe as a coach, including a decade coaching the German national team. John had kept himself in good shape and at the time of the siege was ranked among the top ten players in the world aged over eighty. This was to stand him in remarkably good stead in the hours ahead.

John often dropped into the café after seeing his eye specialist at the nearby Sydney Hospital and had become a regular enough customer to have a favourite table, where he had been sitting that morning. But he was deaf in one ear and had trouble hearing instructions. This contributed to the fact that he would become an increasing annoyance to Monis.

Underlying John's entreaties for release were worries about his family: he was full-time carer to his wife Maureen, whose dementia had made her increasingly dependent on him. He was also a primary support for his oldest daughter, who had had her own health problems. 'They can't afford to be without me,' he kept thinking. He had to give escape a shot if the chance arose.

Louisa Hope's first thoughts were not for herself but for her elderly mother, Robin, now sitting across the table glaring at the gunman. Robin, aged seventy-three, had raised her three children in Moruya, a sleepy seaside town on the New South Wales south coast. She had always been a doer—one of those people who put the heart and soul into country communities. 'When we were kids, there wasn't anything that Mum wasn't involved in,' says Louisa. 'She was a typical country woman, the P&C, sporting clubs, the Labor Party—you name it, she was involved in it.'

Robin had worked hard part time for most of her adult life, in local factories and a bakery, and in recent years had been the carer for her partner, who had had Alzheimer's and passed away a year or so before the siege. Her grief at his loss still lingered. Robin was a feisty soul who, Louisa knew, was going to be highly tempted to give Monis a tongue-lashing at some point in the day. Louisa had to make sure her mother did not succumb to that temptation.

Robin was equally concerned for the welfare of her daughter, who had been living with multiple sclerosis for the last dozen years. The disease had forced Louisa from her job with Macquarie Bank in 2008, but she was a brave and stoic spirit who kept herself busy with work through her Christian network and travelling when her health allowed. Although she was on daily medication to manage the pain of the disease, she was practised in masking her discomfort. Her calm demeanour would be a source of solace for others as the day wore on. Louisa always took great care with her appearance, and shoes were her particular passion. She had a keen eye for an outfit. She would never forget what she was wearing on the day of the siege: a much-loved black dress teamed with her favourite red sandals.

Looking at Monis now brandishing his shotgun jolted Louisa back twenty-seven years to a memory of the only other time in her life when she'd had to confront a firearm. After working as a nurse's aide in Adelaide, Louisa had taken a job with a neighbour who ran a small private detective agency. Soon she was driving around town in her Suziki hatch accompanied by her small white dog, Lucy, serving legal papers and tackling small-scale insurance and household fraud. On her last day in the job, she was given the task of finding a man who was on the run with his child to serve him papers from the Family Court. Working her way through a list of contacts, Louisa narrowed the search to a small milk bar in the city's outer suburbs. Her quarry suddenly emerged from the back of the store, dressed in shorts and workboots—and armed with a shotgun. Later she wondered how she had summoned the presence of mind to talk him into lowering the weapon, but she did. She said she'd leave the matter of the papers for another day, bolted to her car, drove to the nearest public phone and rang the police. The whole time, she remembered, she had been praying fervently under her breath. Now, facing a shotgun for the second time in her life, she was again relying on the power of faith to get her through.

Marcia Mikhael had come into the café with two companions from Westpac, which had one of its major offices diagonally opposite the café. The forty-three-year-old mother of three was an information technology specialist working as a project manager for the bank.

Outside work, Marcia was a fitness fanatic who had been toying with the idea of a second career as a nutritionist and personal trainer. A keen gym-goer for the previous fifteen years, she'd recently become a devotee of 'natural' body building, a lower-key version of competitive body building with less intensive workouts and a strict aversion to performance-enhancing substances. Marcia had found her niche in the Bikini Masters tournaments, where women competed in skimpy two-piece outfits to show off their physiques. In 2013, Marcia had come top in the Bikini Masters division for 'Women Over 40' at the International Natural Bodybuilding Association World Championship in Greece.

On any given weekday, Marcia's job could take her to several of Westpac's main branches. She hadn't planned to visit the Martin Place office that morning, and only changed her schedule at the last minute.

Her colleagues often teased her about her weakness for Lindt chocolate and it was not unusual for her to visit the café three times a week, sometimes accompanied by co-workers Puspendu Ghosh and Viswa Ankireddi. Both were IT professionals in their mid-thirties working under contract to Westpac. When Viswa and Puspendu suggested a trip to Lindt that morning Marcia had initially resisted, insisting she was on a new health kick. Come on, they urged, it would be a Christmas treat. She gave in and the trio headed across the road towards the familiar café doors.

There was a fourth Westpac worker in the café that morning: Selina Win Pe, a senior finance services manager at the bank who was forty-three years old. She was, however, not known to Marcia, Viswa or Puspendu. Selina had caught a bus to the city early that morning, arriving well before eight. Conscious of being due for a meeting at 10 a.m. at the Kent Street branch several blocks away, she decided to duck into Lindt first to collect small Christmas gifts for her senior managers. Always punctual, she had glanced at her watch as she arrived. The time was 9.35 a.m.

The three lawyers with whom Louisa and Robin had struck up a conversation were also regular patrons. Julie Taylor and Katrina Dawson were up-and-coming young barristers, aged thirty-five and thirty-eight respectively, who worked at nearby chambers on Phillip Street less than a hundred metres from the café. The two were close friends and would usually drive in to work together, taking turns to pick each other up from their Eastern Suburbs homes.

That Monday morning it was Katrina's turn to drive. She turned up at Julie's house in her silver Subaru Forester at 8.15 a.m. and the pair headed straight into town. Katrina parked at the Hospital Road car park near the New South Wales Parliament.

Julie had to be in court by 9 a.m. for a brief appearance, so she went to her chambers to pick up her legal papers before dashing off to the courtroom. She and Katrina agreed to meet up later in the morning. The pair were such regulars at the café that Harriette, the barista, knew their orders by heart: Katrina usually had a dark hot chocolate with skim milk; Julie, eighteen weeks pregnant with her first child, was sticking with weak skim latte through her pregnancy. They nearly always shared Vegemite toast. For Katrina, it was a much-loved ritual at the start of her working day. Frequently they were joined by their friend, Stefan Balafoutis, aged forty, who worked two floors above them.

At around 9.20 a.m. Julie got a message from Katrina saying she and Stefan had headed to Lindt, and would she like them to order for her. Yes, a weak coffee, Julie replied. She got to the café at around 9.25, just as her order was being brought to the table.

Julie entered the room wearing a black Angel Maternity dress teamed with a charcoal grey jacket that barely concealed her baby bump. Once her baby arrived she knew she would be able to rely on the support and advice of Katrina, who already had three children.

Katrina was also stylishly turned out, drawing admiring glances from Robin and Louisa as soon as she entered the café. The young barrister came from a family of high-flyers. Her father, Alexander 'Sandy' Dawson senior, was a prominent businessman, president of the Royal Sydney Golf Club and a former managing director of the famous Arnott's Biscuits empire, once one of the country's most iconic brands. He'd stepped down to pursue other business interests after losing a takeover battle against the US food giant Campbell Soup in the early 1990s. Outside the turbulent business world, he and his wife Jane, a sculptor, had raised three outstandingly successful adult children, all now married with children of their own.

The oldest of the three, also known as Sandy, was a barrister (later to become a Senior Counsel) based in the city like his sister. He specialised in defamation law, a field that opened up strong media connections. Among those he counted as a friend was the influential 2GB broadcaster Ray Hadley, whose station the hostages would ring several times as the siege unfolded. Sandy the younger would contact Hadley that afternoon in a desperate bid to see whether the broadcaster had any better intelligence than he about what was unfolding inside the café.

Katrina's second brother, Angus, was the one to whom she bore the closest physical likeness. A senior partner at McKinsey & Company, Angus held combined degrees in Law and Economics, capped with a Masters in Management and Engineering from Stanford University.

As highly accomplished as her two brothers were, Katrina was poised to match, or even outshine, them. At the time of the siege, she was well on the way to becoming one of the leading barristers of her generation.

The circumstances of her birth had given her many advantages, but she worked hard to make the most of them. At Ascham, the prestigious Eastern Suburbs girls' school which she attended, her friends called her 'Tree' or 'Treen' (pet names she kept for the rest of her life), Katrina notched up every glittering prize school life had to offer: prefect, head of the debating team, keen sports player and dux of her final year in 1994, when she became one of only fourteen students across the state to achieve a perfect score of 100 in the Higher School Certificate.

At Sydney University she rowed, played basketball and tennis and competed in the intervarsity heptathlon—all while undertaking a combined Arts and Law degree. She spoke French fluently, and towards the end of her studies spent a semester at the Sorbonne, in Paris. On campus she lived at Sydney University's Women's College, winning a scholarship and becoming elected Senior Student in 1998 by her fellow residents. In 1999 she graduated with first class honours in Law, and somewhere in the midst of this whirlwind of activity picked up a ski instructor's qualification at the northern American resort of Whistler.

Conscious of her good fortune in life, Katrina had a strong social conscience. As a student she carried out pro bono work for the Redfern Legal Centre and the Tenants Union, and she became instrumental in setting up the ASK! Legal Service for kids, run by the charitable Ted Noffs Foundation.

In late 1998 she won a coveted position as a summer clerk at the legal firm, Mallesons Stephen Jaques. There she fell in love with fellow law graduate Paul Smith and they married in 2001. Katrina rose steadily through the firm, completing a Masters in Human Rights Law at the University of New South Wales in 2004. The following year, she picked up another prize, topping the New South Wales Bar exams, and soon afterwards joined the eighth floor at Selborne Chambers as a barrister, where she built up a practice in commercial and insolvency law. It was at Selborne that she met Julie Taylor who, like her, had been a gifted student. Katrina remained at Selborne Chambers for her nine years as a barrister.

Hers had been an extraordinary trajectory. Colleagues would say she made it all seem effortless but, like many of the highest achievers, her natural gifts would have amounted to less had she not married them to enormous application. Her colleague Jason Potts would later quip that her success was born of 'hard work, dedication, determination and, more often than not, sleep deprivation', especially after her beloved three children arrived. She joked to him once: 'I'm so tired that I fell asleep waiting for the water coming out of the hot tap to heat up.'

Despite her unbroken run of academic and professional success, Katrina kept her natural warmth and was a generous friend. At home she would greet guests with 'delicious home-made food', one recalled, while she 'played with the kids, cooked, chatted, danced and sang'. In one jokey email exchange with Julie she wrote: 'I can confirm that I am, in general, really very funny.' In a tribute written after the siege, Potts would quote these lines, adding, 'and she was'.

Katrina's brother Sandy would later talk movingly of his sister: 'I miss her judgment, her love, her happiness,' he told ABC TV's *Four Corners*. 'She was the glue in many ways in the family. We were all very close, we were lucky to be that way . . . But she was the embodiment of happiness and what our family was all about.'

The staff trapped inside the café had one advantage over the customers: a network of pre-existing relationships that would, in small ways, stand them in good stead throughout the siege.

Harriette Denny, the barista, had been at the café the longest, along with Tori and Paolo. Philippines-born, she had been raised as one of six children on Queensland's Sunshine Coast. Like Julie, Harriette was also pregnant with her first child although she had yet to share the news with her parents, co-workers and friends.

She had recently passed the critical trimester mark and, together with her partner Jorge, a stonemason, had spent the previous weekend making Christmas cards as a way of announcing the news. Inside each card was a photo of Jorge and Harriette, dressed in their Sunday best, proudly holding the ultrasound image of their unborn child. Harriette brought the cards into work that morning and stored them in her staff locker, intending to hand them out when she finished her shift. She was particularly looking forward to how Tori would react. Tori loved children and the pair had sometimes joked she might someday 'lease' him one of hers.

Finding herself menaced by a terrorist armed with a shotgun and claiming to have a bomb, Harriette was overcome with fear for her unborn child. She was also consumed with regret about the minor fight she had had with Jorge that morning, and with sadness that she'd not yet told her parents of the pregnancy.

As soon as she got a chance, when Monis gave her permission to visit the toilet under Fiona's watch, she secretly retrieved her phone from the locker in the tiny upstairs staff room opposite the women's toilets and rang Jorge. 'I'm in the building, I'm a hostage,' she told him, weeping while Jorge wept too. 'We told each other we loved each other,' she recounted later. 'Then I hung up on him as I was worried about taking too long.'

As the two young women left the bathroom, Harriette apologised to Fiona for being so 'emotional'. 'Maybe it's because I'm pregnant,' she told her. For Fiona, this would be the only tiny spark of good news in a long, bleak day.

Paolo Vassallo formed the third member of the tight-knit trio with Tori and Harriette. Aged thirty-five, he had been at the café since 2012, working full time as back-of-house supervisor and overseeing food orders, menus and food preparation in the kitchen. Tori was a friend to him as well as a manager, Paolo recalled later: 'There are not many who could do both properly, but he could. He always went out of his way to help you and genuinely wanted the best out of each person. He did that out of his own heart.'

Married with two young daughters, Paolo was now acutely conscious of the fact that he had not said goodbye to his family that morning. As the hours wore on, he became concerned about how his heart would stand up to the strain. With a childhood history of cardiac complaints, he had undergone heart surgery four times by the time he was twenty-seven years old. Escape was on Paolo's mind almost from the outset.

Tori Johnson, the man at the centre of the Lindt team, had grown up a world away from the busy centre of Australia's harbourside city where he now worked. His earliest years were spent at South Maroota, near the Hawkesbury River, north-west of Sydney. Here his artist father Ken Johnson and mother Rosie Connellan lived before moving to the Central Coast. The couple also had a younger son, Jamie, and from the time they were small children the boys were raised to look at the natural world with wonder and delight.

Rosie recalled inventing a game for Tori when he was barely two or three years old: 'At Maroota we would go walking in the bush, but I always worried about him wandering off and getting lost, so I would say to him, "We really need to keep our eyes wide open when we go walking, Tori, because you always need to be able to find your way back home." So he would observe everything, and on the way back I would pretend I didn't know which way to go. We would hold hands, and he would say "Don't worry, Mummy, I will get you home."'

Rosie and Ken encouraged their son's creative streak. 'We would come back from our walks with little treasures, and decorate the table with them,' says Rosie. 'He was always doing little sculptures.' Tori was fascinated by cooking, and later by fashion and architecture. In his teens he designed and built a small cabin on the property where he was then living. It was a source of great pride.

Ken and Rosie separated when Tori was seven. Rosie's new partner, Daniel Piazza, ran a landscaping and nursery business on the Central Coast north of Sydney. Daniel would become a significant figure in Tori's life for the next twenty-seven years. By the time Tori was in high school, Rosie and Daniel's four children—Tori, Jamie, their half-sister Camille and Daniel's son, Julien—were living happily as a blended family.

Tori remained close to his father, Ken, who had chosen his son's unusual Christian name. Long before Tori's birth, Ken had visited Japan and been struck by a picturesque gate he had admired by Lake Akan in Hokkaidō. It was a Torii gate, a traditional Japanese structure that stands at the entrances to Shinto shrines and symbolically marks the point at which human affairs move from the profane to the sacred. From this Ken took the name he bestowed on his oldest son, a name, he would write later, that 'meant the space between the physical and the spiritual'.

At school Tori became a diligent student who, outside his studies, was into 'just everything', Rosie says: 'He would build a stone wall with us, create gardens, and yet he could delicately decorate a salad with flowers. He got into designing clothes at one point: he held a fashion parade in the Gosford Leagues' Club and won the prize for best male outfit. He somehow had the gift of both sides of life, the male and the female. He was just so capable, at every level.'

Rosie learnt that her son was gay not long after he left school. He had begun a hospitality course at the International College of Management in Manly, developed in partnership with the famous Swiss hotel school César Ritz: 'He came up to us from Sydney one weekend and I could tell that something was disturbing him,' Rosie says. 'We went to a little café and I reached over for his hand and said, "We will sit here until you tell me what is troubling you." It took three hours but, when he told me, I said "That is wonderful!", and there was such relief on his face.'

Inspired by an exchange visit to Italy in his mid-teens, Tori yearned to travel. At twenty, he signed up to continue his studies at the University of Hotel Management in Switzerland, also run by César Ritz. It was there he met the love of his life, Thomas Zinn.

The pair became almost inseparable for the next fourteen years. Prior to running the Lindt Café, Tori had overseen a 300-seat restaurant at Cockle Bay on Sydney Harbour, but the job involved long hours.

He took the less well-paid Lindt job to get back his weekends and time with Thomas. Yet, in one of life's cruel ironies, it had been Thomas who began working around the clock in the months leading up to the siege, consumed by a big hotel project that was soon to launch in Sydney. Tori tried to lift the pressure off his partner, taking pleasure in cooking for Thomas, constantly asking Rosie for new recipes with which to surprise him: 'Thomas used to say, "I have six-star food on my plate every single night",' Rosie recalls.

Tori held tight to his hopes of becoming an architect and at night would leaf through architectural magazines or pore over home designs online. One day he was going to build his and Thomas' dream house. He kept a model of it in the lounge room: it would be in the country and there would be a dog, they'd decided. In the run-up to Christmas 2014 Thomas was on the brink of winning his first position as a general manager, and the couple were seeking a hotel posting abroad.

'It could have been a matter of weeks before they would have been gone,' says Rosie. 'We were preparing for this to be our last Christmas with them, because we knew that for the next one they would be established overseas.'

Under Tori's supervision that morning were five other staff members: Joel Herat, Elly Chen, April Bae, Jarrod Morton-Hoffman and Fiona Ma. All were under the age of twenty-three, and Jarrod and Fiona were just nineteen.

The least experienced of this youthful team was Elly, who was only on her third day on the job. Aged twenty-two, she worked part time while undertaking Actuarial Studies at the University of New South Wales. Her parents had dropped her at the station that morning and she had caught the train into the city, arriving at the café at around 8.30. She set to work cleaning tables and taking orders, and had been the first to serve Monis tea when he entered the café.

Joel, a slender young man with a Sri Lankan family background, was also twenty-two; he was in his second year of a Commerce degree. He lived at home with his younger sister and parents, Roma and Bruce. After finding the Lindt Café job online, he was working up to thirty hours a week. He was well known to regular customers and had grown particularly close to Harriette; they would often catch the train home together after finishing their shifts in the afternoon. He was the only staff member to whom she had already confided her pregnancy. Like Paolo, Joel held Tori in high regard, and looked upon him as a mentor.

Jieun Bae, known as April, had been at the café for around a year. She was twenty years old and was studying Visual Communications at Sydney's University of Technology. It was her first day back from holidays when she joined Harriette at the barista's station that morning; hers and Elly's fates would become critically intertwined as the siege dragged on into the afternoon.

The two youngest members of staff, nineteen-year-olds Jarrod Morton-Hoffman and Dentistry student Fiona Ma, would become key figures in the drama engulfing the café.

Fiona, the daughter of a refugee from the Vietnam War, had been working at Lindt for not much longer than Elly. She'd come down from Queensland to visit her sister Helen for the holidays. Helen was already working at the café and had suggested Fiona to the management as an extra pair of hands for the busy run up to Christmas.

Fiona caught the train into work that morning from her sister's place, uncomfortably conscious of the fact that her uniform trousers were still damp from being washed the night before. She'd nearly delayed her journey into work to dry them off, but decided against it. It was one of those tiny decisions with consequences that would reverberate through a lifetime.

Jarrod, a Communications student at the University of Technology Sydney, had worked at the café for around six months like Joel.

He usually took afternoon shifts, but on the morning of 15 December he was covering for an absent colleague. Jarrod jokingly complained to Tori about the early start. 'No, it will be a good day. Everything will be fine,' Tori told him.

Jarrod owed his striking looks to his Eurasian heritage. His maternal grandfather had met his Malay Chinese grandmother while working for the Australian Defence Force in Malaysia. His parents had been in the restaurant trade when they met, his father working as a chef and his mother (who later moved into advertising) working as a waitress. The couple separated when Jarrod was in early primary school. He remained his mother's only child, while his father went on to have two more sons with a new partner. The young waiter had a confidence that was unusual for his age, one of those survival skills sometimes acquired through navigating the complexities of an early life split between two households.

Jarrod had combined high school with casual work since the young age of fourteen, a factor that contributed to his ease in the company of adults. Although he had grown up in the city's affluent Eastern Suburbs, his family circumstances had been modest. He'd attended the local government school in Rose Bay, and gained entry to the selective stream in Year 8. He drifted through the middle years of high school, but during his last two senior years his competitive instincts kicked in and he did very well in his final exams. A brush with the law six months before the siege—the result of a high-spirited night out with mates—had taught him 'what happens when you make stupid decisions.' The siege would teach him another lesson about himself—his capacity for leadership.

Jarrod had not been as close to Tori as some of the others, but, as the day wore on, their mutual respect grew as each sought in their own way to find a solution to the group's terrible predicament.

To Louisa, it was clear Monis badly underestimated Fiona and Jarrod. Fiona was 'remarkable', Louisa said. 'And with Jarrod, he just saw him as a young boy who was a waiter at Lindt; he didn't grasp the full measure of Jarrod's character. He had convinced himself that he had co-opted him, but that was never the case. Jarrod was always one step ahead of him.'

CHAPTER 5

WAITING GAME

Above everything else, Monis craved media attention. Shortly after 10.00 a.m. he instructed Louisa Hope to pick up her mother's phone and call triple zero, getting her to repeat the key demand he'd forced Tori to make at the outset of the siege, with the primary aim of getting the Prime Minister to debate him on air. It was a slow process, with Monis constantly prompting Louisa from the background. The call lasted more than sixteen minutes.

In a second triple zero call, made shortly afterwards, Louisa passed on another message: 'He hopes the police do not make mistakes to come too close, and then we will be hurt, and the other bombs will be exploded.'

Monis told Louisa she'd handled the call well. 'You can be my secretary,' he said. No one was clear whether this was meant to be a joke. Then he told her to try to get in touch with ABC radio. 'I want Tony Abbott to talk to me on national radio so that my brothers who are spread out throughout the city, so that I can tell them not to explode the other bombs,' he repeated.

Louisa did her best to follow the blitz of instructions. 'I realised straight off the bat that the best way to survive this was to placate him; that if we could buy time we would only have to wait a little while and the cops would show up. That's what I thought would happen anyway.'

But she was having trouble finding her way around her mother's phone. Searching for a contact number, she ended up at the *The*

Book Club website instead of ABC radio. Monis' attitude towards her switched in an instant. 'That's not right,' he snapped.

In a flash Jarrod volunteered to take over, ready to seize on any chance to reclaim some small sense of agency, to push back against the creeping sense of paralysis. The outward face he presented to Monis was pliant. Inwardly, he was grimly defiant.

'Very early on I decided I'm either going to live or die on my own terms,' Jarrod would tell me later. 'If I'm going down, I'm going down, but I'm not going to let him just shoot me in the back with my eyes closed, or be left looking out sadly at Channel 7 for the world to see, with all the spectators going "Oh, poor Jarrod! He's died!" I was like, "No, I will go down kicking and screaming, or I will go down plotting my way out with everyone else."'

Taking over the media task also meant being allowed the privilege of keeping his eyes open, which might just marginally increase the odds of survival. 'If he started firing, at least I would be half a second more prepared to run.'

After a while, it became apparent Monis was failing to get anywhere with his demand to be put to air live on the ABC. Now he ordered the hostages to try other TV and radio stations instead.

This struck Jarrod as totally at odds with Monis' supposed stratagem of giving his so-called 'brothers' code words via the national broadcaster. If the brothers were out there waiting for a secret call-sign from Monis on the ABC, how would they know which other stations to listen to if the ABC plan hadn't come off?

Nothing about the situation made any sense. Nevertheless, the young waiter kept up the calls to the media. Although he was pleased to be doing something, it remained a thankless task. Repeatedly he would be put on hold or told that someone was going to call him back, or else Monis would order him to hang up because the person on the other end was asking too many questions.

At 11.36 a.m. Jarrod spoke with the content manager at SBS, Mark Cummins. In an eleven-minute call he explained that Monis wanted to make a public announcement to 'his other brothers of the Islamic State' not to blow up the bombs at George Street and Circular Quay and that he had no other means of contacting them other than over the radio.

Cummins asked Jarrod if the gunman wanted to make the announcement himself. Jarrod said he would consult with Monis. He then called back at 11.59 a.m., but the call was broken off. In time, the hostages would turn their attention to radio station 2GB.

Monis was starting to call the women by name but had come up with labels for some of the men, an effective way of psychologically diminishing them. Tori Johnson was 'Manager', Stefan Balafoutis was 'White Shirt' and John O'Brien was 'Old Man'.

'Those three guys he objectified up front,' says Louisa. 'And I don't think he had quite decided what he was doing with Paolo, because Paolo was in the black Lindt uniform and so in a way I think he just kind of visually grouped him with the kids.'

To Paolo, it seemed Monis was positioning the able-bodied males to keep them at the greatest distance from him. He had already threatened to shoot Tori if he had lied about the three entrances and exits from the café. Now he quizzed the manager about the closed-circuit camera in the room and the single TV set.

Tori told Monis the CCTV wasn't working and that the TV could not receive outside broadcasts, because it was on a continuous in-house advertising loop. Again, Monis threatened retribution if Tori was lying.

Tori had previously been bothered about the lack of CCTV inside the café and had mentioned his concerns to his mother on several occasions. He told her that it had been removed during a recent facelift of the café and not reinstated. It is one of the bitter ironies of the siege that, if the CCTV had been in place that day, it might have saved his life.

The café was a large space with a more elaborate layout than most city coffee places. It had a seating capacity of fifty-two. There was an area dedicated to retail chocolate displays; a section the staff called 'pick'n'mix', where customers could throw their own chocolate selections together; and several counters and cash points. A kitchen and small office were concealed behind a walled-off area running down the opposite side of the room to the Martin Place windows. There was a waiter's station at the back of the room, in the Martin Place corner nearest the lobby doors, tucked into an alcove out of sight of the windows. A small first floor annexe held the women's toilets and a cramped locker room for staff. The men's toilets were down three shallow steps at the back of the room and were more accessible than the women's.

For Monis to maintain control over the entire area and his eighteen captives he would have to attempt to direct every detail of their interactions with each other and the outside world. Most of the hostages were still lined up in the café windows, eyes closed, their hands pressed against the glass. Monis told them they would get 'points' for complying with his instructions, and lose points if they disobeyed. 'He was insisting on no talking, eyes closed, a lot of that, making sure we did not have eye contact or look at each other,' Louisa Hope says. 'It was almost like he knew what he was doing in that regard, like he had practised.'

Harriette was an early recipient of a point, for turning off the Christmas music that continued to trickle through the café speakers. There had been a terrible incongruity in having to stand, weeping, in the café windows with those cheery jingles piping away in the background.

Jarrod was feeling the same way: 'It was just too much: the juxtaposition of being held up by an Islamic terrorist, during Christmas, in a chocolate shop, with the carols running and beautiful red and gold trimmings everywhere and these season's greetings painted on the windows. Part of me was wondering how on earth my English teacher would have analysed such a weird scene.'

Monis allowed Louisa and her mother to remain seated—Louisa because she no longer had her stick, and Robin because of her age and relative infirmity. After a while John O'Brien started complaining that he too needed to sit, as he had a heart problem and was having chest pains. 'Look, I'm eighty-two—I need to see a doctor. Can we get a doctor in here? I could have a heart attack.' This was a ruse. John's heart was fine, but he hoped if a doctor was called in it would give the police a chance to enter. Monis did not take the bait, although he allowed the elderly man to take a seat. But John continued to be more in his face than others, and Monis seemed to mark him down as a nuisance and trouble-maker.

Other hostages were now needing to use the bathrooms and Monis insisted they go one by one, keeping their eyes closed while Fiona guided them. As the day wore on, he would entrust more and more tasks to the young waitress, including getting her to carry around food and water. Why he singled her out she had no idea. But she had been one of the first to serve him when he came into the café that morning and her outward appearance of unflappability was also no doubt a factor.

Fiona had secretly defied Monis in one important respect: she had kept her phone concealed in her pocket. Her role as bathroom escort meant she could now send messages from the toilets and offer her phone to other hostages to do so as well. Louisa wondered if it was the foolishness of youth or sheer bravery that was leading Fiona to take such risks. Most likely both, she thought.

Two hours into the siege, out of Monis' sight, Fiona sent a series of texts to her sister Helen: 'I'm OK . . . not out . . . but not dead . . . I love you guys'. She also sent messages to friends via the encrypted service WhatsApp, complaining among other things that Monis was using her as 'cover'. Yet being kept busy was a blessing of sorts. It was better than standing for hours with one's hands against the window.

There had still been no official response to Monis' demands. Police negotiators had taken up position in a four-wheel-drive parked on Elizabeth Street not long after the siege began, and by 10.40 a.m. they were placing the first of many fruitless calls into the café. Monis was using the hostages as go-betweens, refusing to come to the phone until he could speak with Abbott.

Before long he began blustering to his captives about how they had been abandoned by the government and how much better he was at looking after them than was the prime minister. Just look at how considerate he was being, he told them. They had water and toilet breaks! The old ones were allowed to sit down.

None of the hostages mistook any of this for empathy. Jarrod saw it as part and parcel of Monis' strategy of manipulation coupled with colossal self-delusion, a narrative of victimhood and moral superiority that the gunman had spun for himself.

Marcia described how the ups and downs in their captor's moods kept them all on edge: 'He was crazy throughout the day and he was crazy at night. So one minute he was [making] nice to us, the next minute he was horrible. So he was very unpredictable, and that's dangerous because you never knew what he was going to do in the next second.'

Repeatedly he told them that if anyone died, the hostages' blood would be on the prime minister's hands because 'the government doesn't care, doesn't care if you die'. Jarrod saw him as a kind of overgrown toddler, although infinitely more dangerous. 'He didn't seem to be following any sort of real logic—he was driven largely by anger and emotion.'

Paolo was certain of only one thing: that Monis had no intention of coming out of this alive.

A few of the hostages had concealed their phones from Monis and were using them sporadically and secretively to text friends and relatives during their toilet breaks. Now Marcia found a way to reclaim hers. When Monis had originally ordered them to turn out their pockets and put their bags and phones on the 'manager's' table she'd placed hers, with its distinctive pink flip cover, there too. But she was desperate to get messages out to her family.

On her way to the toilet, she seized a moment when Monis was distracted to snatch it back. Safely in the bathroom, she saw a stream of missed calls and texts from friends and family. Where was she? Was she in the café? Why couldn't they find her at work? She couldn't linger without arousing Monis' suspicion, but she sent a quick text to her niece, her sister and a few others using the same message she had sent to her husband George: 'At Lindt. Hostage.'

Then, to make it less bulky, she took the phone out of its case. She dropped the case in the bin, slipped the phone back in her pocket and returned to her place at the lobby door.

At 9 that morning, Ray Hadley had settled in for his regular three-hour morning show behind the microphone at Sydney radio station 2GB.

Hadley was one of the undisputed kings of morning talkback in Sydney, a top-rating tub-thumper who took a degree of pride in his 'shock jock' label. He had risen to prominence in this hypercompetitive milieu after a diverse career that included stints as an auctioneer and a highly successful sports broadcaster. Hadley's was the go-to program for hordes of Sydney taxi drivers and a generally conservative 'battler' demographic who felt he articulated their take on the world. But he was also an astute networker with high-level contacts across the worlds of sport, business and politics. That network included Police Commissioner Andrew Scipione and Katrina Dawson's barrister brother Sandy.

On that Monday morning, the program started normally enough. Regular guest, then Immigration minister Scott Morrison, came on air. At 9.50 a.m. Rhonda from Ropes Crossing phoned in to wish her partner a happy eighty-second birthday. But then normality evaporated as the first eyewitness reports from the Lindt Café started trickling in, followed by reports of bombs around the city, mass evacuations and news of an Islamic State attack in the heart of the city. The program switched to rolling coverage of the siege, and Hadley—for the first time ever—would remain at the microphone for the next eight hours.

At ten minutes after midday, the station's reception put through a call to Hadley's executive producer Michael Thompson in the studio, saying there was someone on the line claiming to be phoning from inside the Lindt Café. Thompson grabbed the call and found himself talking to Jarrod.

'Why are you calling us and not the police?' Thompson asked.

'I've been asked to call you by the man keeping us here,' Jarrod replied.

Thompson then asked how many people were being held captive and what the hostage-taker looked like, but Jarrod said he was not allowed to say.

Thompson signalled to Hadley that he should come off air and take the call, and was still trying to figure out how to make sure it wasn't a hoax when he was abruptly put on hold.

Then Jarrod came back on the line: 'He says he is going to shoot someone if police don't move back.'

Thompson, every nerve end tingling, handed the call to Hadley.

The veteran broadcaster spoke briefly to Jarrod, but got not much further than Thompson. Then the call went dead.

Jarrod's call had been triggered by Monis glimpsing several members of the tactical operations team, codenamed Alpha, who had based themselves in the empty vehicle loading bay just metres away from the café's fire exit onto Phillip Street. Shortly before noon two team members, given the pseudonyms 'Officer A' and 'Alpha 2' at the later inquest, decided to try and see for themselves what was happening inside the café. They sidled along the wall, with Alpha 2 holding tight to his 17.5-kilogram ballistic shield, which had a small transparent viewing port at the top. Reaching the closest of the café windows, they took turns sheltering behind the shield and peering in.

At first it was difficult to make anything out. The summer sun was high in the sky, and glare bounced off the hard stone surfaces and windows of surrounding buildings. The officers pressed their faces even closer to the window. Now they could make out Monis, with a shotgun in his right hand and gesturing with his left. In Alpha 2's opinion, the gunman seemed to be showing a degree of tactical nous—'like in the movies', the officer would say later. Monis was using hostages as human shields, ducking behind them as he moved around. The officers also thought they could see some kind of wire running from the gunman's backpack, although they saw no sign of a detonation device in his hand.

At that moment, Monis looked up to see the black-clad pair. He immediately ducked and grabbed one of the hostages. A minute or two later, a young woman approached the window bearing a handwritten sign: 'LEAVE OR HE WILL KILL US ALL. PLEASE GO'. Alpha team's leader ordered his two men to fall back at once.

The sign had been written by Jarrod at Monis' direction. Fiona had been ordered to carry it to the window. Not only could she see the police outside as she approached, but she could faintly hear them as well. It was surreal. 'This guy is fucking crazy,' she overheard one of the officers saying.

After first calling 2GB, Jarrod rang the triple zero emergency line and repeated Monis' demand that police pull back immediately or else someone would be shot. He was fearful, and for good reason: Monis had his shotgun at Louisa Hope's back.

It was a difficult conversation, with the emergency operator in one ear and Monis haranguing him in the other. The operator was trying to ask how many attackers there were, but Monis had forbidden Jarrod from answering questions like that. The young waiter tried to drop a hint: 'So I'm trying to say he has not harmed any *one* emphasising the word "*one*", and eventually she must have picked up on it because she said there is one gunman, and I said, Yes.'

Already he was conscious of how much the hostages' fates could hinge on these calls. 'I was worried about screwing it up, and someone else having to suffer for that.'

Half an hour later Jarrod was ordered to make another call to triple zero, saying Monis wanted cars parked near the café along Phillip Street moved. Again, this was accompanied by a threat if the demand was not met.

At 1.18 p.m., according to the station's records, Jarrod called into 2GB again. Ray Hadley broke from the studio and took the call off air. The veteran broadcaster was rattled; he'd never before confronted a crisis such as this. Like Jarrod on the other end of the line, Hadley was worried about making a mistake that might prove fatal.

'It was unprecedented, hostages making contact like that while I'm on air. I was terrified in the middle of it all that I could do something to jeopardise someone's life,' Hadley told me.

Hadley had the number for police chief Andrew Scipione's private line. After this second call from Jarrod, he decided to use it, and rang the commissioner for advice. 'The first thing he said to me was "Ray, I'm on conference, I'm on speaker with the premier," and I said "Well, mate, I'm getting hostages ringing me. What should I do?"' According to Hadley, Scipione told him not to put the hostages on air and not to broadcast any of the gunman's demands.

At 1.26 Hadley returned to the studio and came back on air. He told his listeners: 'Welcome back, I've just had an off-air conversation with the police commissioner because I'm really lost, I need to seek advice. I have been able to confirm that I am talking to a hostage inside the Lindt Café . . . The aim of this is to get these people out safely. The person wanted one of the hostages to come on the radio and talk. I wouldn't allow that to happen. I told the hostage that it would not be in his best interest or my best interest to allow that to happen because I am not a trained negotiator.'

Hadley pitched his next remarks directly at the gunman: 'I would appeal to the people or person holding these hostages: these are people that have nothing to do with what you are arguing or talking about. Mate, you've made your point. Let the people go and come out.'

Hadley's broadcast was being monitored inside the café. In at least two respects it had direct repercussions for the hostages.

At 12.15 p.m. a listener had emailed Hadley stating that the banner Monis had brought into the café was not the Islamic State flag but the more generic Islamic *shahada* flag. At 12.40 Hadley put this fact to air. Monis heard the broadcast, and grew angry. He wanted the message that this was an Islamic State attack to be unambiguous. Why was this being questioned on the radio?

'They just don't understand,' he told Julie Taylor at one point. 'This *is* the Islamic flag. Islamic State wants the formation of an Islamic state. You don't have to have the Islamic State flag to be involved with Islamic State. You don't have to join to be a member. If you say that you support Islamic State and you work for its cause, then you're a part of Islamic State.'

Nevertheless, he added a new demand to his list: that an Islamic State flag be delivered to the café.

Shortly after 1.30 p.m. Jarrod relayed this to a police negotiator. The flag was to be placed on the café doorstep. In return, one hostage would be released. About an hour later, Jarrod called back with an amended offer from Monis: one hostage released for an IS flag, two hostages released for a media broadcast that this was an IS attack on the café. To Jarrod, these shifting demands were evidence that Monis' initial claims about 'brothers' and bombs were invented.

The flag demand would come up repeatedly over the next few hours and the police failure to deliver one would feed into Monis' mounting sense of futility, wounded ego, anger and frustration.

'He kept saying to us, "The media are lying, politicians lie and the medias lie . . . They know what my motivation is, my motivation is and you tell them this, this is an attack by Islamic State on Australia. That's my motivation," Stefan Balafoutis told police later.

Hadley's on-air comments had another impact on events inside the café. The veteran broadcaster had been deeply impressed by Jarrod's composure, and told his listeners so: 'I've been talking to some nineteen-year-old who is really calm.'

Monis did not want calls from the café sounding 'calm'. He wanted the opposite: more drama, more emotional punch. He soon pulled Jarrod off the phones and returned the job to the women.

New South Wales Police had a standard response to sieges. The manuals called it 'contain and negotiate', meaning to clear a perimeter around the siege site, or 'stronghold', and deploy trained negotiators to talk the hostage-taker into surrender or release of any captives. In rare cases this might take days. Sometimes the officers in charge would ask the tactical unit to bring matters to an end if armed criminals were involved and they seemed unlikely to give themselves up.

The police had dealt with hundreds of such standoffs. Sometimes they were the result of a drug crime or robbery gone wrong. More often they were family or domestic violence incidents that had spiralled out of control. Usually it was an individual holed up alone; if there were hostages, rarely did they number more than one or two. Drunk or stoned offenders would frequently fall asleep, and police would haul them out.

But the Lindt Café siege was way off the scale of their previous experience. Never before had New South Wales Police faced a situation with so many hostages, let alone a siege being staged by someone branding himself a jihadi terrorist.

This threw up a particular dilemma. 'Contain and negotiate' held at its heart the possibility that you could strike some kind of deal with the hostage-taker. Yet the federal and state counter-terrorism plans explicitly ruled out making concessions to terrorists, although one clause in the national plan seemed to suggest that minor, non-substantive demands could be met. On the face of it, 'contain and negotiate' seemed completely at odds with key tenets of national counter-terrorism doctrine.

Following standard practice, shortly after 10 a.m. New South Wales police commanders had put a negotiation team in place to deal with the gunman. The team was led by a sergeant codenamed 'Reg', who reported up to an overall negotiations commander identified as 'Graeme'.

Graeme would spend the day embedded at the Police Operations Centre (POC) while Reg oversaw the negotiating team, which by lunchtime had moved out of the four-wheel-drive and into the forward command post set up at the leagues' club. Graeme and Reg were among the few full-time negotiators in the New South Wales Police at the time of the siege; a pool of officers, who had been trained up as negotiators and could step into the role part time if required, were drawn upon as needed.

Reg put a team of around six to eight officers together (numbers fluctuated slightly during the day and night) and tasked an officer codenamed 'Peter' with the primary negotiator's role. Peter kept up near-constant efforts to phone into the café, either on the landline or by trying the numbers Monis had allowed hostages to ring out on. Jarrod remembers the office phone ringing incessantly. Monis would never take the calls himself and only his whim dictated when the hostages were allowed to answer.

The commanders had decided there was going to be no broadcast from the café, and they certainly weren't going to wheel the prime minister out to haggle with Monis. But the police had not come up with anything to offer him instead. After a few hours, it was apparent the situation had ground to a stalemate.

'It was just going around in circles. The same repetitive thing, going on and on again,' Paolo said later. 'Nothing new was being brought to the table.'

There was one exception to the collective mindset among senior police against making concessions to Monis; it occurred early in the siege when Assistant Commissioner Mick Fuller was still in charge. Fuller felt there was merit in exploring with Monis a partial release of the hostages in return for speaking to the ABC. This was noted in Fuller's log: 'ABC request can be done, he [gunman] must stay on phone and release hostages so it can be facilitated.'

But Reg and Graeme did nothing to advance the idea. Graeme would later say it was a 'dangerous proposition' that conflicted with the ban on concessions in the National Counter-Terrorism Plan. He passed these reservations on to Reg, who accordingly did not act on the suggestion either—a fact to which Fuller remained oblivious. At the inquest Graeme denied that he had undercut Fuller's direction, saying that he didn't see it as an instruction at all, but just as part of a discussion. (Fuller would later tell me that he never intended to let Monis on air, rather his aim was to bring an ABC journalist to the POC to kickstart a negotiation.)

In any case, at around midday both Fuller at the POC and Superintendent Allan Sicard at the forward command post were relieved of their temporary command and Pioneer-trained police commanders took over. The new team in charge of the siege response was Assistant

Commissioner Mark Murdoch, running strategy from the POC, and a detective superintendent, who I will refer to as 'Lima', placed in charge of the forward command post at the leagues' club.

Once Mark Murdoch took over from Fuller, the idea of negotiating with Monis over ABC airtime was quietly despatched for good. It would be the first, and last, time any of the police commanders seriously entertained trying to meet Monis partway on an issue of substance.

The siege was starting to take its toll on the hostages, physically and emotionally. Several had health worries.

Julie Taylor had buttoned her jacket up at first, trying to conceal her pregnancy. Later she changed her mind. It was unlikely to be an added danger if he knew, she decided; and perhaps it was better if the others knew as well. Harriette continued to keep her pregnancy a secret, apart from telling Joel and Fiona.

Elly was having increasing difficulty handling the constant tension inside the café. Not long into the siege, she suffered a major panic attack and fell to the floor, hyperventilating and gasping for air. Marcia put her hand up, asking for permission to help and saying she had first aid training. Fiona checked with Monis to see if this was okay. He agreed to let Marcia attend to the young waitress and she showed Elly how to calm herself by puffing into a brown paper bag to help regulate her breathing. 'Think happy thoughts,' Marcia told her. 'You have a family; you will live and get through this and see them again.'

After calming Elly, Marcia moved to help Selina, who'd also said she was pregnant and was lying on the bench showing signs of distress. Marcia sat with her, wiped her face, and helped her slow her breathing. After a few minutes, Selina steadied herself, and Marcia went to relieve Julie who by now had been holding up the flag for close to two hours. Callously, Monis saw in the distress of some of the women another opportunity for ratcheting up the pressure. He wanted to share it with the media: 'Tell them a girl is ill on the floor panicking.'

At around 3.10 p.m., Katrina was ordered to call the police. A negotiator's dictaphone picked her up asking Monis, 'Can I tell him the condition of the room?'

Katrina then gave the police a rundown of the hostages who had health issues: 'There's one lady who's on the floor and she's been vomiting, I think she was in a state of shock . . . um. There's another lady who thinks she might be pregnant and she's also in a state of shock. Ah, and another lady is eighteen weeks pregnant . . . There's a mother and her daughter who are both on medication and there's an eighty-three-year-old man. Ah, he says three people have a heart problem . . . And there are many other people as well.'

The negotiator, Peter, replied, 'Sure, sure. Look I understand that, Katrina.'

Then the call seems to have broken off.

As they stood looking out from the café with the gunman at their backs, the hostages never knew when Monis' wrath might descend on them. At one point Harriette and Jarrod looked at each other over a plate of sandwiches left out on a table next to them. She indicated with her eyes that he should eat something. Abruptly, Monis pounced, waving the gun at her. 'Are you two planning an escape?' he shouted.

'No, no,' they replied, panicked words tumbling out. 'She's asking for a sandwich,' Jarrod said, while Harriette, talking over him, hastily explained she was encouraging Jarrod to eat.

'Be careful,' Monis warned. 'I would have misunderstood that and I would have shot you.'

By mid-afternoon, Paolo, John and Stefan were each quietly having thoughts of escape. Paolo sensed the police not far from where he was positioned at the Phillip Street windows, perhaps only two or so metres away. The sounds coming from the vehicle bay told him there was a group of them, not just the two officers he had seen earlier. He also thought he could make out a sniper in the Reserve Bank building opposite. He started to edge away from the centre of his window, thinking he would give the sniper a clearer line of sight if he could get more to one side.

Monis suddenly grabbed him roughly by the collar and planted him firmly back in the centre of the window pane. 'Here, not here,' he commanded.

But Paolo could not get the idea of escape out of his head. Soon he began furtively glancing towards the door that led up to the emergency exit. There were a few boxes stacked there, but otherwise the way looked clear.

On his next trip to the toilet, under Fiona's escort, he confided to her his urge to flee. He wanted her to come with him, but she said she couldn't: 'I can't leave people behind,' she replied. Wait an hour, she suggested. See if he releases anyone. If not, she would take him back to the toilets and they would discuss it again.

Fiona then led him back towards the Phillip Street windows, leaving Paolo toying with the idea of running through the door alone. But if he did, Monis might conclude Fiona had been in on it too and harm her. His heart was pumping, his mind in a whirl of competing arguments.

Had he given up his last chance to break out? The clock was ticking towards half past three. Events were about to make the decision for him.

Stefan had repeatedly been told off by Monis for not keeping his eyes closed. He was losing points, Monis warned. Stefan was worried:

'I thought, right, he's identified me as the guy with the white shirt who he doesn't like.'

Stefan was sure if any hostages were to be released, he, White Shirt, would not be among them. He wasn't old, sick or pregnant. If this was indeed an Islamic State attack, it was almost certainly going to come to a violent end. He whispered, half to himself, half to anyone who was nearby, 'I think he is going to kill us all.'

John O'Brien had clashed with Monis again. The older man was looking around too much for the gunman's liking. Monis ordered him to come and lie on the floor in front of him. 'It's too hard,' John complained. 'I'm eighty-two years of age and I'm not going to lie on the floor.' Unusually, Monis did not press the point.

John was convinced that he would likely not come out of the café alive either. All afternoon he had been eyeing a clear 'welcome panel' near the front door which partly partitioned off the main entrance from the café. He could see there was a narrow gap about forty centimetres wide between the Martin Place wall and where the partition ended. If he could squeeze through that gap, then maybe he could drop low and reach over to the low-set green button on the right-hand side of the main entrance, thus releasing the front door.

Stefan could see John assessing the gap. After a recent reshuffling of the hostages at Monis' direction, Stefan was now standing close to the elderly tennis champion. He whispered: 'Do you think you can squeeze through?'

John, because Stefan was on the side of his deaf ear, didn't hear him the first time. So Stefan tried again: 'Do you think the green button works?'

John heard him this time, but he wasn't sure. Faking a need to use the toilet, he went with Fiona and asked her if the button would work.

Fiona wasn't sure either: she had only worked there a week, she said. Returning to the banquette John decided it was worth a try. Little by little he began shuffling himself towards the slender gap.

Monis saw him moving: 'Would the grey-haired old man stop. Sit still and keep eyes closed.'

John froze, but not for long. A short while later he resumed his creeping journey towards the partition.

The octogenarian weighed up the risk for the last time. It was, he would say later, the worst few seconds of his life. Perhaps the green button was electronically locked. 'If this doesn't work, if he sees us getting out, then he will probably shoot the two of us in the back,' he thought. Grimly, he urged himself on. He was very close now; he waited until Monis seemed distracted by one of the hostage phone calls.

Suddenly John lunged for the gap and squeezed through as fast as he could, keeping low and reaching up for the green button. To his elation, the doors slid wide and he made a break through the opening, his still-sturdy legs pumping for all they were worth.

Stefan reacted instantly, racing along the banquette, reaching the gap and almost getting jammed for a heart-stopping second or two before he too made it out the door.

The others heard the noise of the doors and look around, stunned.

CHAPTER 6

ANOTHER ESCAPE

Paolo Vassallo, the food supervisor, is still at the Phillip Street window closest to the fire exit when he hears a sharp noise from the main entrance to his left. John O'Brien is streaking past outside, closely followed by Stefan Balafoutis.

The sight plunges Paolo into full flight-or-fight mode himself. Briefly he thinks about trying to escape the same way before realising Monis will now be fully focused on the main entrance. In a split second, he decides to run the other way, bolting for the kitchen corridor to his right knowing that a few short steps from there will take him up to the fire door and out onto Phillip Street.

For the police tactical operations officers, waiting poised for action in the vehicle bay next door, it's a shock to see John and Stefan flying towards them. 'Where the fuck did you come from!' the shield-bearer Alpha 2 exclaims, a jolt of adrenaline now running through the entire team. They're still braced, guns raised, when three seconds later the fire exit door swings open and Paolo comes tumbling out, almost slamming the door in the face of one of the police.

'Get behind me! Get fucking behind me!' Alpha 2 barks at him. Only a few minutes earlier the tactical police team had been denied permission to reconnoitre behind that door. Now it's clear to them for the first time that it opens freely from the inside.

Paolo begs them to go in, to do something: 'Please, what are you guys doing? He's going to shoot someone. You've got to go in, what are you waiting for? If you wait, people are going to die!'

The three escapees have the barest of exchanges with the tactical team members before they're hustled down to the leagues' club, where police investigators and negotiators are waiting to glean their first direct insight into the dynamics inside the café.

The three who've made it out are relieved beyond measure. But for Stefan and Paolo, the escape is bittersweet. They are free, but two of Stefan's close friends are still trapped inside the café, and seven of Paolo's workmates. Better than anyone else, Stefan and Paolo know what those still inside will be going through.

Inside the leagues' club the police teams are working cheek by jowl, manning phones, monitoring TV footage, Greg Parker's images (which are coming to them via a direct feed) and vision from cameras set up by their own technical branch. They confer around the small tables scattered through the upstairs bar area. Numbers are building up and soon there will be ninety or more people occupying the first and second floors of the old club building.

Running down the middle of the main room is the bar, where for decades some of rugby league's biggest names hatched schemes, drowned sorrows and celebrated club triumphs. That this is now the central hub of a counter-terrorism operation is more than a trifle incongruous. Indeed, the whole scene strikes Paolo as something of a 'shambles'. People are talking over each other, and he wonders how anyone can get their thoughts straight amid the clamour. He is surprised at how much he has lost track of time. It's not close to midday, as he had thought, but just after 3.40 p.m.

Paolo is handed over to negotiators and some of the intelligence team, who need to confirm the gunman's identity and learn more about how the hostages are faring. The police show him photos of Monis and Paolo remembers the mole on the gunman's cheek, which shows up in one of the images he is given to look at.

One thing he wants to get off his chest: he doesn't believe Monis' claim that there is a bomb in the backpack. Paolo acknowledges that Monis hasn't taken it off, not once. But it's not settling on the gunman's back in the way Paolo thinks it should do if there was really a bomb in there.

'The way he was moving freely and how the backpack was moving, if there had been something in there I just couldn't see how it would be moving that way,' he tells the officers. In his own mind, Paolo had dismissed Monis' claim of having a bomb.

The police take this on board, but say they can't dismiss the possibility of an improvised explosives device on these observations alone. It worries Paolo that he detects no sense of urgency at the forward command post to neutralise the gunman. He tells the police not to wait, that Monis is going to shoot someone and is not intending to walk out alive. By now the on-call consultant psychiatrist to the police has arrived and is listening in to the debriefings. He decides Paolo is 'babbling'.

The paramedics want to get Paolo to hospital quickly because of his history of heart problems. They tell detectives he can be questioned further once he's had medical clearance. Peering out of the ambulance windows, Paolo thinks how empty the city is. Nothing is moving—just police cars and a few emergency vehicles.

Stefan and John spend longer at the hostage reception centre, telling police everything they can remember. John is briefly examined by a paramedic, but is judged fit enough to undergo a 'hot debrief' with one of the negotiators before being taken upstairs to give a longer statement.

Stefan is elated at being free, but guilt-ridden about leaving Katrina and Julie behind. He impresses on the police the numerous times Monis has directly threatened the hostages. The man never puts the shotgun down, he tells the intelligence officers.

How many are now left in the café? He can't be sure; he was menaced every time the gunman caught him with his eyes open. He estimates around six staff members, perhaps fifteen hostages in all.

He stresses that Monis is fixated on getting the message out to the public that it's an Islamic State attack, and that politicians are lying about his motives. Like Paolo, Stefan is convinced, he tells the police, that Monis has no exit plan.

The escape of John, Stefan and Paolo triggered an immediate tumult in the café. Some of the hostages dived onto the floor or onto the banquette, while Katrina and Selina took cover under a table.

Monis was incandescent with rage and shock. In just a handful of seconds he had lost three of his human bargaining chips. 'The police have helped them. I've got to kill people now,' he ranted. 'Someone has to die now.'

Louisa had been sitting at the table she and her mother had occupied ever since Monis had seized control of the café. She'd heard the slight commotion as John O'Brien hit the green button to open the main door but, because she was facing towards Martin Place, she hadn't seen the men's escape and at first she too assumed the police had helped them out.

Suddenly a hand clamped down on her shoulder, dragging her to her feet. After sitting for so long, it was a struggle to keep her balance. Monis had her in his grip, with the shotgun close to her back. He was positioning her to face the door.

Louisa's mind started racing: 'This is it. If he doesn't shoot me now, whatever cop is about to come through that door is going to shoot me.' She lowered her head, braced for whatever was going to come next: 'I'm praying, just praying. There is a scripture in the Christian texts which says pray without ceasing—I know exactly what that means now.

'Then, quick as anything, Jarrod yells out, "No, they escaped, they escaped!" It's blurry for me now, but I remember Jarrod saying, "Don't kill, don't kill her". He was so quick on his feet.'

Jarrod recalls being less focused on who Monis had seized and more on the overwhelming sense that they were all now in great danger. 'I was in shock,' he says. 'There was this great commotion and I'm thinking, "I've got to stop this guy from shooting us, because he has misinterpreted what has happened. He thinks the police have somehow helped them get out". So I'm not focused on who he is grabbing; I'm just conscious of the fact that we are like sardines in a can with a shotgun to our back. And I know from playing way too many video games that pellets from a shotgun can spray out in all directions and cut down more than one of us.'

The others joined in trying to talk Monis down. And within a few minutes the gunman's threats eased off. Monis told them: 'Everyone thank Jarrod—if you hadn't spoken faster, I would have killed someone.'

With the immediate crisis averted, Jarrod felt relief. But niggling at the back of his brain was also a small sense of resentment. He felt the burden of managing Monis settling more heavily on his own shoulders now that three of the older men had gone.

'After that escape, I felt my role shifted—from trying to figure him out to keeping him under control. When he said, "Everyone thank Jarrod", my thought from that point on was "Well, this is my job now", not so much consciously but subconsciously. I became more vocal after that. And that burden of responsibility, it was something to keep you on your toes. I was OK with it, but also scared with it. Worried that if I made a mistake it would be my fault that other people died. I didn't want to live with that, but at the same time I felt I had to do it. It didn't really feel like a choice.'

Louisa could not understand why the police had not seized the chance to come in. 'I'm thinking, what's going on? Where are they? It would have been a great opportunity for them to come in.'

Monis spelt out the new deal forcefully, and unambiguously: if anyone else ran someone would die, and their death would lie on the head of the person who'd fled. 'You'll go to jail,' he told them. 'You'll be blamed everywhere by other people for running and you will go to jail.'

Jarrod couldn't help a dry inward laugh at this ridiculous legal logic, wondering what the two barristers left in the room were making of it.

Monis, still fuming, told the hostages they were going to have to put up with becoming more tired, because he had fewer of them to move around. 'He was ordering people to stand closer to him,' Elly would tell the inquest later. 'He said "Now I can't be as nice because there aren't as many people to rotate with you. So you're just going to have to stand there and be tired. Maybe I shouldn't be giving you food and water."'

There was no mistaking the sharpened sense of dread among those hostages who remained. A short time later, Louisa heard Monis grumbling to himself, and it chilled her. 'I should have killed that old man; he was a bother right from the start,' she could hear him saying. 'I should have killed him; I was going to kill him.'

Louisa wasn't sure if the others could hear the gunman, but she thought, 'Thank goodness that old man got out.'

Assistant Commissioner Mark Murdoch, the commander at the Police Operations Centre (POC), and Detective Superintendent 'Lima', in command at the leagues' club, were by now firmly settled into their respective posts. The two men would remain in these key positions until close to 10 p.m. It would be their call as to when, if at all, to send in the heavily armed tactical teams to rescue the remaining hostages during their period of command.

Both had undergone specialist counter-terrorism training and were part of the Pioneer cadre inside the New South Wales Police. Yet neither had faced the real thing before. Murdoch, the commander of Counter Terrorism and Specialist Tactics, was a force veteran with thirty-four years behind him. Lima had been involved in many domestic sieges: drunks, drugged-up criminals and domestic violence perpetrators holding a loved one to ransom. All the previous sieges he'd handled had resolved peacefully, except for one case where the perpetrator had killed himself.

Police brought to the Lindt Café siege their standard approach of 'contain and negotiate', which focused on trying to talk perpetrators out from whatever stronghold they were occupying. The underlying assumption seemed to be that the gunman would eventually surrender.

Police Commissioner Andrew Scipione and his deputy Cath Burn continued to pump out reassuring messages to the public: New South Wales Police had the situation well in hand, they said; these officers were the 'best in the world', optimally equipped and prepared for just such an event.

Behind the scenes, however, the reality was different. Lima was finding his 'eyes and ears' at the forward command post far more limited than he would have liked. Despite a number of attempts, police technicians from the State Technical Intelligence Branch had failed to get a listening device into the café, or anywhere near enough to pick up anything useful, leaving Lima to work without the live surveillance this would have provided.

Lima was also finding limits to his ability to access other data. With no computer, he could not access the electronic police logs that were readily available to the officers at the POC. These included the essential 'iSurv' log being used by the tactical police and the negotiators. Nor was he looped into the encrypted radio network of the Tactical Operations Unit (TOU). This meant he could not directly tune in to the observations from snipers posted around the café. Essentially, he was left reliant on oral reports.

His chief sources of field intelligence were: the negotiators' phone calls into the café (but they were frequently left to ring out); intermittent observations from the snipers, which were relayed to him by others; and the interception of the calls being made out of the café by the hostages acting on Monis' instructions. Lima was the man with the primary responsibility for sending in tactical operations if a crisis erupted inside the café, yet he had less information at his fingertips than the commanders several kilometres away at the POC.

The breakout of the three hostages at 3.35 p.m. did little to alter police tactics. Indeed, if anything the 'contain and negotiate' strategy became even more entrenched. Fifteen minutes after the breakout, a scribe recorded in Murdoch's log: 'Need to play hardball with negotiations from now on.'

Just what 'hardball' meant was unclear, given that police had not met and were not intending to meet Monis' substantive demands. The one slight concession they had made was to pull the TOU officers back from the café windows after Jarrod warned someone would be shot unless they did so.

The core negotiating team of around half a dozen officers (under the leadership of their coordinator, 'Reg') had set up in what was normally the gaming manager's office adjacent to the main bar area of the leagues' club. It was cramped, and they were hampered by the constraints of the old PABX landline system.

They were also feeling the lack of the specialist negotiators' truck they'd had for a decade or more. That vehicle, equipped with whiteboards, sound-proof booths and a phone line, had originally been provided by the Commonwealth as part of efforts to ramp up each state's counter-terrorism capabilities. But, after being struck by lightning in a storm in 2011, the damaged New South Wales truck had been sold at auction and not replaced.

The negotiating team were also thrown by their failure to make direct contact of any kind with the hostage-taker. It was something they'd never experienced before. At lunchtime they'd called in expert advice in the shape of a prominent Sydney psychiatrist whose involvement with the New South Wales Police stretched back more than two decades. The doctor arrived at the forward command post in a highway patrol car at around 1.15 p.m. There continues to be a court order forbidding publication of the psychiatrist's name, so I shall call him 'Brian'. A forceful character with a formidable intellect and great confidence in his own opinions, the psychiatrist knew the senior negotiators well.

Brian embedded himself with the negotiators in their 'cell' in the gaming manager's office, where he would be a near-constant presence for the next twelve hours, emerging to join the periodic hook-ups between the two police command posts and observe the debriefs of Paolo, John and Stefan. It was the first time Peter had ever worked with Brian physically present throughout a negotiation.

From very early on Brian formed the view that Monis was unlikely to commit a direct act of violence. He had not been given the full dossier on Monis' history, for example the police facts sheet, which set out in graphic detail the nature of the sexual assault charges. These he saw as acts of manipulative 'seduction'. He came to the belief that the gunman was someone who instead preferred to inflict harm indirectly through third parties (persuading Droudis to murder Helen Lee, for instance).

Brian drew reassurance from the fact that Monis was allowing the hostages water, food and occasional rest periods. This was not, in Brian's mind, consistent with someone who was prepared to kill. Nor were the gunman's actions so far consistent with what Brian knew of Islamic State—although the inquest would reveal he had little expertise in this area to draw on.

Listening to the three escaped hostages, Brian also came to the conclusion that Monis' anger was 'short-lived and followed by an ability to calm down'. Stefan described how Monis had held a gun to the back of one of the hostages when the police got too close to the café windows at around midday. Monis had followed the threat by saying, 'That was very close. I nearly killed you.' In Brian's view for Monis to say such a thing was 'actually quite encouraging' because 'when a gunman says to a potential victim, "I'm really glad I didn't have to kill you, boy! that was close", that's actually not nearly as threatening as you perceive it to be.'

Having decided that Paolo was overwrought, Brian discounted the warnings from the kitchen supervisor that the hostages believed Monis represented an existential threat. Neither the psychiatrist nor the police negotiators had grasped how much the mood inside the café had darkened since the breakout.

Monis was ordering the hostages to draw away from the windows and in towards the north-west corner of the café, furthest from the main door. Viswa and Puspendu were still close to the front. Jarrod was worried that if anyone else made an escape attempt it would endanger them all so he called out, suggesting the two IT workers also pull back towards the centre of the cafe.

Critically, Jarrod had not realised—and would not realise until after the siege ended—that Paolo's escape had been via the passageway and fire door near the kitchen, which were out of sight of the main room. 'I hadn't understood that it was possible to open the fire door without setting off the alarm,' he said. 'If I had, it might have changed my calculations.'

Under Monis' instructions, Jarrod and Fiona began piling chairs on tables, constructing a makeshift barricade around the nook where the gunman was spending most of his time, near the waiter's station. It was a spot that generally kept him away from the windows and out of view of the snipers.

The tighter bunching of the hostages inside the café brought more of them into what Jarrod had privately dubbed the 'kill zone'—the area where they would be most at risk if Monis began shooting or if the police stormed in. There would be precious little time, if any, to run if either of those things happened, Jarrod thought.

Monis had pulled Jarrod off the task of calling media outlets at around 2.30 p.m., partly because Jarrod had not been able to get any message broadcast and partly because of Ray Hadley's comment that Jarrod sounded 'calm'. Through the mid-afternoon Monis had Julie make a few calls, but her voice was too subdued for his liking and he complained she was not assertive enough. Selina and Marcia nominated themselves to take over.

Selina later recalled that, 'I felt that every possible action from Louisa and Jarrod and Julie had been taken to support [Monis'] requirements [without a result] . . . and that if I did not then take responsibility or charge of the situation and speak up with the values instilled in me . . . that we were going to die.'

She took the phone and immediately became more forceful: 'I said, "Just give it to me". I got on the phone and started talking to people, and I was saying, "Fucking do this and fucking do that".'

Monis liked what he was hearing. 'That's what we need,' he said, as if somehow they had all embarked on a joint enterprise.

Between 2.30 and 5.30 p.m. Julie, and then Marcia and Selina, made a flurry of calls to various media outlets under Monis' instructions. These included to radio stations 2GB and 2UE, Channels 9 and 10, and the ABC. With a growing sense that the hostages were being locked out from local media, Jarrod also turned to international outlets. He started trying to source contacts for Al Jazeera and the *International Business Times*. Jarrod suspected, correctly, that Australian media outlets were complying with police requests not to put the hostages live to air; perhaps overseas operations would be more willing to ignore that advice.

Late in the afternoon, Marcia posted a message on Facebook, dictated to her by Monis: 'Dear friends and family, I'm at the Lindt café at Martin Place being held hostage by a member of IS! The man who is keeping us hostage has asked for small and simple requests and none have been met. He is now threatening to kill us. We need help right now. The man wants to [*sic*] world to know that Australia is under attack by the Islamic State. The demands are: 1. Send an IS flag into the café and someone will be released; 2. To speak with Tony ABBOTT via live broadcast and 5 people will be released; 3. Media to tell the other 2 brothers not to explode the bomb. There are 2 more bombs in the city. Please share. He has shotgun and bomb.'

But like Paolo, many of the remaining hostages had come to doubt Monis' claim that he was carrying a bomb around. Monis had warned Fiona at the start of the siege to be careful of his bag because there were explosives inside it. Yet that didn't seem to fit with how careless he seemed to be with the backpack.

Louisa had similar doubts. 'It was just the vibe I got off him, the little inconsistences in what he was saying and the way he was behaving and the look of that bag. That bag didn't look packed. It just looked like he was wearing it the way anybody would walking down the street, no big deal. It didn't look like it was full or heavy or hard to manage.'

Jarrod noted Monis would often rest directly against his backpack when he was sitting down, or sometimes bump it into the hostages as he was moving around. The gun, however, was a different story. It was a very real and present menace. Monis never let it leave his hands, even at times of lower tension in the café.

Increasingly the bathrooms were becoming a place of refuge. The further away from Monis the better, as far as the hostages were concerned. As the day wore on, Fiona or Jarrod would take the hostages up to the women's toilet whenever possible for the few extra minutes of refuge it seemed to offer.

'For everyone the bathroom became this kind of point of respite,' Jarrod says. 'There you could talk to people, explain what was happening. Fiona had her phone, and so did Tori. So they could both get messages out that we couldn't do in front of Monis. Also, it just felt less dangerous to be up there. If the police were going to storm the café, it felt like you would be safer up there, you wouldn't get caught in the crossfire of a marble-encrusted room where shrapnel is going to fly and bounce off every surface.'

Jarrod saw Tori using the bathroom trips to text, maintaining a slender link to the outside world. The manager was intensely focused on doing what he could to prompt some external response to the siege in the brief intervals when he managed to stay out of Monis' sight.

But it was apparent to the others that Monis' animosity towards Tori was undiminished. At one point, when Tori wanted to use the bathroom, Monis turned to the room and asked, 'Everyone, the manager wants to go to the toilet. Should we let him? If he runs away, I'll shoot four people. What do you think?'

It was one of those recurrent moments where the gunman seemed to be toying with them for the sheer hell of it.

Julie asked Tori, 'Are you going to run away?'

'No,' Tori replied emphatically.

In private Tori said the same to Fiona, that escape would put everyone at risk. 'He was feeling responsible for the safety of the staff and the other hostages, he was feeling protective of all those in the café,' Fiona would say later.

Elly Chen had been lying flat on the floor soon after that first escape, partially obscured from Monis' sight by the makeshift barricade of chairs and tables he'd forced the hostages to assemble in the quadrant of the café near the waiter's nook. The escape of Paolo, Stefan and John, and Monis' reaction, had terrified her.

Now she crawled around until she was beneath Table 40, the table closest to the lobby doors, from where Monis had directed Tori to make the first triple zero call. She found April there already, and the pair curled together wordlessly for a while. These two young women barely knew each other, yet each now held the fate of the other in her hands.

The two girls had chosen this hiding place well. Apart from its proximity to the lobby doors, Table 40 was partially screened from Monis' view by virtue of being on the other side of the alcove wall where the gunman was bunkered in. Their position was further obscured from Monis' sight by a large, flat cardboard bear, around 1.3 metres high, advertising Lindt's gold-wrapped chocolate teddies, a popular Christmas treat.

Escape had been on April's mind since the three men broke out at 3.35 p.m. She knew Monis had threatened to wreak vengeance if any more hostages fled, but she was becoming convinced he was going to shoot someone soon anyway. She remembered how, when she was a child, her mother used to tell her 'no matter what the situation, if you keep your cool there is a way out'.

Now April began whispering to Elly that it was her mother's birthday, and that she needed to get home. April still had her phone, so she started contacting friends. One texted back: 'If you can escape, escape and escape with as many people as you can.'

Elly borrowed April's phone and sent a poignant text of her own to her boyfriend, Brendan: 'If I don't talk to you tonight, it's all good. I'll see you on the other side.'

As the afternoon advanced, Monis' attention seemed firmly focused on Selina and Marcia and their attempts to get some kind of breakthrough with the media over his demand for a live broadcast from the café. April decided it was time to seize her chance.

Quietly, she crawled out from under the table, reached up and began to draw down the latch at the top of the lobby doors. Elly coughed to try and cover the slight noise as April worked at it. Bit by bit, the bolt slid free. The girls' hearts were in their mouths.

Jarrod, finally noticing what April was up to, mouthed at them not to go. He was worried about the deal cut with Monis less than two hours earlier. But he could see April was determined. Inwardly resigned now to the girls making their attempt at freedom, he nudged the cut-out bear to a more acute angle, which shielded them even better from Monis' view.

Elly, still terribly worried about the consequences for the others if they fled, agreed with April that the pair would wait until one of the hostages was talking loudly on the phone, hopefully distracting Monis before they tested the door.

That chance came just before 5 p.m. With Marcia or Selina on the phone again (no one was sure later whom), April crawled out from under the table and, still on her hands and knees, pushed open the swing door leading into the lobby.

Elly followed. Gamely, she resisted the urge to run as soon as she got out, instead taking a few precious seconds to close the door as gently and quietly as she could. Then she was out too, following April through the lobby and racing down the stairs that would take them out onto Martin Place.

Other than Jarrod, no one had seen them working the bolts. Monis and most of the other hostages remained completely unaware of their silent disappearance. But Harriette came down the stairs from the toilet a short time later. She glanced under the table and noticed the girls had vanished. Looking at Tori, she tried to indicate with her eyes and with her finger that April and Elly had got out. 'I gave him a little smile and he just looked at me. I think he knew.'

CHAPTER 7

LOST OPPORTUNITIES

The two young women, still wearing their dark brown Lindt aprons, bolted down Martin Place towards the lower corner of the block where a second Tactical Operations Unit (TOU) team had been embedded since late morning. April, her face a mask of sheer terror, collapsed into the arms of one of the tactical men. An alert photographer caught the moment and the shot was soon broadcast around the globe, becoming one of the defining images of the Sydney siege.

The girls were rushed to the hostage reception centre inside the leagues' club, where Elleanor Gillard, the legal clerk who'd been belatedly rescued from Frederick Jordan Chambers opposite the Lindt Café, was still in the process of giving police a statement. She saw Elly and April come in, supported by the police, each young woman sobbing uncontrollably. 'They looked like they would crumple to the floor', Elleanor remembers. 'The people who were carrying them were counting and telling them to breathe. They were carried up another set of steps to the upstairs level—it was very upsetting to see their distress.'

Elly had to be tended to by an ambulance officer. But one of the police negotiators, 'Sasha', soon picked up on a vital piece of intelligence from the young woman—that the café's lobby doors were unlocked, at least for the time being. She dashed upstairs to pass this on to senior commanders.

Like the three men who'd escaped before them, April and Elly could not be sure of the exact numbers left behind in the café and had little more than first names to go on, apart from the staff—unsurprising, given how little chance Monis had given his captives to interact with each other.

The pair looked closely at photos taken by the snipers and at the Channel 7 footage, trying to help police get more clarity around who was still inside.

April reported that Monis' backpack looked full, but she had not seen anything sticking out of the top of it—contrary to the police report earlier that day that wires could be seen protruding from it.

She was less sure of whether Monis had detected them leaving. The girls had made their escape through two sets of glass doors: the art deco swing doors from the café into the lobby, and then a set of outer doors from the lobby onto Martin Place, that were electronically operated. It was this second set April feared might have made a noise as they opened.

Police log entries showed a degree of confusion about whether Monis had actually registered the girl's escape. Some officers were aware there was doubt about the issue; others appeared not.

The message about the doors being unlocked did not filter through to the deputy tactical commander at the forward command post until some two hours later. And the officer charged with planning a possible rescue attempt only realised the doors were unlocked by chance when he noticed them ajar on the CCTV footage from the lobby some time after the escape.

The forward commander, Lima, also said later he could not remember being told that the café's lobby doors were unlocked. He missed seeing the escape on screen altogether. Had he done so, he would have noted for himself how incredibly careful and gentle Elly had been closing the café's rear door behind her.

A police log entry made at 5.34 p.m. seemed to misinterpret these unknowns. 'The fact that someone escaped appear [*sic*] to have frustrated the POI [person of interest]' the entry read. The erroneous narrative developing inside police command was that Monis' bark was worse than his bite.

There was one senior police officer whose expertise and counsel could have been invaluable had he been on duty that day. But that man, Deputy Commissioner Nick Kaldas, was at home on extended sick leave.

Kaldas, head of New South Wales Police Field Operations, had taken leave three weeks before the siege on the advice of his doctors because of a heart condition. But anyone who knew him well also knew the backstory that had sent his stress levels soaring. It was the tale of a bitter feud that had split the force's leadership team asunder. In the weeks leading up to the siege, Kaldas had hit rock bottom. He would later tell Jana Wendt in an interview with Fairfax's *Good Weekend* magazine that he spent much of this period 'sitting in a room with the blinds shut and not wanting to go out'. That this should have been the case at a time when Sydney was paralysed by the first major Islamic-inspired terror attack on Australian soil was unfortunate, to say the least.

Kaldas was the country's best-connected and most internationally recognised counter-terrorism expert. He knew Sydney's labyrinthine Middle Eastern communities better than any other senior officer in the force.

Born in Egypt, where he was christened Naguib by his Coptic Christian parents, Kaldas had grown up speaking Arabic, French and English. The family came to Australia when he was twelve settling in the ethnically diverse inner-west Sydney suburb of Marrickville, where he'd attended the local Catholic school. He'd worked briefly as an insurance clerk before joining the New South Wales Police, where he had now served for more than three decades.

A solidly built, olive-skinned man with an easy manner, Kaldas was a cops' cop, the kind other police would 'take a bullet for', a senior colleague told me. He had worked undercover with the New South Wales Drug Crime Commission in the late 1980s before going to Homicide for a decade, including four years as its boss. Later he'd commanded the Gangs Squad and been the assistant commissioner in charge of counter-terrorism. He had worked closely with the Middle East Organised Crime Squad helping to disrupt Sydney-based Lebanese organised crime gangs.

Unusually for a state cop, he also had first-hand operational experience in the Middle East. In 2004, after the disastrous invasion of Iraq, he'd gone to Baghdad to help rebuild the Iraqi police force for the US-led Coalition Provisional Authority. It was dangerous work, moving around the Iraqi capital under threat from roadside bombs and mortar fire from Islamic insurgents. Five years later, in 2009, he undertook an equally delicate mission for the United Nations, leading a special tribunal investigating the assassination of former Lebanese prime minister Rafiq Hariri.

Kaldas' can-do attitude had won him the admiration of Premier Mike Baird's predecessor, Barry O'Farrell. In 2013, O'Farrell had personally intervened with police chief Andrew Scipione to ensure Kaldas was placed in charge of an operation to crack down on a vicious spate of shootings in Sydney's south-west orchestrated by the Brothers for Life gang. Kaldas won promotion to deputy commissioner in 2007 and commanded specialist operations before being moved to field operations.

It was well known inside the force that for some time both he and fellow deputy, Cath Burn, had been eyeing the commissioner's job once Scipione retired. But the two personalities were as different as chalk and cheese. Where Kaldas was earthy and effusive—'Mediterranean', as he would sometimes joke at his own expense—Burn's professional demeanour was cool and reserved. She was respected for her intelligence and diligence. But she did not appear to inspire the same 'gut' following as he did within the ranks.

Cath Burn grew up one of six children, the daughter of a midwife and lawyer father who had moved on to become a GP. She'd begun studying economics at university before abandoning the degree to join the police force at nineteen. She reached her goal of becoming a detective by the time she was in her early twenties. Burn then returned to her studies part time while continuing to work in the police force, winning a prestigious university medal in Psychology. That achievement spoke volumes about the steely discipline that lay beneath her cool demeanour.

A keen swimmer, whippet-thin in build, Burn had climbed the ranks by way of internal affairs and corporate services and a well-praised stint in charge of the inner-city Redfern Local Area Command. She was promoted to deputy commissioner in June 2010 and in 2012 took over Specialist Operations, which gave her senior line responsibility for counter terrorism at the time of the siege.

In the ordinary course of events, a degree of healthy professional rivalry between Burn and Kaldas would have been natural. But their relations had turned toxic because of a long-festering dispute over a police operation known as Operation Mascot, a saga stemming from events of fifteen years earlier.

Mascot had begun in 1999 as a probe into police corruption. Run jointly by police internal affairs and the New South Wales Crime Commission, its tentacles soon spread to ensnare more than a hundred officers, who were secretly placed under surveillance by their colleagues. An unwitting Nick Kaldas was among those targeted.

Kaldas was furious to discover some years later the scale of the secret bugging he had been subjected to: not just his home and office, but the home of his former wife and their children as well. Many of the surveillance warrants would later be judged of dubious legality and it would emerge that investigators had relied heavily on a corrupt officer turned informant, known as M5, to help them identify targets.

Cath Burn, then a Mascot team leader, had been in charge of handling M5. Kaldas would later accuse her team of proactively putting his name forward to the informant as a possible target. Despite the fact that nothing adverse was ever found against him, Kaldas became convinced the Mascot operation had dogged his career, blocking his advancement at several critical points. (Burn would later complain the saga had blighted her life as well.)

The pressure for an independent inquiry mounted to the point where the state government could no longer ignore it: 'a hundred angry men' demanding answers, as Kaldas put it. Eventually the premier referred the whole sorry mess to the state ombudsman, but that inquiry too was soon mired in controversy. Kaldas accused the ombudsman of going after the wrong quarry, and putting his own integrity under attack again.

In the run-up to the Lindt Café siege the behind-the-scenes warfare was reaching its zenith, with the two deputies barely on speaking terms outside of regular executive meetings. A third deputy, Dave Hudson, frequently referred to himself as 'Switzerland' (a jokey reference to that country's neutral status during World War II). Burn insists that despite the tension, 'We continued to have a professional relationship.'

But the split polarised the New South Wales Police between Burn and Kaldas camps, with Scipione—rightly or wrongly—perceived as favouring the former. One senior officer described the chasm between the two key deputies as 'all pervasive, overwhelming—at times it felt like it was the main issue at headquarters.'

That it had persisted for so long mystified senior people at the federal level who regularly came into contact with all three of the major players. Former prime minister Tony Abbott told me: 'I had good relations with Andrew Scipione, likewise Cath Burn, likewise Nick Kaldas. It was always a mystery to me why people who struck me as highly competent and highly professional seemed to have this Hatfield and McCoy feud going on.'

On the morning of 15 December, Kaldas was at home watching the news about the siege when he got calls from three prominent members of the Sydney Islamic community. They were the Grand Mufti of Australia, Ibrahim Abu Mohammed; the president of the Lebanese Muslim Association, Samier Dandan; and Khaled Sukkarieh, head of the New South Wales Islamic Council. All three offered to help. The Grand Mufti said he would attempt to talk to the attacker and tell him that what he was doing was wrong and un-Islamic.

Kaldas contacted Jeff Loy, the senior officer who was acting in Kaldas' role as Deputy Commissioner, Field Operations, to tell him of the offers. Loy says he passed the information on to other members of the police executive, which included Scipione, the other two deputies Burn and Hudson and later to the man running the Police Operations Centre (POC), Assistant Commissioner Mark Murdoch.

Kaldas waited for a response to the information he'd passed on. None came. By late morning, he followed up with a text to Loy to say that the offers were still on the table. Loy texted back saying he had informed Murdoch, but Kaldas heard nothing more. It was as if the offer had disappeared into a black hole.

Even odder was the fact that news of the Mufti's offer never made it through to the people with arguably the most interest in knowing about it—the police negotiators at the leagues' club and Graeme, the negotiator commander at the POC. Graeme would later admit that not only was he unaware of the Grand Mufti's offer, but that he knew nothing of the prominent Muslim cleric's language, ethnic background or religious affiliation. The failure to hear back about the messages he had conveyed left Kaldas dumbfounded.

The police called a meeting of Islamic community leaders at Campsie Police Station, in Sydney's south-west, on the afternoon of the siege, seeking any fresh information on Monis or possible accomplices.

Later that day more than forty Muslim organisations across the country issued a statement condemning the attack: 'We reject any attempt to take the innocent life of any human being, or to instil fear and terror into their hearts,' the Islamic leaders said. 'Any such despicable act only serves to play into the agendas of those who seek to destroy the goodwill of the people of Australia and to further damage the religion of Islam.'

Senior police, meanwhile, were still struggling with how to respond to Monis' insistent demand for an Islamic State flag. At first the forward command post seemed open to the idea of procuring him an IS banner, and instructed police stations in western Sydney to try and track one down.

Midway through the hunt for the flag, police commanders had a change of heart. What if Monis wanted it as the backdrop for an atrocity? At the leagues' club senior officers discussed the prospect with alarm.

'Can you imagine the news?'

'Yeah, police deliver flag to terrorist who then executes people under it.'

'Do you think it would be a good look?'

'I'd be concerned about the news that police delivered him a fuckin' flag, anyway . . .'

By 5 p.m. a flag had been found and delivered to command headquarters, but by then Assistant Commissioner Murdoch at the POC had flatly ruled out delivering it to Monis.

The hostages were never told the demand was not going to be met, or why. Instead, they saw it as more police stalling, feeding both their and Monis' mounting frustration. 'They never explained it,' Louisa said. 'Later they would argue that they were trying to give us hints, but a straight line would have been better for all of us. It never occurred to me that [concern about execution] was why the police wouldn't give us a flag. He had not displayed knives at that stage, there was only the gun and threat of the bomb. Beheading hadn't even occurred to us.'

Inside the café, Monis continued to turn the screw on the flag issue. He instructed: 'Ask the negotiators "Are you happy not to exchange one life for a piece of linen?"'

While Scipione and Burn continued to assure the public that the New South Wales Police had the best negotiating team 'in the world', it was becoming more evident by the hour that the police negotiators were both poorly resourced and ill-trained for a terrorist event.

By mid-afternoon scores of people were encamped in the public bar area of the leagues' club, now doubling as the forward command post: technical branch police, investigators, an intelligence unit, fire brigade officers, ambulance officers, staff officers, general duties police and, tucked into one corner, a small group of officers from the Australian Defence Force.

At times the atmosphere was what Lima would later describe as 'extraordinarily manic'. Trying to get away from the hubbub, the four core members of the negotiating team sought a quieter space where they could concentrate on trying to get through to Monis.

By now they were set up as best they could in the office of the club's gaming manager—a far cry from the purpose-equipped negotiators' truck they had once had. Reg, the team leader, would later cite the loss of the truck as a reason why his team struggled with the unique challenges of the siege. But, as one negotiator admitted to the coroner, even if the truck had been available, deploying it to the siege site would have detached them from the forward command post and created a whole new set of challenges.

Privately, investigators did not view the absence of the negotiators' truck as the reason for the negotiators' problems. Instead, the ensuing catalogue of errors would come down to poor record-keeping, inadequate training, lack of imagination and dogged persistence with tactics that were clearly unproductive long before the siege ended.

No lateral thinking, for instance, was brought to the task of managing the limited phone lines into the forward command post. Calls to and from the hostages were vital—the only link the negotiators had with the gunman, albeit an indirect one. But the old-fashioned PABX system in the confined space of the gaming manager's office was bouncing calls all over the club whenever the main line was tied up. Somehow it didn't occur to anyone on the negotiating team to restrict all outgoing calls to a mobile and to leave the landline free for incoming calls from the hostages.

The negotiating team was also poorly equipped. Lead negotiator Senior Sergeant 'Peter' revealed at the inquest that he had no access to a computer or iPad, and only a 'little Nokia-type mobile' rather than an iPhone. Reg and Sasha had iPads but they could not access all the data bases being used at the POC.

Peter was also meant to capture his calls with hostages on a dictaphone but would occasionally forget to switch it on or off, later declaring himself 'not real good with technology'. After the siege, investigators found no record of the negotiators' calls made before 1.34 p.m., or after 5.50 p.m.—the calls having been not recorded, recorded over or not downloaded.

There was no attempt by the negotiating team to systematically log each of Monis' demands and systematically track how they were being responded to higher up the chain of command. Something as simple as laminated paper or butcher's paper could have overcome the problem, but no one came up with that solution.

This failure would have major consequences in the final stages of the siege, when police lost sight of a key demand of Monis' to have the Christmas lights in Martin Place switched off. The lack of 'situation boards', or any other means to keep track of demands and responses, would later be heavily criticised at the inquest by an expert review team brought in from the United Kingdom.

Lawyers for Katrina Dawson's family would also later drive the point home, listing all the surfaces where negotiators could, with a little thought, have 'fixed, propped or hung up' a whiteboard, or even large sheets of paper, to keep track of progress: 'wall spaces, a window ledge, a desk, a computer monitor, chairs, boxes, a safe, a filing cabinet, shelving and the back of the door'.

As if he didn't have enough on his hands the negotiations commander, Graeme, was juggling the demands of three other sieges elsewhere around the state while also dealing with the Lindt crisis. A male wielding a machete was keeping police at bay on the mid North Coast; on the far North Coast a drama involving an armed offender was unfolding; and in western Sydney another offender was holed up in a house with a large kitchen knife.

Graeme, who was not at the field post with Peter and Reg but embedded at the POC, would end up working a thirty-three-hour shift, from early on the morning of the siege until well into the next day. Peter, the primary negotiator at the forward command post, was not rested either. He had had only five hours' sleep the previous night but would be left in place as lead negotiator for fourteen hours.

The paucity of Peter's preparedness for a terrorist event would be laid bare at the inquest. As a general negotiator he had received just four weeks' formal instruction between 2004 and 2006, supplemented by field observation. The only structured training he had received in relation to a terrorist attack had been a one week 'skills enhancement' course on Islamic-related counter terrorism in 2009. There had been nothing of that nature since, although he told the coroner he viewed intelligence reports weekly and attended occasional lectures from visiting experts.

Most striking, however, was that Peter had never before encountered a siege with hostages, even though he'd attended a hundred or more negotiations over the previous decade.

The most obvious and overriding failure was not the negotiators' alone. It was the collective decision at the command level to cling to the 'contain and negotiate' strategy without introducing any fresh initiatives for the entire duration of the crisis, long past the point where it was clearly failing.

Over and over the negotiators called the café landline, and called or texted Monis' phone (which he never once answered during the siege) or the numbers that the hostages had been allowed to call from. Whenever a hostage was permitted to answer, the police negotiating team would repeat the request to speak with the gunman. Each time that would be refused. It was, from the hostages' vantage point, an endlessly repeating and dispiriting cycle.

Much later, at the inquest, Graeme was asked whether he could identify 'any single milestone' that had been achieved via negotiation throughout the course of the siege. The only one he came up with was the 'continuation of buying time'.

Islamic fundamentalist terror had been on the radar of every western government since the Twin Towers attacks of 2001. Yet New South Wales Police had seemingly done nothing to adjust or expand their negotiations doctrine to prepare for the reality of a terror attack at home.

As the evening wore on, the tactical commander at the forward command post and his colleague, the tactical adviser at the POC, were the only senior officers who began chafing at the 'contain and negotiate' mantra.

'Contain and negotiate' had come to dominate the New South Wales Police mindset following trenchant criticism in the late 1980s and early 1990s from the state coroner and the legal profession about tactical units using excessive force. The two most notorious cases were those of Gundy and Brennan. David 'Tony' Gundy, an Aboriginal man, was shot dead by police in his inner Sydney home after a dawn raid went wrong in 1989. Darren Brennan received terrible wounds to his face from a police shotgun in a similar raid the following year.

The Gundy death was referred to a royal commission and in 1991 the police tactical units were overhauled and folded into the new State Protection Group. The police chief at the time, Tony Lauer, announced that henceforth 'the use of force will be a last resort'.

The subsequent overhaul of special operations had led to reform in favour of managing high-risk situations patiently and with a view to seeking a non-violent end. That had served the police well in the intervening years, but there had been no fresh thinking about its applicability in an age of jihadi-inspired terror.

This would become glaringly apparent at the Lindt siege inquest, when the late-night forward commander 'Victor' continually referred to 'contain and negotiate' as a kind of 'golden thread' running through the police management of the siege. Time was his 'friend', he stated repeatedly.

The plain fact was that while Scipione had formally declared the siege to be a terrorist incident, a number of his senior officers seemed unconvinced Monis was actually *acting* like a terrorist. Monis did not look like their idea of a textbook kind of Islamic State attacker: he hadn't executed anyone; no one had yet been shot or injured. And Brian, the psychiatrist, stoked these doubts, saying the incident did not fit with IS methodology. He diagnosed Monis as a grandstanding narcissist who was unlikely to commit violence by his own hand and whose primary goal was media attention.

The forward commanders became convinced they were looking at a hostage-taker who was in reality 'displaying behaviours of a domestic siege situation'. Having put this frame around Monis' behaviour, the senior police then compounded their underestimation of his capacity for violence by misconstruing cues from inside the café. Forward commander Victor, for instance, thought that Monis was allowing hostages to use their phones and go to the toilet at will and unaccompanied. He took comfort from the fact that Monis was permitting them to have food and water.

A note in the log of the late night POC commander, Assistant Commissioner Mark Jenkins, noted 'hostages moving around freely, jovial, casual (going upstairs freely)'.

When Monis thrust a gun to the back of Louisa at around 1 p.m., threatening to shoot her if the police did not pull back from the windows, senior officers would later discount this as evidence of an imminent threat. 'In these types of situations threats are made fairly regularly,' the head of the State Protection Group explained at the inquest. Monis was not 'physically assaulting' the hostages. 'There was obviously mental strain but there was no physical assault . . . We were buying time and these jobs do continue for hours,' he said.

Reviewing what he'd heard from senior officers in the witness box, the coroner would later point to deep 'organisational culture' as a factor in this inability of the senior police to realistically assess the level of threat Monis represented, and to think beyond 'contain and negotiate'.

—

At 2GB Ray Hadley was still on air, well past his usual noon sign-off time.

At 2.30 p.m., Jarrod called in once more and said the IS 'brother' was still agitating for his demands to be met. Hadley, again fretting over how to handle hostage calls, asked his executive producer, Michael Thompson, to see if he could get through to Tony Abbott's office. 'I wasn't trying to get the PM *on* air,' Hadley later explained. 'I was trying to get him off air [for some advice]—because generally I get on well with him.'

Thompson texted Adrian Barrett in the PM's press office, saying Hadley was after a private conversation about the siege. Barrett came back with the message that 'we just don't know where this thing is going to go, it's best leaving it to the police who have operational control'.

Hostage Julie Taylor came in on the 2GB open line (the number reserved for talkback callers) at 2.44 p.m. She stayed there only briefly before saying 'hang on, I've got to go' and hanging up.

The most chilling call came in on Thompson's landline. A caller with a strong Middle Eastern accent announced, 'I am the terrorist. I want to speak to Ray Hadley.'

Thompson replied, 'How do I verify that it's you?'

The caller responded, 'Do you want me to kill someone?'

Shocked, Thompson handed the off-air call to Hadley, who judged it to be a hoax. But the call haunted Thompson for weeks; he found himself replaying it constantly in his head, wondering if he had 'nearly got someone shot'.

Thompson and Hadley decided they needed a police officer at the station to handle the incoming hostage calls. They conveyed the request to Scipione and the police media unit. An hour later police negotiator 'Steve' turned up at the studio.

By now Hadley was getting distressed texts from his friend, Sandy Dawson, Katrina's brother. 'Sandy said he thought his sister was in there having coffee with her friend who was pregnant, and he was very fearful,' Hadley recalls.

Just after 5 p.m. a call came in on the station's open line, this time from Selina. Thompson picked it up.

'She said "You're not getting the message, the message needs to get out there, he is going to shoot us one at a time,' Thompson recalls. The executive producer handed the call over to the police officer now sitting alongside them, Steve.

But Selina insisted she wasn't talking to any negotiators and that the call had to go to air live. 'We are inches away from losing our lives! . . . All he has asked for is a flag, a fucking flag, and the police can't even do that! He asked for a flag and a declaration that Australia is under Islamic State attack. The three people that came out haven't made things easier.'

Steve tried to ask her about conditions inside the café, saying, 'Things are happening now to get that type of flag to him.' Selina replied. 'Just do what he wants. He is going to shoot us.' Then she hung up.

Controversially, Steve would later describe Selina's responses as the 'possible onset of Stockholm Syndrome'. When this came out at the inquest, Louisa was barely able to contain her anger.

Just after 6 p.m. Marcia posted on Facebook another warning that 'he is going to kill us'. But the warnings were having little effect on police strategy. Forward commander Victor would later tell the coroner: "There was agitation and there was emotions, but there was nothing to support that the hostages were being mistreated in the sense that I would expect by Monis . . . There was no peak events through the day that caused . . . continual escalation of Monis' behaviour.'

Louisa found this testimony inexplicable: 'Did they miss all the drama that happened in that room when the first three hostages escaped?'

The dogged, almost blind adherence to 'contain and negotiate' acted as a barrier to trying other tactics, such as turning to non-police intermediaries, or seeing if Monis' children could be brought into the picture.

Ray Hadley had finally gone off air just before 6 p.m., to be replaced by Ben Fordham. He told Fordham: 'Don't stuff this up. We are not about chasing ratings here, we are about making sure we get people out of here alive.'

Soon after coming on air Fordham read out a Facebook post by Marcia that included all of Monis' key demands. This was a potential breakthrough, which could have been presented to Monis as the fulfilment of one of his conditions, namely a high-profile media announcement publicising that this was an Islamic State attack.

But the police negotiator at the station, Steve, did not tell the command post about the broadcast. It was another missed opportunity, one that lead negotiator Peter would later admit he could have used as a hook to engage Monis.

In addition to the third parties who had contacted Kaldas in the morning, others had come forward to offer their services. Among them was Mamdouh Habib, who had once been a prisoner in the notorious Guantanamo Bay complex but who was now residing in Sydney.

Keyser Trad of the Islamic Friendship Association offered the association's resources to help make contact with the gunman. He'd had contact with Monis in the past, although he did not know the hostage-taker's identity at the time he offered to assist. 'If we had known who he was, people like me would have been very willing to take the risk [to enter the café],' Trad told the ABC after the siege. 'I am confident he wouldn't have shot me.'

A medico with an Islamic background, a Dr Khan, also rang in to 2GB at 9.20 p.m., offering to go into the café to check on the state of the hostages.

Some of the lawyers who had taken on Monis' many and varied legal cases over the years stepped forward as well. One was barrister Michael Klooster, with whom Monis had talked in the Lindt Café that morning just minutes before he took the hostages. Another was Philip Green, who had assisted Monis as recently as April 2014 on the charge of being an accessory to the murder of Helen Lee.

On the afternoon of the siege, at around 4 p.m., Green and a colleague, Greg Scragg, walked from their Elizabeth Street offices to the corner of St James Road, where plain clothes police officers were stationed at the perimeter of the exclusion zone. They explained to the officers that Monis had been a client of theirs who had accepted their advice in the past. Green said he was willing to try to talk to Monis, and left his number with the police before returning to his office. There he waited until 1.00 a.m. He heard nothing from the police and eventually went home.

A similar experience befell Emanuell (Manny) Conditsis, a lawyer who had represented the Iranian twice, once over the offensive letters Monis sent to the families of deceased Australian soldiers and then again when Monis was charged in 2013 with being an accessory to Helen Lee's murder.

Late on the afternoon of the siege Conditsis got a call from ABC reporter Lorna Knowles, who told him police sources had informed her Monis was the gunman. Conditsis, who was based on the Central Coast north of Sydney, then rang into Sydney police and left a message saying he was prepared to come into the city and intercede with Monis, who had respected him in the past. He urged the constable to immediately convey the offer up the line, and left his mobile number to call back.

At 5.45 p.m. a detective inspector did so. The lawyer repeated his offer. The officer, who at that stage appeared to not know the identity of the gunman himself, took down the details and passed the message upward.

Conditsis sat tight in his office, waiting for further contact from police. None came. At 7.30 p.m. he went home but kept his phone on. By the time he went to bed at 11.30, there had still been no word from police commanders in Sydney. He woke up at 4.30 the next morning to find the bloody end to the siege all over the news. He checked his phone. Still no message. There were no missed calls, except for one from a journalist. It would be three months before a police officer apologised for the failure to call him back.

Conditsis says he has wondered many times since if he could have made a difference. 'I do not have delusions of grandeur,' he says. 'I simply wonder if it was a lost opportunity. Isn't it a shame that we will never know?'

CHAPTER 8

SHIPS IN THE NIGHT

Prime Minister Tony Abbott had a bad feeling about the Sydney siege from the outset. Gathered around the cabinet table in Canberra with him that Monday morning were a number of the senior ministers who made up the government's National Security Committee. Aside from the PM, this group normally comprised the deputy PM, the foreign minister, the attorney-general, the immigration minister, the treasurer and the defence minister. With them in the Cabinet Room were the SCONS—the Secretaries Committee on National Security—made up of the heads of those departments.

The unscheduled meeting had been on the point of winding up when Abbott decided to keep everyone in place to hear from the New South Wales authorities. 'We got the police commissioner and the premier on the line and were briefed by them, and I offered one observation,' Abbott told me, 'which was that this will end badly because this guy is obviously out to make a political point. He had taken hostages, he'd barricaded the café and he'd put up an Islamist flag. Well, that meant it was plainly a terrorist incident.'

The prime minister was keenly aware of the wider international backdrop to the siege. Just six months previously the leader of Islamic State, Abu Bakr al-Baghdadi, had declared himself the head of a caliphate, a fundamentalist religious state harkening back to the early days of Islam. From this base, al-Baghdadi had urged Muslims to join him and 'make jihad' for the sake of Allah.

As recently as September 2014, IS leaders had issued a fresh call to supporters around the world to kill *kuffar* (the plural of *kafir*, meaning 'infidels') wherever they could target them, with specific mention of Australia. And two months prior to the siege, Canberra had raised the national terrorist alert level from medium to high on the advice of the nation's domestic spy agency, ASIO. The head of ASIO, David Irvine, had specifically warned of the risk posed by 'loners', as well as more orchestrated attacks.

In Abbott's mind there was no doubt about the need for urgency in resolving the Lindt Café crisis. 'The point I made was the sooner this is resolved the better. I'm not saying I had the discussion in all its glory at that point in time, but there is obviously a world of difference between a domestic siege, which is essentially a cry for help, and a terrorist siege, which is a desire to make a dreadful political point, invariably by someone who is heedless of his or her own life and the lives of others.'

Abbott says he offered to make military capabilities, including Sydney-based Special Forces soldiers, available almost immediately. 'The Commonwealth wanted to be as helpful as we humanly could be,' he told me. 'I said [to Baird and Scipione], "Look, if you need the [military] commandos' assistance, we'll put them on standby" . . . In Afghanistan they did this stuff all the time. They went into buildings full of armed opponents, they had had an abundance of experience doing this kind of thing.'

The response from Scipione and Baird was polite but pro forma. 'I'm not sure they ever put [that] in so many words. It was more look, "Thanks very much, we'll let you know what we need"', Abbott said.

The PM's chief of staff, Peta Credlin, formed a similar impression: 'The premier said they didn't need it at that stage and thanked the prime minister for the offer.'

Mike Baird does not recall a specific offer of military aid. He told me: 'It was just an update of events, what we were facing. It was part of the protocols to touch base with the PM. There was nothing in the conversation that the commonwealth had this and this, that [they] were ready to deploy. The context was more "anything we can do, let us know".'

Baird's police minister Stuart Ayres does not recall military aid being proffered either. However, according to Abbott's national security adviser, Andrew Shearer, Abbott did offer every support, including Australian Defence Force (ADF) assistance. 'It was very clear that the commonwealth would provide absolutely any support that was required,' Shearer told me, 'and implicitly understood that would include most obviously elements from TAG-East.'

Abbott remained worried. He decided to cancel the Liberal Party fundraiser he was due to attend in Sydney that night and wait the siege out in Canberra. If the New South Wales government changed its mind about the need for federal assistance, he wanted to be sure he was in the right place to get things moving.

The Special Forces unit Abbott had in mind was the Tactical Assault Group-East (TAG-East), stationed at Holsworthy Army Base, around thirty kilometres from the Sydney CBD. Provisionally formed before the Sydney Olympics, the unit was then placed on a permanent footing in 2002, the year after al Qaeda attacked New York's Twin Towers on 11 September 2001. With members drawn from the 2nd Commando Regiment, its primary remit was to respond to terrorist and other high-risk threats on Australian soil. A counterpart unit, TAG-West, is situated on the other side of the continent in Perth.

The men assigned to the TAGs are and were at the time of the siege part of the country's military elite, the crème de la crème of the Australian Defence Force. Many had cycled through numerous tours of duty in Afghanistan.

Their training regimen was relentless, underpinned with 'validation' tests to demonstrate their close combat skills several times a week.

Above all, they were required to operate with precision. Faced with an armed adversary inside a room, TAG-East's standard training regimen at the time of the siege was to be able to take an enemy out with a deadly and efficient two shots to the head.

For the duration of their twelve-month posting, each man assigned to the unit and rostered on duty had to be ready around the clock for deployment with minimal notice. While the unit's base at Holsworthy was nearly an hour's drive from the heart of Sydney, helicopters could get them into town much faster if required.

The unit's ethos of instant readiness meant a headline was enough for the commanding officer to start readying for deployment, even before any orders arrived from the brass higher up. 'Just a news feed could be the trigger,' says a former sniper commander with the TAG. Speaking about the siege, he says: 'They would have been fully ready and it would have progressed a lot further than anyone outside the unit would have realised. They would have had iPads with floor plans, they would have been briefing each other on entry points, they would have had an emergency action plan and a deliberate plan underway. In cases like this, the "rollerball" starts and does not stop until someone tells it to.'

On the morning of 15 December, the intelligence officer from 2nd Commando happened to be monitoring Sky News when he saw the first reports of the Martin Place siege. He immediately informed his counterpart at Randwick Barracks, closer to the city, who scrambled to get a military communications support team together in case police wanted military assistance. Not long afterwards, the commander of TAG-East started calling members back to base.

One group had been on the road since 6.30 a.m., heading out to Singleton three hours north-west of Sydney for long-range field firing sniper practice. They picked up news of the siege on their car radio and within minutes were on the phone to their unit commanders. By 10.30 a.m. they had turned around and were heading back to Sydney.

By mid-morning, the head of the New South Wales Police Special Protection Group was in touch with the army's Special Operations Command asking for a 'liaison officer' to be posted to the Police Operations Centre (POC). A senior Special Forces officer, 'Major S', was installed at a desk inside the centre by 11 a.m. Major S ensured the set-up of a secure communications link with TAG-East. The overall head of the Defence Force, Air Chief Marshal Mark Binskin, was also in touch with the Special Forces head, to ensure, he said later, that 'should this evolve into a broader situation and we got called out for it, we were in a position to do it'.

The military old boy networks were also kicking into action. A former commando used contacts to get a copy of the café's floor plans to TAG-East well before lunchtime and the unit began to set up a mock-up of the café on which it could rehearse possible entry manoeuvres. (The head of the police tactical units would later confess he had no idea where the TAG-East had sourced this information.)

Over the subsequent hours of the siege, eleven ADF personnel would end up at either the POC, the forward command post or the multi-agency Joint Intelligence Group set up for the incident. But their role barely progressed beyond observation. No commandos hit the streets of Sydney. No army snipers were asked to take up positions alongside police marksmen, or to formally advise on how police sniping capability could best be deployed.

The army was not asked for advice (and therefore gave none) on how best to tackle an armed adversary carrying an IED (improvised explosives device). Relevant niche capabilities such as the specialist bomb experts of the army's Special Operations Engineering Regiment were not utilised. One Defence sniper specialist undertook a cursory review of police sniping positions, but retreated for fear of being sighted by the media.

The sole operational contribution the army made came later that night when TAG-East informed the police tactical adviser that it had tested a possible planned intervention ('deliberate action') drawn up by tactical police to rescue the hostages and deemed it viable. As it happened, the police commanders would never end up approving that plan anyway. For all other intents and purposes, the army's operational assistance to New South Wales Police that night would remain virtually nil.

After the siege both sides seemed to run a mile from each other, playing down the suggestion that the military had, or should have had, any role at all. The inquest's senior counsel, Jeremy Gormly, would quizzically remark on the 'striking absence' of steps to 'explore or exploit ADF capability unavailable to New South Wales police . . . their liaison role was almost completely hands off'. The overriding impression was of extreme wariness on the part of the military about being seen to overstep their place.

There were a number of reasons for this caginess. The first was nervousness about how to interpret the federal government's 'call-out' powers, which set out when the army could step in to help a state government. According to Part IIIAAA of the Defence Act, military assistance could only be provided if a state government requested it and if local police acknowledged being overwhelmed. Throughout the evening, not a single New South Wales police commander expressed a view that control of the situation had been lost.

Then there were worries about the type of precedent being set. The army had hitherto never been called out to help combat a terrorist event at home. The closest it had come had been in 1978 when the federal government put troops on the streets of Sydney to help guard the Commonwealth Heads of Government Regional Meeting after a bombing at the Hilton Hotel where visiting dignitaries were staying.

The last factor was perhaps pride, although the police submissions to the coronial inquest vehemently denied this. But it was clear most police commanders did not seem comfortable with the army being on their turf that night, and vice versa.

There were a couple of notable exceptions to this. The tactical adviser (a superintendent) at the POC was on good personal terms with the army major posted into the police operation. He would later testify that he had seen the Defence liaison presence on the night as laying the ground for possible army involvement 'should we be in a position for Defence Force assistance to civilian authority'. In his view it was important to get the Defence liaison officers 'ahead of the game as much as we could'. He, the tactical commander and the head of the State Protection Group appeared to be the only senior New South Wales police officers holding that view.

Reluctance to get the army too involved was a long-standing attitude within the police force. After the siege, a former federal agent recounted a conversation he'd had with a senior New South Wales police officer several years earlier: 'He told me "We will never do a handover to the ADF, because we might as well resign our commissions".'

These constraints had a notable impact on the patterns of interaction between the Defence liaison officers and senior police. By around 9 p.m., for instance, two sniper experts from TAG-East—one of them a highly experienced sniper coordinator with four military tours of the Middle East under his belt—had taken up liaison positions at the forward command post at the leagues' club. The police tactical commander briefed them on arrival. They met some members of the police team and spoke briefly with one of the negotiators. But they kept such a low profile that the deputy tactical commander, who was charged with assigning the New South Wales Police sniping teams, didn't even know that army sniping experts were present.

The deputy would later tell the coroner: 'I was aware that there were two members from the Australian Defence Force in the Forward Command Post. I didn't know who they were or what their qualifications were.' He confirmed that he had not held any conversation with them.

Chief Superintendent Lima, the afternoon/evening forward commander, said he was unaware there were any ADF officers on his patch at all, although the late night forward commander Victor contradicted this, saying Lima had told him of their presence. Victor had previously been part of training scenarios where police handed over to the military under the relevant sections of the Defence Act. Indeed, he later told investigators, 'that is something that we test and train for', and that 'technically we can do a joint assault'.

But on the night of the siege, Victor viewed the Defence people as being there in the role of observers only, not as a resource for the police to draw on. He described them to the coroner after the siege as 'silent partners' 'in an informal role, gaining situational awareness . . . reporting back to their command'.

When it was put to Victor that the military had far more experience in dealing with adversaries armed with bombs than the New South Wales Police, he begged to disagree: 'I think the ADF . . . would have had the same problem as us dealing with a person in a confined space with an IED. I don't think they would bring anything to the table.' Nor did he concede that army liaison officers might have had a valuable role in advising police on what military resources were available to help resolve the siege. 'I don't agree with that position, Your Honour. They're actually there in an informal capacity.'

State and federal bureaucrats had drawn up manuals with hundreds of pages, laying down the many ways in which their agencies were meant to seamlessly coordinate during a terror attack. None of it seemed to count for much on the night.

Part of the problem lay in what long-time insiders say had been a falling-off in joint counter-terrorism training between the military and police, as the police switched focus to counter-terrorism investigations, and the Defence hierarchy focused more intently on operations abroad. Commonwealth resourcing for routine national counter-terrorism exercises had been significantly scaled back after 2011. And the machinery for testing combined command, control and co-ordination mechanisms between the states and the Commonwealth, and within states themselves, had also lost momentum. The last big joint exercise had been Operation Black Angus in 2011, devised around a scenario of multiple shooters firing automatic weapons into a crowd at Sydney's ANZ Stadium, the former Olympic Stadium at Homebush Bay.

The exercise had cost hundreds of thousands of dollars. It was meant to showcase how well the first responder agencies of government, federal and state—plus the supporting intelligence and emergency services—could work together to confront the scourge of terrorism. The Lindt crisis exposed a very different picture.

There was one vital capability police certainly knew they were lacking, and that was surveillance from *inside* Monis' lair. From the early stages of the siege, they desperately needed 'ears' and 'eyes' inside the café.

Providing covert surveillance of a live crime scene generally fell to a specialist unit within the New South Wales Police known as STIB (State Technical Investigation Branch). Well before noon, police forward commander Lima had begun pressing STIB to get covert audio and visual monitoring of the interior of the café.

But the New South Wales police technicians had no success. They installed extra cameras around the perimeter, including at Channel 7 and at the Reserve Bank. From Elizabeth Street, they climbed via a window into the legal chambers across the lobby from the café, and installed a camera angled towards the lobby doors on a bookshelf. At 3 p.m., not long before Paolo, John and Stefan escaped, a STIB officer was told to try to penetrate the café via the fire doors on Phillip Street. But that attempt was abandoned when the forward command ordered the tactical team not to reconnoitre inside the fire door for fear of what that might trigger inside the café.

At 6.15 p.m., acting on information coming from the escaped hostages, Lima asked his tactical commander if there was any way of getting surveillance devices smuggled into the café via the women's toilets. Not viable, he was told.

Someone checked whether the ADF had a better surveillance capability—another small exception to the general attitude that night of keeping Defence on the sidelines—but it too came back with no options.

With evening coming on, it became even more urgent to get a solution. Greg Parker, the Channel 7 cameraman, compensated for the encroaching darkness by cranking up the 'gain' feature on his camera, which had a similar effect to that of night vision goggles. It 'literally illuminated dark spaces,' Parker said later. 'Monis thought he couldn't be seen but we could track his movement every time he moved past a window.'

Still, the police needed better visibility and monitoring of what was going on inside the café. So, finally, the New South Wales Police turned to the Australian Federal Police (AFP) for help. By around 6 p.m. AFP technicians arrived and began setting up and testing their own audio equipment.

By around 7.15 p.m., they were having some success. With access to more sophisticated technology than their state counterparts, they managed to get a covert listening device in a position to pick up some of the conversation inside.

This was a far from perfect arrangement. The audio feed could not be sent directly to the New South Wales Police, but had to be transmitted in the first instance to an AFP listening post (the location of which was suppressed by the coroner). From there an AFP officer monitored the feed and sent summary reports through to one of the New South Wales investigators, who passed them on to the negotiators at the leagues' club on Phillip Street.

This cumbersome chain of communication had many drawbacks. The listening device did not provide a live feed. Its recordings were transmitted as a series of audio files that travelled, in blocks, to the listening post. The audio feed was on delay, so the interactions between

Monis and the hostages inside the café were not being picked up in real time. Sometimes the delay was two to three minutes, sometimes longer. At one stage it blew out to twenty-nine minutes.

Much of what was said was barely audible. And it was hard to replay the feed to double check.

'It was just the worst possible way to transmit the most critical information,' an expert told me later. 'It was one person listening, with no guidelines as to what to listen for, who was not trained to listen for mood but for an event, and at the same time is trying to transmit the gist of what he is hearing by text.' Yet some of the New South Wales police commanders remained under the impression during the duration of the siege that the listening device product was 'live'.

Eventually the AFP asked the New South Wales Police to take over the role of monitoring the device themselves. One of the New South Wales negotiators, 'Steve', came to the AFP listening post at around 9 p.m. From midnight he, and later an officer who came to relieve him at 1 a.m., were left alone to perform a job that should have been performed by at least two people: listening to exchanges inside the café, assessing them and transmitting short summaries. He also had to juggle other tasks while trying to monitor the audio, including answering unrelated telephone calls. Lima requested more resources to help the negotiator, but they were never provided.

Just after midnight, the device failed to transmit anything at all for close to half an hour, a period when negotiators missed three critical calls from hostages.

Behind the scenes, despite all his public assurances of having a 'world class' team on the job, Commissioner Scipione was becoming keenly aware that he had a problem. He had, after all, once been second in command of the Specialist Services Group (of which STIB was a part) earlier in his policing career.

More than twelve hours into the siege, at 10.37 p.m., he sent a message to his deputy, Cath Burn: 'Catherine,' it read. 'I have had a quick chance to talk to the SSG [Special Services Group] team that were forward tonight and it has become apparent that we should be preparing a fresh bid for any new equipment that is necessary. Can you please make sure we get some advice . . . as to any new electronic imaging/audio/intelligence gathering equipment that we may need for the future. I will need this soon . . . See you bright and early in the morning.'

It was a rare admission of inadequacy that only came to light at the inquest twenty months later, long after the siege had ground through to its fatal conclusion.

If getting a listening device that could transmit from the café was proving hard, getting visual surveillance of the interior was even harder. In fact, STIB never managed to get a set of 'eyes' into the café.

Why this should be remains one of the great unexplained mysteries of the siege. And it would have a critical impact, particularly on the fate of Tori Johnson when the siege reached its violent climax in the early hours of the following morning.

Lima would later concede how much harder the surveillance shortfalls had made his task. 'A lot of things we were working with . . . were really against us,' he admitted. 'The fact that we didn't have [surveillance] capability within the stronghold was very difficult . . . Not getting eyes within the stronghold made it a very difficult set of circumstances to deal with.'

One striking fact emerged at the inquest, however. The domestic spy agency, ASIO, which had unparalleled expertise in this area, offered to help STIB on the morning of the siege, but its offer was knocked back. This hidden bombshell lay buried among 400-pages of final submissions prepared by the three barristers assisting the inquest, led by senior counsel, Jeremy Gormly SC. It did not become public until May 2017. In a section of their submission headed 'What video footage did STIB obtain?' Gormly and his team wrote: 'It is noted that ASIO contacted STIB and offered assistance at 11.30 hours. It seems that that offer was *not* taken up.'

The coroner found this aspect of the police operation mystifying. It was 'not clear' what had come of ASIO's offer to STIB, he would find. There was no evidence to indicate 'that the offer was taken up, progressed or otherwise responded to by the NSWPF [New South Wales Police Force]'.

STIB was never called to explain itself at the inquest. It was dropped from the witness list because the inquiry was running over time. However, some of its officers did provide statements. The STIB commander nominated 'live' media coverage as among the 'constraints' his unit encountered. 'This made approaching the café to deploy technical surveillance resources difficult, as we were unaware of what media platforms the offender may be utilising to view the live broadcast', he said.

Gormly remained deeply unimpressed. The statements provided by STIB officers, he said, were 'in many respects inadequate'. They contained factual errors, lacked attention to detail, were inconsistent with one another and 'taken as a whole, were a poor and unsatisfactory account for the State Coroner of what occurred'. 'To the extent they were called upon, it is difficult to escape the inference that STIB, not unlike the negotiators, lacked the ability to rise to the occasion and meet the legitimate expectations that the NSW police force had for them.'

After the siege, the New South Wales Police maintained that 'the lack of surveillance was not for want of trying'. Its submission to the inquest insisted that the 'technology was not available to either the NSWPF or partner agencies and cannot properly be the subject of criticism'. When I asked why ASIO's offer to help had not been accepted, the only response was to refer me to the coroner's report.

One expert with knowledge of ASIO's capabilities was stupefied at the police claim that 'partner agencies' could not provide the necessary surveillance. 'If the New South Wales Police didn't ask, how will we ever know? ASIO's technology is far and away better than what any of the police forces have,' the expert told me. 'Why would you have knocked them back? ASIO have the technology, the skills and the capacity to do that on a routine basis. They wouldn't give their equipment to the cops. They will not do that because it's classified, but they would have put their techs on the job. Why the New South Wales Police proved incapable in that respect, I just don't know.'

A senior lawyer told me: 'The New South Wales Police did not have the capacity and should have. The commonwealth did have the capacity and volunteered it, but it was rejected.' Another source with long military experience said: 'The police know how good ASIO is. The first thing I would have done is have the ASIO Technical Support Unit in there, in a heartbeat.'

Late night commander Victor would later speak of his disappointment at the limited technical resources he was given to work with during the siege. He said he couldn't 'talk about it in open court', but 'some of the things . . . that I asked for weren't available to me'. The commander of the police tactical unit said much the same: 'I would have expected it [surveillance from inside the café] to be achieved and was disappointed in the result.'

Either way, the situation made a mockery of the promise embedded in the National Counter-Terrorism Plan that the Commonwealth's technical response capability existed precisely to help state police with surveillance at the scene of a terrorist incident.

As subsequent events were to show, a covert camera with a view into the café could well have saved Tori Johnson's life.

Two and a half years later, Abbott's chief of staff would reflect on all this with regret. 'There is so much capacity and expertise at the commonwealth level and I'm not convinced the two connected well enough during a point of crisis,' *The Australian* reported Peta Credlin saying. 'What worries me is these standing committees all talk about inter-operability, information sharing but it occurs at the level of senior officials.'

During the crisis, she pointed out, none of those bureaucrats were 'actually the ones standing on the footpath at Martin Place'. 'During the siege, did the operational police have the experts giving them the advice they needed? Did we give operational police everything else they need—artillery, equipment, communications kit, legal authority? I'm not sure—AFP, ARMY and ASIO where were they?'

The Dawson family would also lament the fact that despite the army's internationally recognised capability in dealing with IEDs and armed adversaries, and despite the proximity of TAG-East, police did not appear interested in exploring the potential of niche ADF resources that might have helped resolve the siege.

It remains one of the many sources of sorrow and frustration for the bereaved families.

Over at the State Crisis Centre, the politicians and their aides seemed blissfully unaware that police were struggling with a lack of specialist expertise.

'That stuff, ASIO, the army, was never really mentioned,' recalls John Redman, the media aide to Police Minister Stuart Ayres. 'The advice was always the New South Wales police force have got this. We've got the best people, we've got the best this, we've got the best that, it never felt like really a legitimate option getting the army in. It didn't feel like it was being seriously considered and in hindsight I don't think it was. The message from the police leadership to us was that they had the best people doing it, that was the term they used quite a bit throughout the day—that the people that they've got on this are the best, we have the best.'

Premier Mike Baird says that from what he observed at the State Crisis Centre there was 'an incredible confidence in the capabilities [of the New South Wales Police]. They were incredibly professional; to a man and woman they were united in doing everything they could to get everyone out, to keep the city safe.'

Back in Canberra, Prime Minister Tony Abbott was being kept abreast of developments by the head of the AFP, Andrew Colvin, and by Abbott's national security adviser, Andrew Shearer.

In the late afternoon, Shearer briefed the prime minister that the terrorist wanted to talk to him. 'My response was "Look, if the people in charge of handling the siege think it would be helpful, of course I am happy to talk to this guy in any way, shape or form"', Abbott says. Shearer conveyed the offer to Colvin, adding that the PM's office would be guided by advice from the professionals.

But there was little doubt about what that advice would be: such a major concession to Monis would have flown directly against the key tenets of the federal and state counter-terrorism plans.

While not wanting to turn to the army for help, New South Wales police leaders could see they would have to make some relief arrangements for their front-line assault teams, who had been up since the early hours. Should the siege drag on through the night and into the next morning, as police commanders were expecting, replenishment from within their own ranks was going to be difficult, given the other incidents occurring around the state. Therefore, Scipione turned for help to the AFP in Canberra and to the Queensland Police.

Queensland's equivalent of the New South Wales Tactical Operations Unit was its Special Emergency Response Team (SERT). At 3 p.m. on the afternoon of the siege, SERT was put on standby. Formal approval for the team to deploy to Sydney came at around 7.40 p.m.

and it climbed aboard two planes—one for the men and another for their gear. The Queenslanders touched down at Sydney Airport at around 10.30 p.m. and made their way to the POC in town.

The AFP had its specialist tactical unit on the ground in Sydney by a similar time. Both teams stowed their gear in the basement at the POC while they were briefed by the officer designated as the New South Wales relief tactical commander.

At 11.45 p.m. the reinforcements from Queensland were sworn in. The men put on ballistic vests and helmets, picked up New South Wales Police radios and ensured their weapons were loaded. An advance party—comprising the relief tactical commander, the senior AFP team member and the head of the SERT team and his deputy—headed for the leagues' club.

But by the time they arrived at the forward command post it was already 1.40 a.m. Before they could step in to relieve their New South Wales counterparts, the tragic final act of Monis' self-scripted drama had already commenced.

There seemed no great eagerness on the part of those in command to rush into a handover to the interstate police, despite the risk of fatigue among their own tactical teams. A dictaphone recording at the leagues' club picked up a senior officer saying that the New South Wales 'guys' would want to hang around at the siege site because 'I don't think our PTG [Police Tactical Group] wanna handover to an interstate PTG'.

'I think it would be fuckin' embarrassing.'

'Yeah,' another officer replies. 'We're the biggest and baddest in the country, mate.'

Quizzed about this comment at the inquest, Lima dismissed it as a joke, an example of insider 'black humour', which was 'simply showing the respect for our own PTG'.

The legal team for the New South Wales Police was also quick to quash any suggestion that 'professional rivalry and pride' might have been a factor in delaying rotation of the tactical police. To suggest otherwise was 'insulting to both the interstate PTG officers who travelled from other states to relieve the New South Wales PTG and to those officers who were planning for their integration into the teams at the stronghold,' they told the inquest.

But the POC commander, Murdoch, made it plain that he never envisaged using interstate police for any planned intervention in the crisis. 'It wasn't our intention to use either the Queenslanders or the people from the ACT in a team that we would use to assault the café,' Murdoch told the inquest.

The families of the victims would later see all this as a sign of hubris, and a failure of sensible fatigue management. Mike Baird takes issue with the charge of hubris. 'What I sensed was professionals who had trained all their lives for this moment,' he told me.

Tony Abbott, however, had caught a whiff of the tribalism that ran inside the New South Wales Police Force. Two and a half years later, sitting in his electorate office not far from Manly beach, the former PM mulled over whether a greater willingness to engage with what the federal government had to offer might have improved the outcome.

'Understandably the state police wanted as far as is possible to do it for themselves. And I guess, given that it was the first time they had done anything like this, some weaknesses, some clunkiness, was exposed,' he said. 'With the wisdom of hindsight, arguably some army snipers might have been useful. With the wisdom of hindsight, an army team to storm the building might have been useful. That said, I am not in any way critical of the tactical police, who were operating in circumstances that they had never previously experienced, and under very restrictive rules of engagement. [But] were we to have another incident of this type, I suspect the commonwealth's offers of assistance would be more readily accepted.'

Andrew Shearer, who took up a senior post in Washington when Abbott lost the prime ministership, agrees with his former boss. 'In the military they talk about "seams" between different commands, areas of ambiguity and potential weakness,' Shearer tells me. 'And I think what we saw that night was this seam between the commonwealth response and the state response that was a point of weakness, a point of ambiguity about who was really responsible and how capable different people were and so forth. You'd like to hope that we have all learnt a lot and that seam is now much more robust.'

CHAPTER 9

LENGTHENING SHADOWS

The tall shadows of surrounding office blocks were lengthening around the café as late afternoon crept towards evening. The hostages were beginning to despair. Hopes that the police would find a way to free them—hopes that had risen after the escape of Paolo, John and Stefan at 3.30 p.m.—had come to nothing. Monis was still refusing to negotiate directly with the police and still controlling the hostages' every interaction with the world beyond the café, except for the odd covert text message some were managing to send from the toilets. They would have to continue to navigate through this crisis themselves.

The first escape had forged a tighter understanding between the hostages who remained. 'That really galvanised us together, I think,' Louisa says. 'Although many of us were strangers to each other, we also understood instinctively that we had to operate as a group if we were to survive. There was a very definite sense that we were in this together and this was the way we were going to have to go. All of our collective efforts were around pacifying and cajoling [Monis], to stop him killing one of us while we waited for the police to come.' The next major flashpoint, they feared, would be when Monis discovered Elly and April's covert escape.

The gunman was regularly getting the hostages to check online news sites received via smart phones in the café. But batteries were running flat. For now, no information was coming in from the outside world. As evening approached, Monis asked Joel and Jarrod to go and look for a phone charger so he could get the news back up.

They pretended to search, but came back saying they couldn't find one. Look again, he ordered. After stalling a bit longer, Jarrod eventually returned with a charger and Monis ordered him to read the top stories aloud. It was striking just how obsessed the gunman was with monitoring media depictions of the attack.

'The one thing he really wanted, more than anything, was to hear that they were reporting him as an Islamic State operative,' Jarrod says. 'That was the one thing. Along with that was his increasing obsession with getting the Islamic State flag. The other thing I noticed was that he had stopped talking about the bomb. It was like he'd abandoned that as kind of a bad plot line.'

The top story Jarrod read out was about Uber outrageously overcharging people who'd fled the city as police began evacuating the blocks around the café. Some were being slugged a minimum of $100, the *Sydney Morning Herald* website reported. The ride-sharing company was suffering a huge backlash on social media.

Jarrod hesitated as he came to the next story. As he'd feared, it was now being reported that five people had made it safely out of the café. 'Keep reading,' Monis ordered.

The young man made a split-second decision. If the gunman discovered April and Elly had slipped the net, the consequences could be fatal for those who remained. So he decided to self-edit the bulletin, changing 'five' to 'three' escapes. 'I just started subbing in replacement numbers,' he says. 'That meant changing every news story on the other sites as well; there were heaps of them.'

This was a significant risk for Jarrod. He'd gained a degree of freedom of movement because Monis had come to trust him. That freedom was paying off in small ways. On his trips to the kitchen, for instance, Jarrod had begun slipping small business cards under the internal rear door leading to the fire escape, hoping police would find them. On them he had drawn pictures of Monis' gun and various internal maps of the café, showing the makeshift barricades the hostages had been forced to erect and where the gunman had positioned himself. Should Monis discover that Jarrod was doctoring the news reports, that freedom would evaporate in an instant. Worse still, Monis might decide to exact violent retribution.

Coverage of the siege would later become a source of particular ire for Louisa, who felt the authorities and news outlets were giving little thought to how it might affect the hostages' parlous position. Earlier in the day, Assistant Commissioner Mick Fuller had told the police media unit to ask Channel 7 not to broadcast close-ups of the café. Greg Parker's images, invaluable to the police, were being patched through to the forward command but not to a wider audience. The public wouldn't see his pictures until the evening news of 16 December, when the siege was over. But those precautions were not enough.

'Everything that the media were reporting and saying was coming into the room, and it was affecting what was happening in the room,' Louisa recalls.

Monis had repeatedly made it plain he wanted police well back from the café. Yet some journalists were reporting police positions, inadvertently giving Monis the very information most likely to enrage him. 'Police maintain a very heavy presence outside there,' one ABC reporter told his audience in a broadcast that was picked up by the listening device inside the cafe. 'They've been sort of hugging that wall just near where we saw those hostages, ah, leaving the scene earlier this afternoon.' Nor was local media the only problem. 'I recall it was late at night when we heard the BBC reporter telling the world that she could see the police surrounding the café in Sydney,' Louisa says. 'I was utterly terrified, he'd made it plain he didn't want the police anywhere near the café and it directly put our lives at risk.'

Sitting in his office in Canberra, Tony Abbott was having similar qualms. 'I was watching the live telecast on Sky and I remember thinking, "If Monis has got access to a TV, he is watching the police doing whatever they are doing, and drawing his own conclusions about what is likely to happen." And I thought, "Well, I wonder how helpful that is."'

Louisa resolved that, if she survived, she would highlight the extra risks the media coverage had sometimes created for the hostages. Yes, there was a right to know. But how could that trump someone's right to live?

The hostages still did not know Monis' name. He'd divulged no personal information of any sort. At one point one of the women referred to him as 'the terrorist' when making a call at Monis' direction.

After she'd hung up, Monis asked: 'Do you think I'm a terrorist?'

'I didn't know what else to say,' she replied.

He turned to the others. Did they think he was a terrorist?

'We go, "No, no". But what else do we call you?' Louisa says.

'Call me Brother—Brother ISIS,' Monis replied.

Inwardly this sickened them, but no one was going to argue with it.

'It wasn't going to be a smart idea to challenge it,' Jarrod says. 'Within his hearing, we always voiced our agreement with what he was saying, joining in criticism of the prime minister and pandering to his opinion of the situation. We had no choice.'

As the evening drew on, Monis finally heard for himself that the media was reporting five, not three escapes. Angrily he began demanding an explanation. Jarrod's heart was in his mouth. They had to come up with a diversion, and fast.

Suddenly one of the group declared that the claim of five escapes was a media lie.

'Yes, yes!' the others piled in. 'The media's been lying all day! Journalists tell lies to make the police look good!'

After an angry few minutes, Monis seemed to buy the explanation. The fact that he had never done a proper head count contributed to his confusion.

'There were so many young Asian women with long dark hair in the café—that was just a fact. He missed that second escape, and at first I had missed it too,' Louisa says.

By now, too, the hostages were getting better at figuring out how to ride the currents of Monis' emotions, and how to play to his obsessions.

Jarrod says: 'If we had just said to Monis "They're lying" when the five escapes came on the radio, he would have said "Don't lie to me". But by playing off his own ideology—like, "You know how the media works, they just work with the police to make you look like a fool"—he was more likely to agree with that. It was almost now a matter of using his own words against him.'

Jarrod now knew the rear café doors into the lobby were unlocked. He began, in small and unobtrusive ways, clearing a path towards that exit.

Earlier he had quietly placed the large cut-out bear at an angle to help screen Elly and April's escape. Now he nudged it to make it fall over, giving him an excuse to prop it back against the wall and out of the way.

'If no one was going to come and save us any time soon, we knew we were going to have to start thinking about saving ourselves,' he says.

Quietly he let Fiona in on what he was thinking. Every time one of the pair passed that section of the café, running the various errands Monis sent them on, they would nudge a table here, a chair there, trying to make small inroads in the furniture barricade. It was hardly a clear path to freedom, but it was doing something.

They let some of the others in on the plan during trips to the toilets. 'I spent a lot of time in those bathrooms taking people up and down,' Jarrod says. 'It was just two cubicles and a space at the basins. But it was a good place for people to come to feel safe, just for a little bit. I knew if he started shooting we'd have more of a chance up there.'

Monis' impatience with the police negotiators was growing. The endless media-go-round was becoming tiring for everybody.

'It seemed that every contact that was made, it was the same routine,' Louisa says. 'Go through the switchboard; get put through to the newsroom. The newsroom going "Oh, I don't know what to do . . . Yes, we'll take . . ." Then, "No, we won't take the statement." And the negotiators coming back, "Can we talk to him?", and one of us here saying "No, he won't talk."'

In the late afternoon, the police negotiators decided they would reveal to the gunman that they knew his identity. They called through to the café, asking to speak to 'Sheikh Haron'.

Monis' reaction was swift: 'That's not me. Hang up now!'

He instructed the hostages to shut down communication and not to answer any further calls, and expressed open contempt towards the lead police negotiator, Peter. 'If Peter calls, ask him "Where's the flag?"' Monis told them. 'If he says there's none, tell him to fuck off.'

Jarrod offered to try and print 'a hundred flags' if he would 'let the pregnant lady go'. Monis wasn't buying that either.

It had still not occurred to any of the hostages that the reason police were not providing a flag was because of apprehension Monis might use it to stage an atrocity.

Marcia later spoke eloquently of their collective frustration: 'He's asking for a flag and a phone call. If that hadn't been done for the whole day, it wasn't going to happen. So I knew [now] his demands were not going to be met. There was no negotiation for the whole day; it was just me on the phone trying to get a flag . . . trying to get Tony Abbott to give us a call. That didn't happen. And not being able to accomplish *anything* for hours and hours and hours; it made me feel very hopeless.'

The public messaging from police and politicians was not helping matters. Every time a senior figure took to the airwaves—fudging the gunman's demands or claiming police had contact with the café and that negotiations were proceeding—Monis grew more irate.

This had first become apparent at lunchtime, when Tony Abbott had given a press conference in which he'd said the hostage-taker's demands were unknown.

Shortly afterwards, police intercepted a phone call Jarrod made from the café: 'The brother would like to ask why is the prime minister being dishonest and saying that he does not know the intentions of the brother and his motivations. Why is he not telling the truth?'

At two press briefings, at 4.45 p.m. and 6.45 p.m., Deputy Commissioner Cath Burn repeated the claim that police had been in contact with the hostage-taker, generating further consternation in the café.

Desperately seeking a different way to deliver Monis the audience he was demanding, the group came up with the plan of posting videos to social media. 'It was like a brainstorming session, everyone coming up with ideas of how to get him what he wanted, which was to be in the press and on the media,' Louisa recalls. 'So everyone was trying to brainstorm these ideas: "YouTube! Good idea! Facebook, great, yes, yes! Make YouTube videos, post it to Facebook. That's how we'll do it, that's how we'll get the truth—his version of it, anyway—out there!" Who had that original idea? I couldn't tell you.'

Monis latched on to this plan with gusto. This would grab the outside world's attention, elevate the profile of Islamic State, put the siege centre stage. The women had to go in front of the camera, he declared. That would give it emotional punch. 'We should get the women to do it, because they will listen to them . . . You just tell the truth, but this is what you got to say . . .'

A macabre casting session ensued. Monis selected Marcia, Louisa, Selina and Julie as his mouthpieces while he sat on the banquette with his gun over his knee, relishing his role as director. Joel was to be the cameraman, recording it all on his iPhone. Viswa was to hold up the flag as backdrop.

At one point Monis attempted a lame joke, referring to the physical appearance of the Indian-born IT manager: 'You can see Viswa's face in the video. They probably think he is the brother.'

The others made a show of polite, awkward laughter. Joel quipped back: 'You can take his clothes and get away if you want to.'

It was demoralising that they had to stoop to this. But at least it kept Monis focused on something other than threats and rants.

Julie Taylor would later recall this as a time of relative respite: 'We were all [absorbed], including Monis, with making videos and trying to get them onto the internet . . . People were calling news agencies who appeared to be open to airing the video; and [getting them] uploaded to YouTube and Facebook. It took a very long time and it was a period when Monis wasn't threatening anyone or being aggressive, I guess because everyone was trying constructively to help, I think that it distracted him from threatening us.'

Louisa was thankful the younger hostages could figure out how to get the phone videos uploaded. 'The kids were on it, they were working it through. Thank God, because I think all of that prolonged our lives.'

Joel uploaded the four recordings, labelling the files 'SYDNEY HOSTAGE SPEAKING PART 1 TO 4' and giving them Lindt hashtags. He had continued to harbour fantasies of being able to plunge his hidden Stanley knife or the scissors into Monis if he got the chance. But just as Jarrod had earlier, he pictured the consequences if he failed: 'I played it out in my head. If I miss—and there was a good chance I could miss, you know—that he could kill someone then and there. He had a shotgun that was sawn-off.' The bullets, Joel worried, could spray anywhere. In his heart he knew it was not worth the risk.

In any case, Monis eventually told Fiona to take Joel's apron off. Joel handed it to the gunman, who laid it on the bench. Inwardly, Joel breathed a sigh of relief—Monis had not seemed to notice the blade and the scissors in the pockets.

On the fourth floor of the Channel 7 building, opposite the café, Greg Parker and the sniper had been joined by a third person—senior reporter Chris Reason, who had only just returned to work that morning after a precious six-month break with his family. Now, like Parker, he found himself at the centre of the most extraordinary news event of his career.

Channel 7 management had persuaded police to let Reason back into the building at around 5 p.m. He was the only journalist in the country allowed to cross police lines that night. The briefing officer gave him a stark warning: 'If there is a bomb in the backpack, if it does go off, you will hear it before you feel it. Duck under a desk, dive to the floor, because this whole place will be shattered glass.' Under the agreement, he would do one live cross for the main Channel 7 bulletin at 6 p.m., and then leave. Police looked through his viewfinder to ensure the background would give away nothing operationally sensitive. Then they left him to it.

Six o'clock came and went, but no one had come to get him. Reason stayed on. He estimates he did thirty to forty live crosses that night, not just to an Australian audience but to audiences around the world.

Greg Parker remained glued, hour after hour, to his camera with the powerful lens. The view into the café was very clear. 'Once dark fell and Monis turned the lights off it became less clear but it was still possible to make him out; the cameras could see his shape, his movements, the gun and the backpack,' Reason says. 'Sitting with the sniper in the dark, watching the horror only 30 to 40 metres away, I knew everyone was hanging off every piece of information we could offer—including, most likely, the hostages' families and friends.'

Family members had been slowly trickling into the forward command post at the leagues' club from late morning.

Harriette's sister-in-law, 'M', drove down from Newcastle to rendezvous with Jorge, who was her brother and Harriette's partner.

She found the roads into the city blocked from the north side of the harbour, so she caught a ferry across to Circular Quay and ran up to St James Station, where she found Jorge sitting disconsolately on the kerbside, still in his work gear.

Jorge told her that Harriette (or 'Yetty', as the family called her) had managed to send him a few texts. But none of the general duties police standing guard around the outer cordon seemed interested.

'I can't believe they didn't want to know!' M recalls. 'I thought maybe it was the way Jorge presented, still in his hi-vis shirt, maybe that was why they didn't take any notice. So I went up to one of the TOU [Tactical Operations Unit] guys and showed him the phone. They checked our ID and then we were thrown into a police car.'

The car took them the long way around, via Redfern and back to the forward command post set up in the leagues' club. There at last they met with detectives and discussed the phone messages.

Jorge explained that Harriette had access to her phone because she had left it in the upstairs locker room, opposite the women's toilets, before she started work. She had obviously secretly retrieved it after going to the bathroom. He was convinced, from the tone of her texts, that Monis was unaware she had access to it—and that therefore they could trust her information.

But the police were unpersuaded, and discouraged Jorge from seeking details from Harriette. 'When she called, I asked her: "Can you see any wires coming out of the bag?" And she went: "I don't want to talk about that, I love you." And the police in the background are going: "No, no, don't ask her any questions." They believed he was listening to all the phone calls.'

Jorge told the police he had done the stonework inside the café and could get in touch with the architect if they needed blueprints of the shop fitout. A car was sent to get the plans. Then they waited.

At around 3 p.m. police decided to move the swelling number of family members and friends from the forward command post to a suite of rooms at the old King Street complex of the Supreme Court, a short walk along Elizabeth Street towards Hyde Park. But it soon became apparent that there was next to no information available to them.

A detective sergeant briefed them in broad terms about how the siege was being managed, stressing that if they received any messages from inside the café they should immediately alert police. The police team was 'actively negotiating' with the gunman, they were told. But, like Cath Burn, the detective sergeant did not explain that there had been no direct engagement with Monis.

At half past five, Selina sent a text to seventeen friends and members of her family re-stating Monis' demands. A few minutes later, Marcia posted on Facebook: 'he is going to kill us'. Alarmed relatives called the emergency operators on triple zero. At 7 p.m. Marcia texted her husband along the same lines: 'I'm scared, he is going to kill us.'

Shortly after this, Paolo Vassallo received a vital piece of intelligence from inside the café. At the time he was lying in a bed at St Vincent's hospital, surrounded by an electronic chorus of beeping machines and heart monitors. Now physically safe, emotionally and mentally he was plagued by thoughts of what his colleagues were still enduring. At 7.05 p.m. he heard the ping of a text coming in. It was from Tori: 'Tell the police the lobby door is unlocked. He is sitting in the corner on his own.'

Paolo immediately yelled to one of the detectives to come over. He showed him the text and made him promise to pass it on to the police commanders straight away.

This was the kind of news Paolo had been longing for ever since his escape. He was convinced police would see this as the chance to end the ordeal for his colleagues.

Later, Paolo would think sadly of the false hope that must have entered Tori's head at that moment.

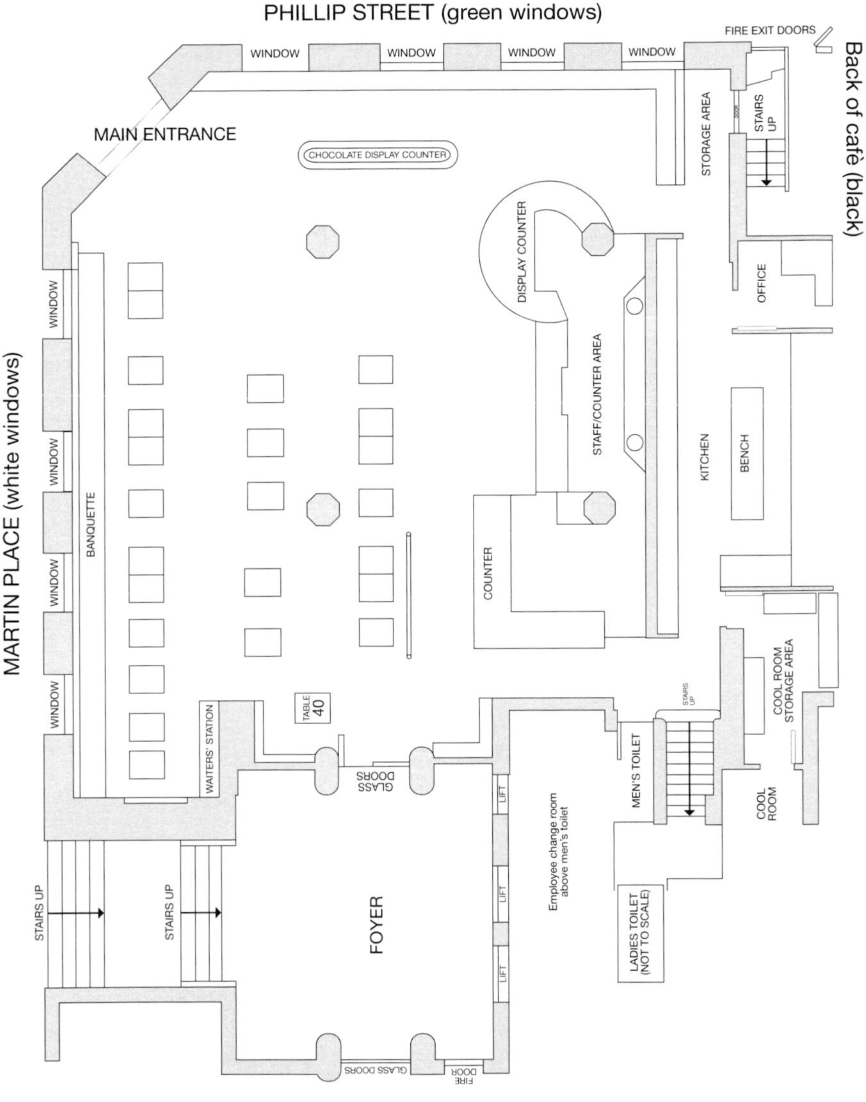

Layout of the Lindt Café, adapted from *Inquest into the deaths arising from the Lindt Café Siege: Findings and recommendations*, State Coroner of NSW

Man Haron Monis dressed as Shia cleric in 2010. (KATE GERAGHTY/FAIRFAX)

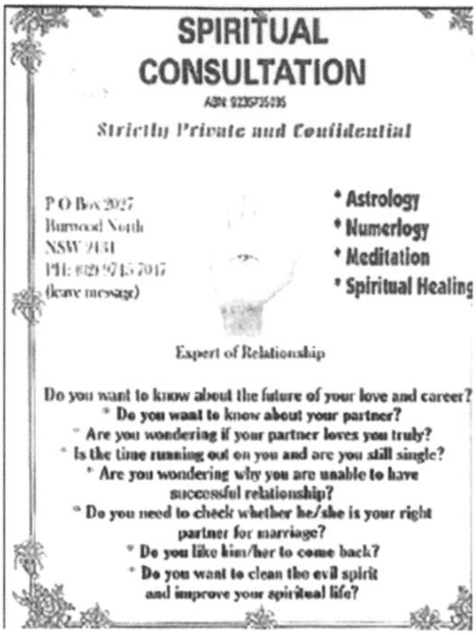

An ad for Monis' spiritual healing service. (CORONER'S COURT OF NSW)

A screenshot of Monis inside Lindt Café during the early stage of siege.

(Top and above) Hostages with hands up against the café's Martin Place windows.

Hostage Joel Herat unfurling Monis' *shahada* flag.

The siege attracted huge domestic and international media coverage.
(ANDREA FALLETTA/NURPHOTO VIA GETTY IMAGES)

Tactical police wait at the corner of Martin Place and Elizabeth Street, a block below the café.
(FAIRFAX)

Premier Mike Baird, flanked by Police Commissioner Andrew Scipione.
(DANIEL MUNOZ/GETTY IMAGES)

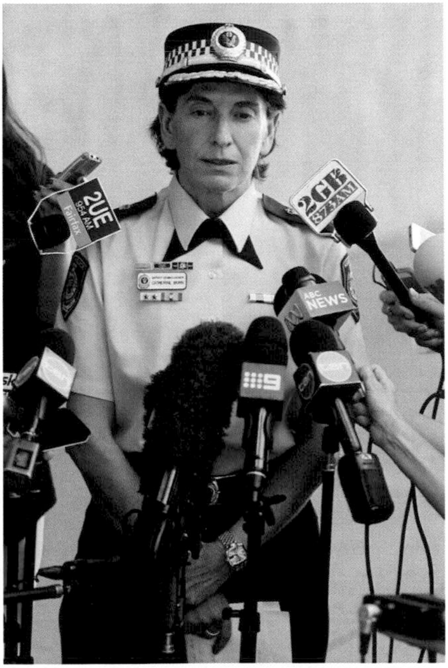

Deputy Police Commissioner Cath Burn.
(JOOSEP MARTINSON/GETTY IMAGES)

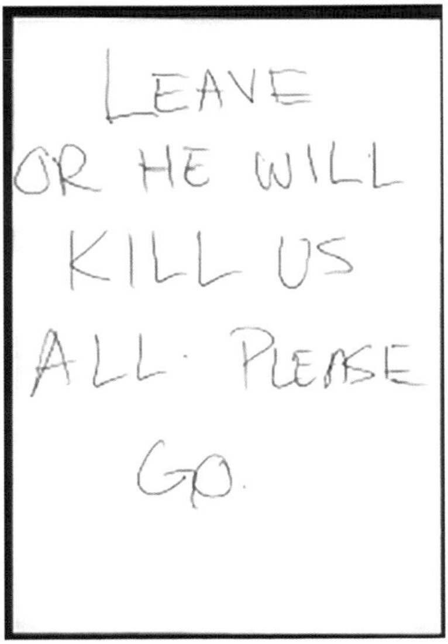

The sign held up by Fiona Ma, warning off the police. (CORONER'S COURT OF NSW)

(Left to right) Harriette Denny, Julie Taylor, Viswa Ankireddi and Joel Herat flee the café at 2.03 a.m. (JOOSEP MARTINSON/ GETTY IMAGES)

Heavily armed tactical police outside the café. (DON ARNOLD/ GETTY IMAGES)

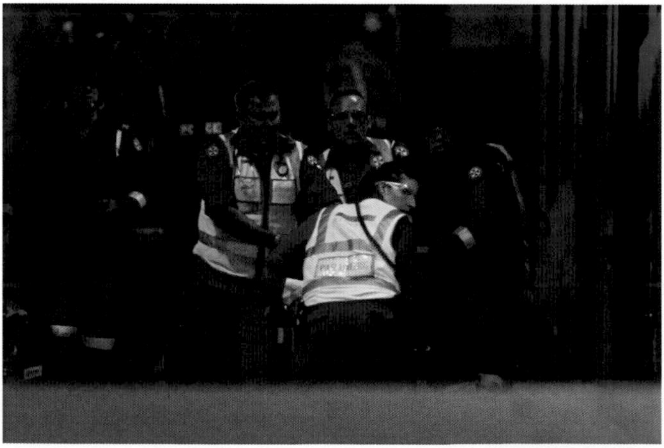

Paramedics bring wounded hostages from the café after the police emergency action. (ANDREW MEARES/ FAIRFAX)

The image of hostage April Bae in the arms of a tactical officer made newspaper front pages all over the world. (MARK METCALFE/GETTY IMAGES)

Memorial pictures of Katrina Dawson and Tori Johnson in the sea of flowers. (WILLIAM WEST/AFP/GETTY IMAGES)

Hostages Fiona Ma and Selina Win Pe visiting the sea of flowers in Martin Place. (DON ARNOLD/GETTY IMAGES)

Reunited. Hostages Louisa Hope and Jarrod Morton-Hoffman at the first anniversary remembrance service. (JAMES ALCOCK/FAIRFAX)

At around 7.38 p.m. one of the snipers in the Westpac building caught a glimpse of the top third of Monis' head through a tall narrow window of the café the police had dubbed 'White Window 4'. (The windows along Martin Place had been designated 'white' and those along Phillip Street 'green'.)

White Window 4 was furthest away from the entrance, up towards the waiter's nook, where Monis had been trying to stay out of sight. He was sitting below the black *shahada* flag.

Confident at first that he had identified Monis correctly, because of the headband bearing Arabic script, the sniper, 'Sierra 3.1', radioed his sighting through to the deputy tactical commander at the leagues' club. The three snipers at the Westpac post conferred quickly: if they were to take a shot, one would breach the Westpac glass to make a hole for Sierra 3.1 to shoot through. The third man would come in with a simultaneous shot.

They recorded an image of what they could see of the gunman—the crown of his head framed in the lower portion of the window—and sent it back to the forward command post. The tactical commander queried how solid the identification was. What if a hostage had been made to wear the headband as a decoy? And if Monis was sitting close to other hostages, what if a bullet passed through Monis and into one of the others?

The snipers remained unaware of the text Tori had sent to Paolo at 7.05 p.m. (which he also sent to Lindt manager Alistair Keep at 7.40 p.m.) describing Monis' location as 'sitting in the corner on his own' inside the café.

Also worrying the tactical commander and his deputy was whether the snipers had a clear legal right to take a shot. According to their training, a shot was only justified if any of the hostages were in imminent danger. What did that actually mean? Was it demonstrably the case at this point in the siege? What kind of evidence would they have to stand and provide in a courtroom?

One of the snipers would later tell the inquest, 'What I believe is if we had chosen to shoot the offender at [that time] and kill him, we'd probably be sitting here right now discussing whether to charge Sierra 3.1 with murder or not. That's my thought.'

On top of that was the difficulty of shooting through glass and then being sure that the shot was instantly lethal, achieving what the snipers called 'flaccid paralysis' so there could be no reflex movement that might trigger a bomb.

By the time they had gone through all of this, the opportunity had slipped away. The coroner would later take the view that the snipers, indeed all the front-line police, had had the legal authority to use lethal force against Monis from the early stages of the siege.

Katrina asked if there was still any food. By now it had been getting on for ten hours since the start of the siege. Some, like Jarrod, were not hungry. Others thought they could manage something.

Monis told Fiona and Jarrod that he didn't want ham or chicken. Jarrod assured him he would find an alternative. 'I'll even change my gloves; I won't serve you anything that's been touched by ham,' Jarrod told him. In his head he was thinking quite the opposite—that he wouldn't mind smearing bacon all over Monis' victuals.

Fiona went to the kitchen and ferreted out croissants, quiche with salad, and brownies. Jarrod walked around with a big bucket of Lindt chocolate balls.

Monis continued to follow radio coverage of the siege. The reporting only seemed to agitate him further. Julie remembered him saying, 'The police are lying. Politicians are lying. I might have to shoot someone so that they take it seriously.'

At 7.59 p.m., Monis ordered Fiona to switch the lights off inside the café. Soon afterwards, he heard a live broadcast of a media conference being held by Andrew Scipione and Premier Mike Baird.

Baird praised the 'outstanding' efforts of the police and their professionalism. Monis started talking back at the broadcast: 'Be professional, what have you done, what have you done?' the gunman muttered angrily to himself.

Scipione then went on to lavish praise on the negotiators as 'the very best in the world' and to say that 'we have got contact with him'. Monis bristled again: 'He said he has contact with me?'

A short time later the covert listening bug picked up Monis still grumbling, 'I'm sorry, but both of them are wrong, wrong. Bad things happen.' Then the transmission faded into inaudibility.

Monis now ordered the hostages to stop answering calls from the police negotiators and to switch off the few phones he had been allowing them to use under his direction.

British police experts, who later reviewed the conduct of the siege, queried why the New South Wales Police negotiating team was not given the chance to help shape the public messaging from Scipione, Burn and Baird. The only explanation given later was that it seemed no one had thought of it at the time.

Another opportunity to try and hook Monis into direct dialogue had been lost.

There was one small improvement as the darkness closed in: the hostages no longer had to keep holding up the flag. Jarrod suggested it be taped up onto the glass—a suggestion Monis accepted.

Monis began to keep Julie and Selina close by either side of him. According to Julie, Selina had earlier claimed to be pregnant, and everyone could see that Julie was. That made two prize human shields in his eyes.

Julie was again turning over in her mind the prospect of escape, but judged it to be as dangerous as ever. She wanted to keep her unborn child safe. Yet she was also worried about being wounded or worse, particularly if the police came through the door with their weapons blazing. She knew very well that sitting next to Monis carried with it the risk of being injured or shot in crossfire. 'There's no way he can be expecting to walk out of this alive,' she thought.

Harriette was also consumed with thoughts of keeping her baby safe. She didn't want to die. She wanted to be a mother, to bring her child into the world and nurture it. Being made to sit in the group drawn even closer around Monis increased her apprehension. And being surrounded by chairs, stacked on top of tables as he had ordered, felt like a form of suffocation—like the last slender route to escape was being blocked off.

Most of the hostages continued doing their best to fly under Monis' radar, with one exception: Louisa's mother, Robin. A straight-talking, down-to-earth countrywoman, Robin had stood up earlier in the afternoon to demand that she be allowed to visit the toilet and that her daughter receive the medication she needed.

After that outburst, Monis summoned Louisa to come and sit near him in the alcove at the rear of the café. 'Come here,' he said. 'Why do you need medication?'

'I have MS,' she told him.

He didn't know what MS was, so she started explaining the disease to him, speaking as conversationally as she could.

'I thought it might make a point of human connection,' Louisa recalls. 'He asked where my medication was and I said in my handbag. Which one is that, he asked, and I pointed it out. He said, "Pass Louisa's handbag. That red one—pass it. Okay, have your medication." I popped out my pills and used the water bottle and sat it on the table.'

Monis made a big show of these occasional gestures of solicitude. Again, he would proclaim how much better he was treating the hostages than was Tony Abbott. But these moments did nothing to allay the constant sense of threat that prevailed inside the café.

Robin was not to be kept in her place so easily, even by a man armed with a shotgun and possibly a bomb. Later she got to her feet again, challenging him for keeping her, a seventy-three-year-old, as captive. 'And how old are you?' she demanded to know.

To Louisa's surprise, Monis told her his age: fifty. His patience with the older woman was beginning to wear thin, however. When Robin sat down again, Monis said to Louisa: 'Tell your mother to keep quiet.'

Louisa didn't want any more provocations: 'I spoke to her directly, "Mum, you are an old lady. You must keep quiet—no more now, no more to be said." And I'm giving her the look and trying to keep control of her. That became pretty full-on in itself. The greatest challenge emotionally for me was being in the café with my mother. Her presence—and my need to try and protect her as best I could—influenced my actions both in the café that day and every day thereafter.'

Robin continued to seethe, but did so away from Monis' earshot. 'I would like to spit in his face,' she told Jarrod and Fiona on one visit to the toilet, giving them a rare laugh.

Monis' enmity towards Tori, which had been overt from the beginning, seemed to become more entrenched as the evening wore on.

'He had started to form a relationship with some of us in a kind of way—with Jarrod and Fiona, and with Selina—but it was open animus towards Tori, that was obvious,' Louisa says. 'And Tori did not try to engage him. He pulled back and he sat with Robin because she was agitated.'

Time was grinding on. Now that night had come, many of the hostages were losing all sense of how long they had been there.

It was so quiet they could hear the faint beep of the lights changing at the pedestrian crossing outside on the empty street. Every hour or so the café's large industrial ice machine would drop a load of ice into the silence. This would make Monis jump each time he heard it, as though he thought the police were breaking in.

His paranoia extended to the wall behind his back in the waiter's nook where he had stationed himself out of sight of the windows. 'What's this made of?' he demanded to know, banging on it.

Jarrod had not the faintest idea, but tried to wing it yet again. 'It's plywood with wood behind it, and then there is brick and then there's insulation and marble on the other side. I swear it's really strong—they can't break through it,' he assured Monis.

Harriette, as she followed this exchange, was amazed yet again at Jarrod's ability to dream up stuff like that on the spot.

At one stage Monis pondered aloud what the café would look like if he blew up his bomb. 'Who would pay for the damages?' he asked.

Harriette says: 'I don't remember anyone saying anything back. I just remember Monis answering his [own] question and having a little laugh, saying the insurance company would pay for it.'

Monis had no exit strategy as far as the hostages could see. It was something Stefan had warned police of when he first escaped the café.

Marcia started pressing the gunman on what would happen to the rest of them if he let some hostages go in response to his demands being met. 'If you're going to let five people go if you talk to Tony Abbott, and two people if the media says it's an Islamic State flag, and one if they give you a flag, what's going to happen to the rest of us and what's going to happen to you?'

Monis ducked the question: 'Don't worry, I have a plan for myself.' What that was he never told them.

The strain was taking its toll on them all by now—even Jarrod, who threw up from the stress on one of his trips to the toilet. But he knew he had to keep an outward appearance of calm: 'I washed myself off, dried my face and thought, "Back to work".'

Later he would reflect on why he had not attempted to escape earlier, as the other five had. There were so many opportunities he and Fiona had when they were in the kitchen together. The fire door was so close. But every time he thought of escape, it came with discomfiting feelings of guilt: 'I don't think I would have been able to deal with that afterwards, deciding that my life was worth so much more than anyone else's; that I would be willing to sacrifice an entire room of innocent people just to save my own skin.'

Jarrod also felt a certain immunity, which he put down to 'youthful arrogance'—a conviction that somehow he would come out all right, and therefore owed it to the others to stay and help de-escalate things inside the café.

Fiona and Tori used the refuge of the bathroom to discuss yet again what would happen if anyone else escaped. Tori was very clearly against; like Jarrod, he believed it would put the lives of others at risk. All three of them knew that Monis had a keen awareness of their individual presence in the café, and that they would be instantly missed if they tried to sneak out or make a run for it. Fiona would make a point of telling the inquest later that Tori felt a responsibility for the others, as she did herself.

Louisa was still convinced that help was surely on its way: 'It never occurred to us that the police weren't coming. I just assumed, "Okay, we will be here for a little while. Let's sit this out and the cops will come soon, any minute now." Right to the end, it never occurred to me that they didn't have a plan to come and get us.'

CHAPTER 10

THE LONG NIGHT

Night was well and truly upon the café and the lights had gone off inside. The tactical team was well aware Monis wasn't making contact and that his demands were not being met. They could hear occasional observations from the snipers over the secure radio network. None of them could predict how this would eventually play out, but they couldn't see much sign of progress.

Officer A, on standby with other members of the Alpha team inside the vehicle bay on Phillip Street, had been called to a number of sieges in the past, although nothing on this scale. 'We [were] told during the hostages escaping that he was becoming more and more agitated, so it was my opinion it wasn't going very well,' he would tell investigators later.

His day had begun at 4.45 a.m. when he'd risen to catch the train to work. Shortly after 10 a.m., he and other members of his team had arrived at the café. Officer A's gear, which weighed between 25 and 30 kilograms, included a Glock pistol worn in a holster, his M4 assault rifle with three magazines, three stun grenades (known to the men as 'flashbangs' or 'stunnies'), his bullet proof vest, radio, helmet, headphones, gloves and night vision goggles. Now the men were trying to conserve energy as best they could, knowing the order to 'stand to' (assume action stations) could come at any moment.

The snipers in the buildings nearby were also having to maintain constant vigilance. Their surveillance role had become even more vital because of the failure of New South Wales Police technicians to get covert vision from inside the café.

The police marksmen had taken up three positions. The two-man 'Sierra 1' team was inside the Reserve Bank across the road on Phillip Street. 'Sierra 2' remained embedded on level 4 of the Channel 7 building beside cameraman Greg Parker. And the 'Sierra 3' team, comprising three snipers, had taken up a position on level one of the Westpac building, on the diagonally opposite corner.

All snipers were less than 60 metres from the café. This presented no problem in terms of range, given the men were trained (the coroner was told) to hit something the size of a dollar coin from 100 metres. The bigger problems were visibility and the challenges of shooting through glass.

Each of the sniper posts had drawbacks. The Channel 7 hide had good vision into the Martin Place or 'white' windows, but the station's glass frontage was effectively bulletproof, making a shot from there nigh impossible.

From the Reserve Bank, the view into the Phillip Street (or 'green') windows was obscured by Christmas advertising decals plastered over much of the glass. The only section of the café the team there could see into was the window closest to the fire exit, a part of the room Monis never went to.

That left the Sierra 3 team in the Westpac building with both a good view and the best theoretical possibility of taking a shot should the opportunity and justification arise. Yet even here there were problems. The Westpac glass would have to be breached first before a shot could be fired, running the risk of alerting the gunman. And the 'breacher'—the tactical team member charged with making a hole for the snipers to aim through—was worried that the glass would craze, compromising the marksman's ability to take an accurate shot.

One of the tactical officers had scouted other locations around Martin Place earlier in the day to see if there was an outdoor hide where a sniper team could set up without being seen from the café. No good sites had been found.

For all these reasons, as well as uncertainty about when a shot would be legally justified, a sniping solution to the siege had been pretty well ruled out early on. But their watching and observing role through high-powered telescopic sights remained critical.

The head of the tactical teams, 'Tango Charlie', knew the lengthening stalemate presented a problem for his men. Fatigue would eventually become an issue. But he was more concerned about the lack of options he was being given to work with.

'Hope is not a strategy,' Nick Kaldas used to say to his senior officers. Yet at the Police Operations Centre (POC) hope so far seemed to be the dominant, and maybe only, strategy.

The senior commanders appeared to be adhering to the belief that Monis would eventually crack and surrender. If the worst occurred and hostages were suddenly deemed to be at imminent risk, the police would have to storm in with little notice.

Tango Charlie, a chief inspector and TOU commander at the forward command post, was unhappy about this. He had tagged Monis a terrorist from the beginning, and did not believe the gunman had an exit plan. A veteran of twenty-five years in his field, an active member of the Army Reserve with experience of scores of domestic sieges, he knew that if Monis did not start letting hostages go, and negotiations remained stalled, the siege was only going to end in one of two ways.

The first was by way of a police 'emergency action', or 'EA'—storming the café because a crisis had erupted and it was no longer an option to stand by and watch it happen. The second option, much preferred by Tango Charlie and his men, was a planned rescue attempt, known in the lingo of the assault teams as a 'deliberate action' or 'DA'.

Having a DA in hand meant they would be able to choose when to enter the café, not wait to respond to a crisis triggered by the hostage-taker. It meant picking a time when Monis was distracted or when they judged his guard to be down, or at some other point when they held the advantage. Hopefully they might pick that moment so well the hostage-taker would not have time to aim and fire his shotgun or detonate the supposed bomb in his backpack. In Tango Charlie's mind, it was definitely the lower risk option.

But only one person had the power to approve a DA that night, and that was the commander at the POC. Between noon and around 9.30 p.m. the man occupying that position was Assistant Commissioner Mark Murdoch, who later handed over to Assistant Commissioner Mark Jenkins. Neither of them approved the DA handed up to them by the tactical teams.

The emergency action plan had been drawn up early in the siege, within the first hour and a half. But devising the deliberate action plan was a more complex business and Tango Charlie had asked one of his most experienced operatives, 'Delta Alpha', to take on the task.

That officer had done so carefully. He'd cased the building, studied the entrances and exits and considered some potential covert entry options. This included an examination of an internal vent that ran from the roof of the building down to the café, but it was too narrow and even trying to clamber in would make too much noise, the officer decided. He discounted it as a viable option.

Delta Alpha went back to the idea of a planned assault, working out how many men would be involved and what equipment they would need. He also sought the input of the sniper teams.

When the draft DA plan was complete, Tango Charlie looked it over, asked some questions, suggested a couple of refinements and declared himself happy. At around 7 p.m., he presented it to Lima, the forward commander at the leagues' club at the time, who sent it on to the POC for approval. Nothing came back down the line.

Through the remainder of the evening, both Tango Charlie and his deputy pursued the unresolved matter of the DA on several occasions, only to keep getting it bounced back unapproved.

It was deeply frustrating. No one had told Tango Charlie the plan was unworkable. No one had raised any objections to any aspect of it. 'I believed that it was a viable plan [that] should be well considered,' he would explain later at the inquest. 'I had an interest because I preferred my men when they did enter, if it was necessary, I would have preferred they do it as a DA, not an EA.'

What made the knockback even more baffling was that a DA could never have been launched just on the strength of approval alone. That was only a first step, which allowed the tactical teams to rehearse a planned assault safe in the knowledge that this would be the plan they would follow if it got through the second stage. That second stage was called 'authorisation', and only when a DA had received both approval *and* authorisation was it a live option.

The failure to clear even the first hurdle sent the plainest possible signal to the tactical teams that early intervention was not on the cards for the top commanders.

'I asked at various times as to what was the status or the outcome, whether it [the DA] had been approved, authorised or no action, and I was advised . . . that the current strategy was not going to be deviated from and the deliberate action had not been approved,' Tango Charlie said. This was unprecedented in his long experience: never before had he been on a high-risk operation where a police commander had rejected a DA.

The to-ing and fro-ing went on right through the night. Soon after midnight, POC commander Jenkins briefed Jeff Loy, the most senior officer now left in the State Crisis Centre. Jenkins told Loy there was no DA plan because he'd been advised the tactical police would not be able to enact it without 'probable loss of life' and that 'they couldn't get it under the loss of two or three lives'.

Yet the officer at the POC responsible for briefing Jenkins on the DA plan would later testify differently. That officer, given the codename 'Tactical Adviser', said he never told Jenkins there would be 'probable' loss of hostages' lives if the DA was actioned, although he couldn't absolutely guarantee a safe outcome.

One of Britain's leading experts on armed policing, who reviewed the siege for the coroner months later, declared himself baffled by the failure of the senior police commanders to sign off on the DA. Deputy Chief Constable Simon Chesterman told the ABC's *Four Corners*: 'The plan was a good plan. It had been worked up by some very professional and experienced officers. It had been briefed, it had been rehearsed by the Australian Defence Force . . . It was their best chance of resolving the siege with minimal damage and injury. Can you imagine being in a situation where you're responsible for those people's lives and you haven't got the best possible plan in place? I would have been screaming out for it.'

Another source of friction came at around 8 p.m. when Tango Charlie learnt he had not been consulted about a plan to start toughening the tone of the negotiators' text messages going into the café. He pushed back, saying he should have been consulted. Any attempt to provoke Monis ran the risk of having consequences for his men, poised for action just metres from the café. The plan was dropped.

But this wasn't the only instance of poor communication between the Police Operations Centre and the forward command post. The forward commander, Lima, had contacted the POC in the late afternoon to remind them that he had to be 'kept in the loop' about command decisions.

In truth, he was finding that he had far fewer technical resources at his disposal than he expected. He had no automatic access to the live electronic logs being used by other senior police that night. In fact, he was having difficulty getting any IT capability at all into the leagues' club. When asked during the inquest whether he felt at a 'significant disadvantage' by not having access to real time events during the siege, his reply was unequivocal: 'Yes.'

He also had an inexperienced scribe and was getting no significant information from the listening device after it was deployed soon after 7 p.m. He didn't see any Channel 7 footage until 8 p.m. and missed the broadcast of both the escapes at 3.35 and 4.55 p.m. And because of the paucity of phone lines, conference calls between the POC and the forward command post were taking place around a mobile phone at the leagues' club end.

More insidious were the parallel chains of command and communication developing at both the leagues' club and the POC, not helped by the plethora of different commanders on deck that night. One senior officer later told the inquest the night had become a 'commander-thon.' As the Dawsons' legal team later observed: 'In the midst of attention and resources dedicated to establishing who would be in charge . . . the practical capacity of officers on the ground was overlooked.'

Part of the difficulty was that very few of the senior New South Wales officers had experienced a crisis, that is an unplanned event, where both a POC and a forward command post were in operation. Tango Charlie would testify he'd encountered nothing similar in his twenty-five years of service with police tactical operations teams.

The cracks were beginning to show, and nowhere did this manifest more starkly than in the bungled response to Monis' demands that the Christmas lights in Martin Place be turned off.

Darkness had fallen. Monis was getting agitated about the light streaming in from outside through the high narrow Martin Place windows. 'What light is this?' he demanded to know.

Jarrod told him they were Christmas lights, although in fact they were mainly the reflections bouncing off the mirror-ball effect festive banners the city council had strung on poles along Martin Place. One of those poles was right outside the café.

Monis told Marcia to call the police and get the festive lights turned off, but not all the street lights. Those he wanted kept on so he could see any attempt by the police to sneak up on the café.

As instructed, Marcia called the police negotiator Peter at 8.38 p.m. to say the 'brother' wanted the 'flashing blue Christmas lights' turned off. It was the first time in some hours that Monis had made a new demand that was not a political demand. Potentially it held the prospect of a trade-off.

The lights bothered him repeatedly as the evening wore on. 'He wanted them off completely, he wanted us in total darkness. Every time he was told that the lights couldn't be turned off, he got increasingly agitated,' Fiona said.

But instead of police seizing quickly on the lights demand as a bargaining chip, what followed degenerated into a debacle. Reg, the negotiation coordinator, relayed the demand to the POC for a decision, but he failed to inform either of the forward commanders, Lima or Victor. Nor did he fully brief his superior, Graeme. He did, however, raise the matter with a detective sergeant at the forward command post, who in turn contacted Nick Speranza, a supervisor for energy company Ausgrid, just after 9 p.m.

Speranza made some inquiries inside the company and then phoned back to say he could send out a team to shut down the Martin Place lights by making an adjustment to connections in a nearby substation. The Ausgrid team assembled at their depot at 10.30 p.m. Two vehicles stood at the ready to drive into the city, but after waiting around for fifteen minutes or so, they were sent home again because no decision had yet come back from the POC.

The commanders who had taken over at the field post and the POC between 9.30 and 10 p.m., Victor and Jenkins respectively, remained oblivious to the lights demand and would remain unaware of it for the next two and a half hours. Soon after midnight, the issue suddenly forced its way back onto the agenda. Monis had continued to raise the issue, with growing irritability and insistence. Selina, growing distraught, called the emergency line on triple zero, having failed to raise any of the negotiators.

'The person who is holding us hostage has kindly asked the lights at Martin Place be switched off,' Selina told the emergency operator. 'They are glaring into the Lindt Café. He doesn't want any lights here. We asked for this request two to three hours ago. If not done as soon as possible, he will start to kill us . . . I need you to switch the lights off as soon as possible or he is going to hurt us.'

At home, Speranza got another call from police. It was now 1.40 a.m. Yes, he could send another team out, but did they not know that one Ausgrid team had been deployed earlier in the evening and sent home? The police said they would phone him back. They never did. The 'Christmas lights' would remain on until the end of the siege.

Reg would later explain that he had been waiting for his negotiations commander, Graeme, to get back to him on the matter, while Graeme insisted he was unaware Reg was expecting a decision from him and that he thought the lights had simply come up 'in conversation' with the hostages. The litany of errors was magnified by the listening device failing altogether for around half an hour just after midnight. This was the very time when the hostages were frantically trying to place a series of calls to the negotiators about the lights—calls that were never answered because the entire negotiating team was in the middle of a handover to a relief team.

It was no small error. The inquest's senior counsel, Jeremy Gormly, would later describe the lights saga as 'comprehensively mismanaged'. He speculated that if the listening device had been working at that time, it might have alerted the police twenty minutes sooner to the fact that the issue had been lost sight of earlier in the evening.

'In the circumstances, an additional twenty minutes may have permitted police to make definite arrangements for the lights to have been turned off and to contact the stronghold to request something in return,' Gormly said. 'The failure in [listening device] capability at such a pivotal time created a real loss of opportunity.'

The lights debacle would be held up by the Johnson and Dawson families as emblematic of the fundamental problems that dogged the siege response.

By late on the night of 15 December, the unfinished matter of approving a DA was still bouncing back and forth between the POC and forward commanders.

At 9.45 p.m. a series of meetings occurred to formalise the handover of the senior command from Murdoch to Jenkins. An entry in the police logs noted Jenkins still had to be briefed on the outstanding DA request. But even before that briefing occurred, Jenkins received a late-night phone call from Scipione just as the commissioner was wrapping up for the night and preparing to leave the State Crisis Centre for some rest. In that call, the subject of a DA came up. Who said what to whom during that conversation would be contested after the siege.

The call, at 10.57 p.m., was short, no more than four minutes long. At Jenkins' end, a police scribe took down the following note: 'DA plan to occur as last resort—COP'. In police speak, COP stands for Commissioner of Police.

At the inquest Jenkins first ascribed the remark that a DA would only be a 'last resort' to Scipione. But in the witness box two days later, he changed his mind. He said that, on reflection, it was 'highly likely' that he, not Scipione, said those words because his scribe would only have been able to hear his end of the conversation. However, he gave no further explanation of the context in which the words had come up.

Scipione, who gave evidence nearly three months after Jenkins, insisted he had only rung Jenkins as a kind of 'welfare check'. The police chief remained adamant he had never used the words recorded by Jenkins' scribe. Indeed, to have done so would have run counter to his own assertion that he never gave any orders throughout the siege.

'I didn't use the words "DA plan to occur as a last resort" because I had no reason to make that recommendation to him,' Scipione told the coroner bluntly. 'That's not an area where I would in any way play a role. They were his words; they weren't my words. I didn't have enough information to form a view. It wasn't something I was required to do.'

Twenty minutes *after* concluding the phone conversation with Scipione, Jenkins was presented with the resubmitted DA plan by the tactical adviser at the POC. The adviser was unaware of the phone call with Scipione. Like Tango Charlie, the tactical adviser was keen to get the DA approved so the men could start rehearsing it. But, like Murdoch before him, Jenkins declined to approve it. At the end of the conversation, Jenkins in effect told the tactical adviser, 'I understand my job, just go and do yours.'

Jenkins would later tell the coroner that he never approved the DA because he formed the view that it would be 'very very very risky'.

Asked at the inquest if he had ever told Jenkins or the tactical adviser that the DA would be 'very very very risky', Tango Charlie's reply was unequivocal: 'No, I did not.'

The DA was such a delicate issue that the army liaison officers at both command posts found themselves stepping around it as gingerly as if it were an unexploded landmine.

The army sniper present at the leagues' club told investigators after the siege that he looked over an 'incomplete' DA plan just after midnight but was at pains to stress that he did so just for 'situational awareness'. During the ten-minute conversation, the pair discussed possible risks to hostages and what 'additional specialised assets' the TOU team had. 'I was very careful during this conversation [with the police] to ensure that the TOU planner did not think we were trying to take over his plan or be critical of it,' the army sergeant said.

At the POC 'Major S', the senior army liaison officer, sat in on some conferences held among senior police. At around 6.30 p.m. he learnt of the plan to prepare for a possible handover to Queensland and Australian Federal Police operatives should the siege drag on. Major S reported this back to the army's Special Forces operations command, who then came back with an offer for the incoming interstate police teams. Once they reached Sydney, they could if they wished familiarise themselves with the café by using the mock-up TAG-East had constructed out at the Holsworthy Army Base.

This offer was never taken up. By the time the Queensland and federal officers had arrived and been sworn in, it was already approaching the early hours of the next morning.

The overall head of police tactical operations also asked Major S if the Special Forces would take a look at the still unapproved DA. It was sent through to TAG-East for review. Replying via Major S, TAG-East advised that the DA plan was 'tactically feasible', but this advice did not appear to make any difference—Jenkins' decision not to approve the DA remained in place.

For the police, the darkest shadow over the entire night was the bomb. It was indeed the overwhelming reason the top commanders later cited for not approving a deliberate action plan. Repeatedly in the witness box, they said they feared sentencing their own men and the hostages to death if they sent them in and Monis triggered an explosive device.

It was preying on the minds of the TOU men as well. One later described how his buddy had shown him a picture of his daughter on his phone as they waited out the long hours in the vehicle bay. 'He said, "Mate, what if we don't come out of this?" We were just thinking of the worst case scenarios, the shotgun wasn't my biggest concern, the bomb was the . . . petrifying thing.'

Given the bomb lay at the root of so much police decision-making, it would have seemed essential to glean as much early intelligence as possible about Monis' bomb-making skills, if they existed at all.

Monis' credibility in this respect had already been dented by the failure of police search parties to locate any of the supposed bombs the gunman had claimed his 'brothers' had planted around the city.

The next obvious place to look for clues was at his unit in Denman Avenue, Wiley Park. The gunman might have left traces of internet searches on how to source materials for constructing a home-made improvised explosives device. Perhaps there was physical evidence of such materials having been stored there. Maybe police would find a suicide note, or some other pointer to his ultimate intentions. All these were compelling reasons to search the flat as soon as possible. As the UK expert Chesterman later pointed out, 'the greatest threat was the backpack . . . any intelligence around whether that was a viable IED or not would have changed the course of the strategy'.

But the authorisation for the search was not given until 3 p.m. and it would be many more hours after that before police finally entered Monis' unit. The inquest later picked over why the delay—which could have been critical—occurred.

Police had placed the unit under surveillance by mid-afternoon, but held off making an entry because there was a woman present who they suspected to be Monis' partner, Amirah Droudis.

By 8.30 p.m. that night they still had not moved in. They explained this by saying they feared Monis might exact retribution if he knew the search was taking place. They were also concerned Droudis might copy his tactics and trigger her own siege, given that she was on bail for the murder of Helen Lee. Strangely, 'darkness' was also recorded in the police logs as a reason not to launch the search.

At 9.40 p.m. Droudis got into her black Jeep Cherokee and drove away from the unit. Officers stopped and searched her and only when threatened with a forced entry, did she finally give the police access to the flat at close to 10.30 p.m.

An hour later, at 11.30 p.m., the senior commanders at the POC were told nothing of interest had been found, a message that was confirmed at 1.30 a.m. after a further two hours of searching. No evidence of bomb-making materials or access to them had turned up.

But this news was never conveyed to the men who arguably would have had the most interest in hearing it: the members of the tactical teams on standby to storm the café.

CHAPTER 11

JUST SEVEN REMAIN

The café had gone into shutdown, with the lights off and Monis blocking any further calls to the police negotiators. Between 8.40 p.m. and midnight there would be no engagement at all between the hostages and police. The only exceptions were the call made by Marcia asking for the Christmas lights to be turned off, and a second call she made at 8.42 p.m. telling police to pull back from the windows. 'He can see you,' she warned, alluding to the indistinct reflections of some of the tactical officers in the polished stone of the Reserve Bank opposite.

The negotiating team mistook the apparent lack of activity from inside the café for calm. Peter, the lead negotiator, would later explain that 'there was no indication that the stronghold was at an agitated state; we believed that . . . we were still going to come back the next day, so that was still progressing'.

Between 9 p.m. and 1 a.m. Steve, the police officer who had been left in charge of communicating intelligence from the listening device, sent twenty-two text messages back to colleagues in the negotiators' cell conveying snapshots of what he took to be the mood inside the café. The picture he painted was reassuring.

'[Monis] Speaking very calmly, inquiring as to their welfare,' he wrote in a breezy text at 9.30 p.m.

'Positive response to news coverage,' he texted in another despatch, at around 10.00 p.m. 'Police have decided not do to anything, that is good news. Selina asking to be allowed to talk to us.'

A little later, Steve noted that 'a female was crying and vomiting'. On any ordinary interpretation this might have been read as a sign of extreme stress, but Steve reported that the woman's symptoms had 'no overt cause'.

What Steve was seemingly not picking up on were some of the more alarming statements from Monis coming through the surveillance device: that there was little point allowing the hostages further interaction with police negotiators, for instance. Or that the lead negotiator, Peter, 'could not be relied on for anything'.

Until midnight, Steve was working alongside an officer from the Australian Federal Police. After that he worked on alone, trying to interpret and then convey by phone or text the essence of what the device was picking up. At 1 a.m., the job passed to his colleague 'Mick', who also soldiered on with the job alone. It was an enormous responsibility lying on the two men's shoulders. Inevitably, it left the police operation resting on precarious foundations at a critical point.

By 10 p.m. Mark Jenkins (widely seen as a protégé of Deputy Commissioner Cath Burn) had relieved Mark Murdoch as commander of the Police Operations Centre (POC). The handover was formalised in a joint teleconference between the POC and the forward command post at around 9.45 p.m. Murdoch advised Jenkins that he believed a peaceful outcome could be achieved.

Following the briefing Jenkins was in no hurry to move the dial on police strategy, which remained firmly set on contain and negotiate.

Down at the family reception centre, loved ones and friends were getting increasingly anxious about the stalemate. At 10 p.m., Tori sent a text to his family: 'I'm still alive. Very scared.'

Rosie Connellan asked police if she could answer her son. 'They said, "You had better not"', she recalls, her voice breaking. 'And so I didn't even get back to him, I didn't even message him, and I am heartbroken about that, I will never get over that one. I should have gone on the phone and demanded to speak to Monis—it would have been more than was being done by the people we hoped were doing something.'

In the negotiators' cell at the leagues' club, Peter and the psychiatrist, Brian, were weighing up Monis' capacity for violence. 'Does he have the ticker for it?' Brian pondered. 'A wounded narcissist is a dangerous specimen, because they take the defeat very personally, and whoever it is who has defeated him becomes his ultimate enemy.'

They discussed the fact that Monis had procured the death of his ex-wife through the lover, Amirah Droudis. 'He is not a violent man as such, he just likes a bit of power . . . would that be right?' Peter ventured. 'I don't think he does [have the ticker] because he got his missus to kill his other one . . . *he* doesn't do it, he gets someone else to do it.'

Within a few hours, this assessment that Monis was 'not a violent man' would prove to be tragically wrong.

Jarrod was worried that with the media no longer talking to them, 'we were slowly losing our value as living hostages'. He believed Monis was taking stimulants to try to keep himself alert. It was getting well into the evening and the gunman was showing no signs of flagging.

Monis ordered Jarrod and Harriette to make tea for everyone and Jarrod quietly urged her to come with him into the kitchen to do it. No need, Harriette replied—tea was already available in the barista section of the café.

Jarrod insisted, whispering, 'I want to go to the kitchen, I want to pretend to get teas, so that we can open the back door for the police to come in.' This scared Harriette. The fire door exit might be alarmed, she thought, and she didn't want to put it to the test in front of a man wielding a shotgun.

The pair also conferred in whispers about whether they could drug the gunman, perhaps with sleeping tablets— but neither of them had any. At 9.30 p.m. Jarrod asked Monis if he should call the police again about switching off the Christmas lights. Monis said it would be a waste of time. 'How many times I said about IS flag. It does not make difference one time or ten.'

At around 10.30 p.m. Monis started ordering some of the hostages to ring their families, particularly those with children. The order terrified Harriette, who was convinced these would be their last calls. She started frantically weighing up who she would ring to say goodbye to—Jorge, or her family.

Monis told Viswa Ankireddi to call first. After Viswa had hung up, Monis demanded to know why he hadn't spoken to his young daughter.

'They just think she'll come to the phone and cry. She can't stop,' the IT worker replied.

'Why would she be scared?' Monis chided.

'Because he is not there,' Marcia explained.

Jarrod chipped in: 'It will make her more sad.'

Marcia's call was next: 'Did you have a good day?' the others could hear her saying. 'I love you, just remember that, I love you very much. I'm going to be fine, don't worry . . . I'll be home soon. Okay, sorry I love you.' Then she had to hang up.

Marcia broke down. Her oldest son, Daniel, then aged twenty-one, had been pleading with her not to sound like she was saying goodbye: 'Stop it, Mum, stop it. Everything is going to be okay!' Puspendu wanted to leave his seat to comfort Marcia, but he didn't dare make the move.

It was Katrina who tried to ease Marcia's distress. 'She picked me up from the floor and gave me water,' Marcia said later. 'All she said was "Are you okay?" Nothing else, because we were not allowed to talk. But she stayed next to me with her hand on my leg, to comfort me.'

Julie Taylor asked permission to phone her husband, but Monis told her to wait until Tori had called home. This was to prove a particularly painful moment for the manager.

When Thomas answered the phone, he was immediately worried that Tori was putting himself at risk. He kept the call brief: 'Why are you calling me? You shouldn't be doing that.' Thomas told Tori he loved him and that all the family were nearby to support him. 'And I told him, "Don't do anything silly", and hung up.' Later, there were so many other things he wished he'd had the chance to say.

The call left the manager in tears. Monis was giving Tori the 'third degree', demanding to know who he had spoken to, whether he had children.

'We heard everybody's phone calls to their family,' Louisa says. 'It was hard listening to them. One of the Indian guys told us he had spoken to his wife, and she was sobbing so much that he could barely speak to her. And Selina—I think she was talking with her mother. She was giving directions about her cat, and what to say to whoever else . . . She seemed to be giving her mother instructions. And in that moment I thought, "My God, this woman is saying goodbye to her mother." But even in that moment she was utterly in control.'

Katrina called home as well; her young children were in bed and she did not want them woken.

Learning of the calls, one negotiator interpreted the development as Monis 'using family to intimidate'. But a text message from Steve gave a more benign impression. At 11.25 p.m., he reported Monis saying: 'Hopefully by morning everyone home. After Tony Abbott calls, everyone happy, go home.'

Viewed this way, the negotiations commander, Graeme, saw the calls to families as a positive sign. Both he and Reg, the negotiations team leader, thought hostages were calling loved ones to let them know they would see them the following day.

But in Jarrod's mind Monis' directions to call family had a more sinister and manipulative intent. Jarrod hadn't been asked to place a call, nor did he want to make one. 'I didn't call my family because in my head I was sure that I would speak to them tomorrow,' he told me. 'Making a call like that would have felt to me like a last rites sort of thing, like the last meal before you die. And I'm thinking "I don't want to die" . . . I'm *not* going to call up and say, "Sorry guys, I'm not going to see you tomorrow." No, I am like, "I will talk to you in person."'

Viswa's thoughts were for his wife and daughter. 'I was mentally preparing for the fact that I could be killed at any time . . . I was very sad.'

After the siege, British police expert Deputy Chief Constable Simon Chesterman told the inquest that the Monis' orders to some hostages to call loved ones should have raised a red flag straight away. He told the coroner: 'Separating people off and telling them to phone home would indicate the threat to those people has just gone through the roof.'

Sometime after 11.15 p.m., Monis told the hostages he needed to urinate. But he was not going to risk a trip to the toilet. Again they put their heads together to come up with a solution.

He would need a bottle, but not one with a narrow head. Someone dug up an old sauce bottle and he relived himself under the table, with no attempt to excuse himself to the women present. Then he handed it to Fiona to take to the toilet and empty.

At around 11.25 p.m. the listening device picked up Monis grumbling to himself about not shooting John O'Brien and Stefan Balafoutis earlier. 'I feel bad I didn't shoot White Shirt man, because I had the chance,' he said, adding a few seconds later, 'The Old Man as well.'

As midnight approached, the hostages noted their captor was becoming increasingly paranoid. He suspected the police were listening in on him; he was jumping more often at noises; he kept sending hostages to the windows to report on what they could see outside.

Rather than the late hour inducing a calmer atmosphere, as the negotiators were hoping, Jarrod felt fatigue was rubbing everyone's nerve endings raw. The gunman's mood swings were growing more pronounced. 'The changes in his behaviour and emotion seemed to just flip, almost like a switch,' Jarrod says. One minute he would accept an explanation about noises he thought he could hear in the kitchen. Then, in the next instant, his temperament would just change, and he was saying "Don't lie to me. I'll know if you are lying to me. If you're not honest to me, you are guilty. You will not survive this."'

Monis announced he wanted to smoke, and asked Jarrod and Joel if there was any way he could light up in the café without activating the sprinkler system.

Jarrod tried to persuade him that the best place to have a cigarette safely was inside the industrial freezer. There was only one sprinkler outlet in there and they could put Glad Wrap over it. 'It's very easy to close, you close the whole thing,' Jarrod told Monis. Secretly the nineteen-year-old was hoping that if he could lure his captor inside the freezer unit, he could slam the door and trap him inside.

This plan was unintentionally sabotaged when someone else proposed the simpler solution of smoking into a bottle. Monis liked the sound of that better. He had his cigarette and then handed the reeking bottle to Jarrod, who trapped the smoke by putting a towel over it and dumping the whole lot in the sink.

During his trips to the kitchen, Jarrod would check to see if there had been any response by police to the messages he'd scrawled on business cards and pushed under the fire exit door.

'The original purpose of the cards was to see if there was a police officer on the other side,' Jarrod says, 'so I could push through and he might push back. Just so I had the knowledge that, if the worst came to the worst, we'd be able to open that back door and they would be able to come in immediately. But once I'd put the second or third card there and got no response, I figured there was no one there, or else they were there but had orders not to interact with us.'

His cards with their hastily scrawled maps and poignant directions ('you are here'; 'he is here') lay undiscovered by police until after the end of the siege.

Now Monis was harping on again about the blue Christmas lights outside that were still reflecting too much light into the café. He'd wanted them switched off hours ago, but nothing had happened in response. It was nearing 1 a.m.

'Street lights are connected to the main frame,' Jarrod started explaining to him. 'They are not meant to go off, the same way that the traffic lights don't go off.'

Monis was struggling to get his head around what Jarrod was telling him: 'Which mainframe, what mainframe?' he fumed.

Jarrod replied, 'The mainframe is the electrical grid that we use.'

'The government can do anything it wants,' Monis insisted.

Jarrod was thinking to himself how much harder it was becoming to wrangle the gunman. The techniques that had worked over the preceding hours—pretending that they were on his side, being biddable—were no longer proving effective.

A number of the hostages were losing hope that they could collectively stop him from committing an act of violence. 'I thought if nothing was done, we'd probably all be dead in the morning,' Joel recalls. 'Nothing was happening to try and get us out.'

Between 12.30 a.m. and close to 1 a.m., Marcia made a sudden flurry of calls from the café to the negotiators' line to convey Monis' resurgence of anger about the lights.

None of them were answered. Why this happened was never clear. However, the most likely explanation according to the coroner was that the entire negotiation team was engaged in a handover to a relief team at the time, and simply didn't hear the calls. Louisa vividly remembers how the failure to get through fuelled the rising mood of desperation. 'It was staggering that there was no answer on the number the negotiators had given us to call them. There was collective disbelief. We all had one of those "what the . . .!" moments; at that stage of night it was putting us in mortal danger.'

At 12.48 a.m., Selina rang triple zero saying the hostages had been unable to get through to police and that their attacker was demanding they douse the lights within fifteen minutes or she would be shot.

Shortly afterwards, Monis could be heard complaining about this: 'I wish you not tell [*sic*] fifteen minutes to them . . . Now that we have just fifteen minutes it will be very bad . . . fifteen minutes to go . . . before they ring me up.'

Selina was exhausted. 'Brother, I have helped you so much. Yes, I have,' she said.

Monis kept urging the hostages to post his demands on social media. They were having mixed success. The video files the hostages had shot on their phones were large. Monis was getting increasingly impatient. 'Try Twitter, try YouTube, or Facebook,' he told them. 'Try overseas media agencies again.'

At around 1.30 a.m. Monis changed tack. Perhaps he should release one person as his emissary, he began saying.

The listening device recorded snatches of this new plan. 'The person who is released really needs to be fair . . . to contact media, to contact human rights and say, "Look what happen there—one flag, one phone call can save them",' Monis was heard saying. 'And to tell the truth—whether I have been nice to you or not. Not just to tell lies.'

But he was adamant the plan had to be broadcast in advance, so the police could not portray a release as an escape. He began mulling aloud about who he should choose to walk free from the café.

Selina and Jarrod were early volunteers. Monis demurred. Fiona and Jarrod had been 'loyal' and deserved release, he said, but it would be better if 'someone sick goes now . . . sick or older or something here, and then you young guys go out'.

Jarrod then suggested that Robin or Louisa should be allowed to leave as both could be relied on not to endanger the other. Monis ruled that out too.

Katrina spoke up next, suggesting it should be Julie: 'Julie's pregnant and she can talk to people.'

'How many months?' Monis asked. Four and a half, Julie told him. 'She's going to find out tomorrow if she is having a boy or a girl,' Katrina added.

This didn't sway Monis in the slightest. It seemed to them that the gunman was enjoying this cruel lottery.

Meanwhile, Marcia was frantically trying to get through to newsrooms—any newsroom—to tell them of this fresh plan. Given it was the dead of night, she was having little success. Monis suggested she try the BBC or CNN, but Jarrod said he'd already tried that and had been unable to dial out of the country.

Marcia could be heard on the listening device telling Monis that if he let Julie go, then Julie could explain for herself that she had been released and that it wasn't necessary for the media to have been advised in advance.

Monis remained adamant: the release would only happen if it was publicly declared beforehand. In a last desperate bid to find an avenue for him to announce his plan, Marcia tried radio station 2GB again.

The call was picked up by an overnight producer. Marcia explained their dilemma: 'He is going to release one of the hostages right now but, before he does that, he wants to make sure that it is actually on the radio, saying that this person will be released.' Monis could be heard in the background saying, 'Otherwise the politicians will say the lie and say ran away.'

The station placed Marcia on hold. A minute later she could be heard via the listening device frantically pleading with the 2GB staffer on the other end of the line: 'Can I tell you . . . the police is doing nothing. They have lied to the media, saying that they have been negotiating with the brother for the whole day. They have not negotiated, they have not done nothing. They have left us here to die. They have left us here to die and you won't even take a message!'

The producer said she was sorry, but she would have to route the request to a police negotiator. Then she terminated the call.

All hope gone now, Marcia reported back to the café: 'They are not allowed to take any messages from us. No radio station is allowed to take any messages from us.'

Monis' next words, at 1.44 a.m., would signal the siege's turn into its final and darkest phase: 'All the media are not allowed to take any message . . . So then don't worry. There no point to release one person at the moment . . .'

Critically, news of this change of heart never reached the police commanders, either at the POC or the forward command post. Tori and Katrina had less than half an hour to live.

Since the hostages had been ordered to make their calls home at around 11 p.m. little had been heard from inside the café except for the two desperate calls from Selina to the emergency operators on triple zero.

At the old Supreme Court building, families were still pushing desperately for information. But a senior officer advised them to go home, saying the wait could run into days.

Jorge recalls a senior policewoman telling them, 'Look, we have got the best negotiators in the world, we are negotiating with him, we just have to wait it out. If you have somewhere to stay nearby do that, we will get your numbers and get you in as soon as we know.' After one of the officers told him it 'could take hours . . . even weeks', he went 'What? Weeks?' 'It made me crazy,' he said.

Some family members and loved ones left; others were determined to wait it out. Jorge's boss Max had arrived earlier in the evening and now went home to get Jorge some clothes and food (as a diabetic Jorge needed to eat at regular intervals to stabilise his blood sugar levels). When Max returned to the Supreme Court family reception centre with a duffel bag for his employee, no one in authority asked to search it.

This worried Jorge's sister, herself a mother of three: 'I kept asking, "Is this place safe? Has somebody checked it top to bottom?" Because we are sitting ducks here. What sort of news would that make, the families of all the hostages, if they bombed this place!'

At 1.43 a.m., Thomas Zinn's phone sounded an incoming message alert. It was a last text from Tori: 'He's increasingly agitated. Walks around when he hears a notice [*sic*] outside with a hostage in front of him. Wants to release 1 person out of good faith.' Then came a second message: 'tell police'.

Zinn immediately passed the message to one of the police liaison officers, who passed it to a negotiator, who passed it to a colleague, who recorded the call in a log.

That's where it stopped. The news of Tori's text went no further.

Jenkins at the POC didn't hear of it. Nor did forward commander Victor. Neither the night negotiator, Matt, nor his colleague Darren B. recalled seeing the text.

Contrary to Tori's warning about Monis' growing agitation, the police instead remained convinced that captor and captives were somehow settling down for the night. The night commander, Victor, would later tell police interviewers: 'I had a conversation with [the psychiatrist] where he fundamentally said that look, things have quietened in there. It looks like they appear to be going to bed, putting their heads down, lights are out.'

At 1.35 a.m. the command group held a meeting at the POC that reaffirmed their collective view that Monis was probably settling in for a rest, with the most likely scenario being a resumption of activity in the morning. The log entry for 1.50 a.m. reflected that assessment: 'Dr thinks settling stronghold, probably better he [Monis] has a rest . . . never hurt anyone, facing serious charges probably goes to gaol for a lengthy time, could be building credibility for gaol.'

So 'stable' did police commanders decide the situation had become that, as the clock ticked towards 2 a.m., they were in the midst of final arrangements for the New South Wales Police tactical operations team to begin handing over to the relieving Queensland Police. Indeed, at about 1.55 a.m., Jenkins would describe himself as the most 'optimistic' he had been all night about the prospects for a peaceful end to the siege.

But Monis' patience was about to run out.

Jarrod had feared that there was a crisis brewing from around midnight. Monis was jumping at every noise and demanding reports ever more frequently about what hostages could see from the windows. Far from growing drowsy, Monis was desperate to stay awake.

'I was thinking we are hitting the end game now,' Jarrod recalls. 'It was totally ridiculous for anyone to have thought it might settle down. If he had had a partner with him it would have been a different story, but he was on his own. The minute he falls asleep I could take his gun and shoot him in the face. It was like the sand was running out through the timer, we were running on vapour.'

Marcia, too, could sense the end was drawing near: she wanted it, but was dreading it at the same time. She knew the only way now was for Monis to be killed. But how, she wondered, could that possibly happen without anyone else being harmed?

Robin and Tori were sitting on the banquette behind Louisa, holding hands and occasionally talking in whispers. Louisa could faintly overhear Selina and Monis conversing. She could not hear what they were saying, but Selina seemed to be pleading.

According to Selina, Monis was telling her: 'Your government doesn't care about you. I've given you food, I've given you water, I've let you go to the toilet. So, you know, I need to kill one person.'

She responded with horror: 'I couldn't believe that he was asking this of me, and so very quickly I asked him, "Please don't kill anybody".'

At around 1.45 a.m., the hostages discovered that their videos had been taken down from YouTube (the police had succeeded in having them removed half an hour earlier).

Julie was the first to pick this up. 'I think there might be a problem with YouTube,' she said. Marcia confirmed that the videos had disappeared. Monis was already irritable and jumpy. This made things worse. 'Even your message is not allowed to be on YouTube? What happened to democracy and freedom?' he complained.

'Once we had all realised that the videos had been taken down and saw Monis' responses to that, there was an overwhelming sense of frustration and defeat,' Louisa recalls. 'We felt we'd run out of options.'

Joel suggested reposting them, but Monis replied, 'No, they will delete again.' Jarrod chimed in, assuring Monis that there would be 'mirror' copies of the videos circulating. At 1.55 a.m., the listening device picked up the hostages and Monis discussing whether to make a new YouTube account. Julie offered to do it. But before they could put this into action, something outside the café grabbed the gunman's attention.

Just before 2 a.m., Monis leapt to his feet and grabbed hold of Selina. He said the noises were happening again, and that he could see reflections in the granite walls of the Reserve Bank opposite, where something seemed to be moving.

'I need to go check the door now,' he said.

Fiona Ma was in the toilet with Robin. Monis ordered them out.

'Why is it taking so long?' he demanded.

Fiona emerged with Robin and delivered her back to the banquette near Louisa and Tori.

Selina was crying. She could feel the gun pressed against her.

He ordered Jarrod, Selina and Fiona to form a human shield around him and told them: 'We go together. Go front . . . No. No. No. Fiona . . . Jarrod, you can just go front around me, around me, around me.'

Jarrod was afraid that if Monis got as far as the kitchen exit and opened it, he would find the miniature maps Jarrod had drawn on the back of the business cards: 'I knew if he found those cards we were dead. Like I was one hundred per cent going to die if he finds those cards. I had literally drawn on them where the barricades were, the people, what his gun was like . . . It was a How to Storm the Café kit and there was no way I was going to be able to explain it away.'

As Jarrod was worrying about this, he noticed activity outside the café: a group of four or five police officers in black with military-grade weapons. He could make out their reflections clearly in the highly polished stone of the Reserve Bank across the street. Had Monis seen them too? Perhaps he hadn't, not clearly, as surely he would have reacted by now.

From her position near the waiter's nook, Louisa was also watching closely. She noted with anxiety that it was the first time—during all that day and night—she had seen Monis walk out of the room into the kitchen annexe.

Marcia began whispering, almost chanting, under her breath: 'Shoot him. They have to shoot him.'

Monis now made a fateful error. He told Jarrod to turn back and stand watch near the lobby doors, and then he kept moving towards the Phillip Street side of the café. Fiona was slightly to one side and in front of him at gunpoint, while he gripped Selina on his other side.

Fiona caught sight of the black-clad officers' reflections as well. Monis said urgently: 'Do you see that? Can you see that?' She pretended she couldn't, recalling only too well that the last time he had seen police he had threatened to shoot someone.

Selina was crying as Monis pushed the two women into the area near the fire escape door. They were now completely out of sight of the others left in the café.

As Monis moved out of sight with the two women, Louisa became consumed with panic. 'When he left Jarrod at the lobby doors, I am thinking Monis could do anything to those two girls—he could sexually attack them, he could kill one of them. Maybe he is going to execute one of them in the kitchen, away from all of us. I thought he could do anything. I'm going "Holy shit, what else can I do?". I close my eyes and I'm praying away like a mad thing.'

In the corridor on the café side, Monis was getting Fiona to stack up boxes against the fire door. They weren't going to offer much in the way of a barricade, Fiona thought. There was hardly anything in them.

He ordered her to stack them higher. She kept going.

Katrina, Julie and Marcia were still where Monis had left them, Julie on the bench and the other two in the back corner tucked between the waiter's station and the Martin Place wall. They were puzzled by the strange rustling sound coming from the corner where the gunman had marched Selina and Fiona. Was Monis making something? What was he up to?

The three women looked at one another, terrified. 'Oh, my God! He's going to shoot someone,' Marcia said.

Cameraman Greg Parker and the snipers in the surrounding buildings caught a glimpse of Monis' sudden burst of activity. A minute or so earlier, Chris Reason had been thinking of grabbing a catnap. He had moved towards a nearby sofa and kicked off his shoes, and was texting his boss when Greg called him over to have a look. 'Mate, something is happening.' He raced over to look though the monitor. From the Channel 7 building they could see Monis walk to the corner of the room near the fire door with several hostages, his gun at the ready. This was the area of the café the police had designated the 'black/green' corner ('black' being the kitchen wall, 'green' being Phillip Street). They could see Fiona Ma piling up boxes. They could read the signs of fresh agitation inside the café.

The images from the Channel 7 camera were beaming back to the forward command post and the POC. The commanders were getting information from the sniper radios as well.

The spotter in the Reserve Bank building called in to the tactical commander: 'Yeah, Sierra 1, a number of people inside have moved towards that exit on the green, green/black corner.' The time of the call was recorded as close to 2.02 a.m. The sniper would later reveal his worry that an execution might be imminent. 'I was of the belief that he was going to, ah, either execute them or move them out to that fire exit, because it seemed strange that he's started to move into this position when he hadn't been there all day or night,' he told investigators two weeks after the siege.

'I could see things were escalating inside and from the two hostages that he had moving into that corner of the building, they were very distressed. You can see they weren't just walking normally. They were quite agitated and hands up, hands down, heads down, crying . . . It looked like he had the firearm to the back of their heads or back of their necks.'

Jarrod stands rooted to the spot, but his mind is in a state of tumult. He is mentally exhausted from the hours of dancing around Monis' paranoia, trying to ride and shape the turbulent currents of the gunman's moods.

He thinks attempts to placate Monis are now finished. He can hear shuffling coming from the emergency door to the fire escape. He is on tenterhooks, in case Monis finds the notes he has pushed under the door. He mistakes the purpose of the boxes being shifted: he's sure it is to open the door, in which case the gunman will almost certainly find the cards and it will be 'definite death', not just for Jarrod but for some of the others. No help is going to arrive, he thinks. Now is the time, perhaps the very last chance, to make a break for it.

Jarrod knows the lobby doors are open, that they were left unlocked after April and Elly had slipped out unnoticed. He has known this for nine hours, but not acted on it before: 'My thought was that, if we wait for them to storm the building after he shoots someone, it's going to take too long and some of us will get shot before it happens. And if he opens fire on us, then we will get caught in the crossfire. So I'm like, "We may not get this opportunity again. They are not going to come into the café until someone is dead or gets shot." I reckoned we could get out eight or nine, which was most of us. It seems horrific now, doing basic arithmetic on people's lives. I did feel guilty about leaving Fiona and Selina, but at the same time thinking there was no way for it to be perfect. And I thought, if we got out we could tell the cops they need to go in now, because he was going to freak.'

Joel and Harriette exchange glances with Jarrod. Both are staring at him. Harriette bumps Joel and whispers to him to move his leg: 'Turn around so you can run towards the door.'

Puspendu is also watching closely, and nudges Viswa. Viswa is sure he silently tapped Katrina.

Julie remains oblivious to the silent signalling taking place among some of the others.

Jarrod thinks 'Now!' As he runs a glass goes flying to the ground, then he pushes through the lobby doors and is out into the foyer.

Joel grabs Harriette by the hand, dragging her with him. Viswa and Puspenda follow and Julie Taylor—sitting further from the door—now snaps into action, following on the heels of the rest of the group, almost by instinct. 'I wasn't conscious of anything really except that it seemed to me that everybody between me and the door was running for the door. And I just saw a lot of people move and I followed them,' she said later.

Marcia misses the moment. She has her head lowered onto her arms, which are folded on the table in front of her. But she is too wedged in to move anyway.

Katrina didn't follow either. The last time Harriette looked over she had been sitting with her eyes closed, her chair back against the wall, legs stretched out in front of her. It was very quiet, and very cold. Thinking back on it afterwards, Harriette wondered if Katrina had been dozing. But Julie remembers locking eyes with Katrina in the minute or two before Jarrod led the breakout. Perhaps the sound of the shotgun made Katrina think it too dangerous. 'I think we were all terrified,' Julie said.

The crashing of the glass brings Monis out of the corner, screaming: 'What's that?'

At 2.03 a.m., the group of six escapees have made it into the lobby. They are running towards several interior steps that lead to where the outer Martin Place doors are. But now *those* doors won't open. Jarrod tugs on them frantically. He is thinking he's going to die right here, in this foyer, like one of those films where someone drowns in just a tiny bit of water. Behind him he can hear Joel scream: 'He's chasing us!'

Jarrod sees what looks like an emergency button. He presses it.

Thank God, it works. The doors open and then they are all tearing through them, adrenaline surging through their bodies.

Suddenly there is a crack! Glass explodes behind their heads as Monis discharges his shotgun towards them, and it hits somewhere above the lobby doors.

Julie, at the rear, slips in her stockinged feet but she manages to pull herself up and keep going. Shattered glass is showering around her. She senses, rather than sees or hears, a bullet zinging past on her right-hand side somewhere above her head.

Jarrod's mind has been whirring ever since he burst through the outer doors onto Martin Place. Now he runs wide, so he won't obstruct the police line of fire if Monis is behind them.

Jarrod, Joel, Harriette, Julie and Viswa run down the slope towards Elizabeth Street, where police and ambulance crews are waiting. In the panic Puspendu shoots off on his own across Martin Place and in the direction of the dark harbour.

Until a few moments ago, Monis was holding the lives of the thirteen remaining hostages in his hands. Now just seven remain.

CHAPTER 12
THE STORM BREAKS

Fiona is still near the first exit stacking boxes when she hears a sound like a glass shattering. She remembered April had left a glass in front of the lobby doors earlier in the day. She thinks it must be that although she's not sure, because from where she is standing now she can't see beyond the kitchen wall.

Monis hears the sound too. He lets go of Fiona and Selina, and charges back into the main room.

Louisa, eyes closed, is still praying feverishly for Fiona and Selina. Then she hears a loud, sharp 'bang', opens her eyes and notices most of the others are no longer in the room. As far as she can tell, it is just her, Robin and Tori left in the main chamber of the café. She does not see Katrina behind her and has lost track of Marcia in the gloom. She has a split second in which to decide what to do next.

'I never heard them scream or anything like that,' Louisa remembers. 'I hear a bang of some kind, open my eyes and they are all gone! And there is myself, and Tori and Mum still sitting there. So then I get up to go, and I'm halfway to the lobby door and I turn around and see that Robin and Tori are not coming. What the hell! They should have been coming—Tori should have been up and out and pulling her along with him. That's what I assumed was going to happen. But it was dark; I couldn't make eye contact. So, when I realised they were not going, I literally spun around on my good foot and I thought, "I can't go without Mum, and I'm not going to give him the pleasure of shooting me because he thinks I'm running". So I laid down on the floor right there.'

For the second time that day Monis is suddenly on top of Louisa, yanking her up by her bra strap through her dress.

'He's telling me to get up, get up and I'm saying, "I'm trying, I'm trying—my leg," and trying to pacify or placate him. And I see Marcia, and she is sitting on her back haunches, terrified, and trying to cover her sobs with her hand. Thank God he didn't see her, thank God. And Katrina, I had no idea where Katrina was—I thought she had got out.

'I'm thinking, "okay, I'm ready; he's going to kill me for sure". But if he's going to kill me, I'm not going to give him any provocation. He will have to do it deliberately.'

Monis is demanding to know how she got there, away from her chair. 'I said "I fell". It was easier to lie than explain that I'm just lying here waiting for you to murder me.'

He drags Louisa away from the corner and towards the centre of the room. He makes Robin stand to his right and Louisa to his left. His attention is fixed on the front door. He is braced for the police to enter. But nothing happens. Running on rage, fatigue, frustration and humiliation, he is now a tight ball of roiling emotions. He is close to snapping point.

'Tori is still sitting on his chair,' says Louisa. 'And then he calls Tori over, points the gun at him and says to him, "Manager, kneel down with your hands on your head".'

When the hostages break out, the New South Wales Police assault teams are still in position. They are waiting for the handover to the relief teams from Queensland and the Australian Federal Police (AFP) that will now never happen.

There are four tactical teams now stationed close to the café. Alpha team is standing by in the vehicle loading bay, just past the café on Phillip Street. Charlie team is on high alert inside the fire stairs off the lobby. Delta team is across the foyer from the café, in the book-lined ground floor library of Frederick Jordan Chambers. The four-man Papa team has split between the Alpha and Charlie/Delta groups. If the emergency action is triggered, the plan is for the teams to try and make simultaneous entry through the front and lobby doors of the café.

When the sharp crack of a shotgun rings out at 2.03 a.m., the shield-bearer for Alpha team calls out: 'Shots fired'. The group tenses up like a tightly coiled spring. They know the time to act must surely be nearly upon them. The possibility of the bomb hangs like a dark shadow in the back of each man's mind.

There is a split-second debate over what they've just heard. Was it a door slamming, one of them asks? 'It's not a fucking door slamming, it's a shot fired,' Alpha 2 insists. 'Mate, we've got to go, we've got to get in there.'

Officer A's radio has gone down. He is now relying on 'buddy comms'—the incoming radio traffic passed on from the team member next to him. He grips his M4 carbine, a weapon which carries his name on it. Officer A has never shot a man before. Every nerve in his body tells him that is about to change.

The snipers in the buildings around the café are also radioing in what little they can see and hear. Those in the Westpac building see the group of six hostages fleeing through the lobby doors. They hear Monis' first shot and see the muzzle flash inside the café. They radio in: 'Shot fired'.

Their colleague in the Reserve Bank building across the road, Sierra 1.3, grabs his breaching shotgun and prepares to break the window glass so his partner can take a shot at Monis if a clear opportunity presents itself.

In the darkened Channel 7 building, the Sierra 2 sniper is also watching like a hawk.

'I hope no one else is in there . . . 'cause he must be pissed,' he observes as they watch the escaped hostages running down Martin Place.

In the fire escape, adrenaline is coursing through Charlie team as well. Everyone is braced for action. Still, no order comes.

At the leagues' club, night forward commander Victor has summoned his core team for a meeting at 2 a.m. They are gathered around one of the small tables in the bar room, discussing what to do about getting the Martin Place Christmas lights switched off and nailing down the impending handover to the relief teams from Queensland and the AFP.

One of the senior New South Wales Tactical Operations Unit (TOU) men is briefing the interstate commanders on the details of the emergency action plan (EA). They have sworn in the relief teams standing by ready to start a phased take over from the TOU officers, who have been on duty now for close to seventeen hours.

Victor gets on the phone to Jenkins at the Police Operations Centre (POC). Jenkins is considering switching off the lights outside the café as demanded by Monis, in return for the release of female hostages.

At 2.03 a.m. the senior officers' group has barely settled into the discussion when they hear a commotion from the other side of the bar room, where the screens are. 'Something's going on there,' Victor's offsider calls out.

They hurry over to look at the live broadcast. They are only just absorbing what is on the screens when they hear the sound of screaming from downstairs. It is the escapees, led by Jarrod and Joel, who are now entering the hostage reception area on the floor below.

Tango Charlie and his deputy leap onto their radios, trying to get feedback from the sniper posts. The new night lead negotiator, 'Darren

B', is signalling that he's getting nothing through on the listening device that can explain what has just happened.

Victor instructs his men to call the POC, to see if they have the ability to play back the footage of the hostage escape. He talks to Jenkins: 'Mate, some hostages have got out.'

'Yes,' Jenkins says, 'we're watching it.'

It's still not clear to them whether there are five or six. Puspendu has momentarily confused things by running across the plaza in a different direction from the others.

There is one pressing question the police need to answer. Did Monis fire at the hostages and miss? Or did he aim deliberately high, over their heads, as they scrambled through the lobby doors?

The hostages themselves have no doubts on this score. They impress on the debriefing officers that Monis has fired *at* them, that none of them doubts the gunman was trying to hit them.

But a different impression takes root in the minds of the commanders. The consensus at the POC leans towards thinking the shot must have been deliberately high. Yet again, the impetus to take decisive action slackens.

Later the inquest will hear that a sawn-off firearm tends to ride high at the moment it is fired, especially in the hands of someone unfamiliar with it. Jenkins, however, thinks differently—it is his belief, he testifies later, that the upward recoil only happens after firing.

Victor is crunching through the arguments for and against sending the tactical teams in or holding off for a while longer. He takes the view that Monis does not seem to have lashed out after the 2.03 a.m. escape, and that the situation is already de-escalating. Above all, in his mind looms the threat of the bomb. What if Monis is just trying to bait them? What if he is luring them in so he can blow the lot of them up? This will be a key justification he will later offer for the failure to act when Jarrod leads the breakout.

Victor makes a decision. He says to Jenkins, 'We're not at EA. It's not the emergency action. No EA. It's not the EA.'

Inside the café, an enraged Monis is barking a string of orders at Tori. The listening device picks up some of it. The time is close to 2.04 a.m.

'Manager, stand there. There, there, there—don't move!' Monis demands.

Two minutes later, at around 2.06 a.m., his orders take an even more ominous turn: 'The manager, put your hands on your head. Hands on your . . . You will not move, alright? Don't move!'

Tori is in terrible peril. He is weeping. But the delay on the listening device means no one is getting this information at the police end. In fact, the delay in transmission at this time is between four to five minutes.

Observations from the sniper posts are Tori's last remaining hope. Although the café is in darkness, the marksmen can see enough with ambient light and their scoping and night-vision equipment to make out some activity in the café, even though they have no way of hearing Monis' words.

Sierra 3.1, the sniper stationed in the Westpac building, sees Tori reposition himself near White Window 2, the second window along Martin Place from the entrance. He sees Tori turn towards the entrance and drop down on his knees, before interlocking his fingers on top of his head.

Both Sierra 3.1 and his companion believe they make a radio call transmitting the critical observation back to the commanders at the forward command post and the POC, that a hostage was now on his knees. Incomprehensibly, tragically, that call—if indeed it was ever made—is never received. The final chance to save Tori Johnson has been lost.

Louisa can hear Tori sobbing as he continues to kneel on Monis' order. But the young manager composes himself, and the sound of his weeping stops.

Monis is pumping himself up. He's doing what an athlete might do before sprinting off the blocks in a race, Louisa thinks. 'He is rolling his shoulders and adjusting his gun. He is sort of shuffling, moving his feet from side to side. He's kind of preparing himself—he's scanning the front of the café, the doors and the windows on the Phillip Street side, and he is clearly expecting the police to come in.'

Tori has become 'very still and quiet', Louisa says. 'He wouldn't have known that Monis was going through that process of preparing his gun, aiming directly at him, because he was in front of Monis and he wouldn't have seen him.'

Somewhere between five and seven long, slow minutes tick by with Tori on his knees. Louisa cannot hear another thing inside the café apart from Monis' shuffling and him telling her and Robin to keep quiet.

Fiona, Selina, Katrina and Marcia haven't breathed a word. Monis tells them: 'Don't move. If you don't move you are safe, alright.' Marcia, flat on the floor, has her eyes glued to a white fluorescent strip on the back of Monis' backpack. As long as she can see that strip, she thinks, she and Katrina are safer, because it means he is facing away from them.

Then suddenly, and without warning, he fires a second time. The sound ricochets sharply off the marble pillars and café walls. The gunman has fired off into the high right-hand corner of the room, as if he's trying to lure the police in, daring them, taunting them to come and get him.

Tori flinches and drops down at the second shot. Then he steadies himself on his knees again.

Relief temporarily floods over Louisa. 'He hasn't killed Tori,' she says to herself thankfully. 'I think then "Perhaps he's not going to do it". But inside I have this constant internal dialogue going on, worrying about what he's going to do next. Surely, surely the police are coming now. God in heaven help us.'

To her alarm, Louisa now sees Monis reach into his cargo pants pocket, apparently to reload. He is starting to shuffle and scan the front of the café again. He is saying to her and Robin, 'Keep your eyes closed, keep them closed'.

Louisa prays.

With their sights trained on the café, some of the snipers register Monis' second gunshot.

The Sierra 3 team in the Westpac building see Tori drop briefly from view, then rise once more to his knees. Again, the team believes it called in the fact that a second shot has been fired—an observation also called in by at least one of the TOU officers on the ground. But there are problems with the tactical teams' radio network, and it seems to be cutting in and out. The TOU radio log records an unidentified officer saying, 'Tango Charlie, you are weak and unreadable'. The timing is appalling: once more, the snipers either fail to or are unable to transmit a vital piece of information, this time the news that Monis has let off another shot, a sign that the situation inside the café is deteriorating with every minute. The message never makes it to the command posts.

Fiona has taken refuge in the tiny office next to the kitchen. She does not know Tori is kneeling. She is frightened Monis will come back to find her. She is hoping the police will enter, but she cannot see any sign of impending rescue. She knows Monis will now be bent on vengeance of some kind. If she is going to leave before that happens, she will have to find a way out herself.

Crouching down behind the chocolate station that sits just outside the kitchen, she inches her way back into the main room to attempt to see what is happening. She tries to keep low—'crouch running', as she calls it—but she can't see much. Then she hears the crack of the second shot, the sound bouncing off the hard café walls and floors.

She remembers something Jarrod had said to her earlier in the day, something about Monis only being able to get off two shots before he had to reload. Sure enough, now it sounds to her like he is reloading. She has no idea who is left in the café. Perhaps it's only Selina and her now here with him.

The sound of Monis reloading the gun removes any last hesitation Fiona has about what she now must do. She makes a dash for the Phillip Street door, presses the green button and is out.

Sierra 1 sees her burst out of the door at 2.12 a.m. 'We've got a runner,' he calls over the sniper's radio network. And then she is scooped into the arms of the TOU and she is screaming at them: 'He can see you out there!'

Tori Johnson has less than two minutes left to live.

At 2.10 a.m., the senior people inside the forward command post are easing off their state of high alert. Although it is just seven minutes since the escape of Jarrod's group, the deputy tactical commander finds time to upload the emergency action plan onto the iSurv data log.

At the POC, the picture is similar. Momentarily turning his focus away from the café and the forward command post, Jenkins is sufficiently reassured about the gunman's seeming lack of response to the group escape to place a call into the State Crisis Centre.

By now, police chief Scipione and his deputy Cath Burn have left the Crisis Centre with plans to come back at dawn. In charge is Acting Deputy Commissioner Jeff Loy, alongside Deputy Premier Troy Grant, himself a former police officer.

So convinced is Jenkins that the situation has de-escalated, he tells Loy the police have been having a 'really positive last hour until that point' with some progress on negotiations around the Martin Place lights. He passes on to Loy the collective assessment that the shot fired at 2.03 a.m. was deliberately high over the heads of the escaping hostages.

None of the senior commanders read Monis' firing of his shotgun as a critical turning point in the siege. Later, at the inquest, the deputy tactical commander will be asked point blank: 'Do you accept that as at 2.03 a.m. the danger levels to the hostages remaining inside the stronghold had increased substantially?'

'No, I don't,' he will reply.

—

Monis has fired off two shots now, but there's still no reaction from the police assault teams he knows are outside. He is scanning the Phillip Street side of the cafe, agitatedly swinging his gun from side to side.

Louisa has been made to stand so close to him that his backpack slams into her when he moves. 'He was waiting, absolutely waiting for the police to come in,' Louisa says. 'He kept saying, "Keep your eyes closed, nothing will happen to you." So I've got my eyes half closed, half open. I'm trying to maintain my balance, but I can see what's going on.

'He's rolling his shoulders, adjusting his gun. He's doing it all again, and I'm telling myself that he didn't do it last time, he didn't shoot Tori, so he won't do it again, no, he won't. And then—bang!—he did it. Tori fell forward with a thud, his hands still behind his head. Monis had done it, he had assassinated Tori.'

Monis shows no emotion in response to the atrocity he has just committed. He reloads. He pulls back into the far corner of the café, where Marcia and Katrina are still trapped. He is still scanning, swinging the gun from side to side, waiting for someone to come through the doors.

More than half a minute ticks by, an interval that seems to Louisa and Robin to go on forever. 'I am waiting for either me or Mum to be called over, to be told to kneel down,' Louisa recalls. 'We were convinced we were staring down the barrel of us being next.'

Alpha team has been poised for minutes now in a tightly packed 'stack'—the formation that will carry them into action. They are lined up according to the role each man will play: the breacher, the shield man, the shooter, the back-up officers.

In the lead is Alpha 2, the shield-bearer. If and when the order comes, his job will be to run forward with the ballistic shield and protect the breacher, who will have to blow open the glass so the others can enter.

Some have phoned their wives and partners, wondering if this will be their last conversation with loved ones. But fear of the bomb now has to be pushed to the back of their minds; this is what they train for every day of their working lives.

The third, fatal shot rings out. It is 2.13 a.m. This time there is no breakdown of communications as the snipers call the stark news over their radios: 'White Window 2, hostage down, hostage down!'

Alpha's team leader, Officer B, calls out: 'Get ready, boys! We're going to do this.'

Hearing 'hostage down', Tango Charlie, the tactical commander, gives an immediate order to storm the café: 'Echo Alpha! This is Tango Charlie—commit the EA! Commit the EA!'

The forward commanders watch their screens anxiously, but there seems to be no response from the Alpha team. Radio gremlins have struck again.

Tango Charlie prepares to repeat the order, but his deputy steps in and repeats the agreed codeword three times.

Now, at last, they see Alpha team surge forward.

If Monis truly has a bomb, Tango Charlie fears he might have just sent his men to their deaths.

Alpha team, joined by two members of Papa team, bolt out of the vehicle bay next to the café. The Papa men run to the closest window along Phillip Street, attempting to break the glass with a breaching weapon so they can toss in a stun grenade. The glass holds firm, so they run to join Alpha team now breaking through the front entrance. Officer A is sticking close behind the shield man, Alpha 2.

Officer A has his gun over Alpha 2's shoulder, seeking out the target. The light source on his helmet picks Monis out from the gloom almost instantly. Officer A can't see any hostages, but he sees Monis looking straight back, shotgun pointed directly at him.

'There's the cunt! There's the cunt!' Alpha 2 shouts. 'Shoot him!'

Monis fires twice, but the shots go high and Officer A has already locked onto the target. He aims at the gunman's upper chest and fires, then keeps firing as he moves up to Monis' head. Monis is starting to buckle, but hasn't released the shotgun.

Officer A keeps shooting, his trigger finger unleashing seventeen bullets in the space of a few seconds. The café reverberates with the onslaught—not just the roar of the gunfire, but the sound of the stun grenades being hurled through the doors by other members of the tactical teams.

Officer B fires off five bullets, but a shot or shrapnel or flying glass grazes his upper cheek near his temple and he falls to the floor.

'Get the fuck back up,' Alpha 2 yells at him. Officer B is 'shitting myself' after being struck, but takes cover and gets back up.

Officer A is trying to make himself heard above the noise of the stun grenades, which are still flying into the café. He calls for the others to stop. 'It's enough,' he shouts.

'The terrorist is down!' he yells, over and over, until he is hoarse.

The shooting is over by the time the combined Charlie/Delta team bursts through the lobby doors. They have not achieved simultaneous entry with the Alpha men. Later the police and families will argue about whether that delayed entry by the second tactical group could have affected the outcome. Either way, it's almost certain that by the time Charlie/Delta team gains entry Monis is already dead.

—

The police entry plunges the five remaining hostages—Louisa, Robin, Marcia, Selina and Katrina—into the middle of a maelstrom. Blinding light suddenly obliterates the darkness, while the sound generated by the SF9 stun grenades, the 'stunnies', is staggering. Purposefully designed to disorientate, each stun grenade sets off nine separate explosions. To the hostages' ears, it sounds as if an entire army is coming through the door.

Marcia and Katrina are on the floor, lying parallel. Katrina puts her hands to her face; Marcia has curled into the foetal position.

Louisa has the sensation of being caught up in something like a catastrophic car accident. 'There is shrapnel coming up from everywhere. Everything seems to happen in a split second—all the bits are flying everywhere,' she says. 'I wanted to shout out "Stop, stop!" but I didn't, because I thought Monis mustn't be dead yet. Otherwise, why would they keep going? They can't still be shooting up for no reason!

'I've fallen on the ground again, flush with the bench under the windows. I'd covered my eyes with my hands and it just kept going and going, and I thought to myself: "Well, I've survived this whole day, but you're gonna die here and you might as well watch." So I dropped my hands.

'Then I felt this piercing pain in my foot and I was aware that the straps of my favourite red sandals were missing. Part of me was thinking "How am I going to get those repaired?" while the other half is registering the pain. And then the whole thing finally stopped. One of the tactical guys was suddenly on top of me, saying, "You're safe, you're safe." And I'm thinking, not so safe, really. But I'm aware that I'm still alive—and that Tori, that beautiful young man, was dead.'

Selina is lying on the floor in a state of shock near the kitchen. She has been braced for Monis coming back to find her ever since the other hostages fled. And then she hears and sees 'shit shattering everywhere. I'm thinking, "Please kill him, please kill him." There was so much light and banging. There was screaming from outside. It felt like ages.'

Marcia feels terrible pain in her lower legs. She knows she has been hit, but she suppresses the urge to scream. All she's thinking is, 'Please, God, I need to get out of here alive.'

The sound and fury comes to an end. With their torches penetrating the gloom, Officer A and Alpha move to where the body of Man Haron Monis lies sprawled. A large portion of his head has been shot away, blood pooling on the floor. Unquestionably, the attacker is dead.

One of the TOU men tells Louisa she has to leave immediately. 'Can you walk?' he asks.

No, she says. She tells them that she is wounded in the foot. He asks whether she can hop, which she attempts with enormous effort. Her stomach has taken shrapnel as well, but she doesn't feel that yet. She starts awkwardly hopping towards the door, but two of the men lift her bodily and out onto the street.

She has lost track of Selina and Marcia, and her mother. She does not know that Katrina Dawson is lying mortally wounded in the furthest nook of the café.

'Get some fucking medics! We need some fucking medics in here, now!' Alpha 2 yells.

Later, a year later, Louisa would finally discover why Tori had never got up from the bench where he was sitting with Robin.

'It was close to the first anniversary after the siege,' she recalls. 'We hadn't really talked about the events in the café much. If it came on the news, we would talk about it in the abstract, not in a personal way. And on that particular day I had a chance to put it to her [Robin]: "Did you not see me go to run out?" "Yes," she said. And then I said, "Why didn't you and Tori run with me?"

'And Robin replied that she told Tori, 'You go, you go". That she was elbowing him, and he said, "No, I will stay".

"Tori made a choice,' says Louisa. 'Tori had the opportunity to run, without a doubt. He chose to stay with Robin, and he was assassinated. If that's not sacrificial love, I don't know what is.'

CHAPTER 13

LOSS

Louisa is now out on the street, desperately waiting for news of her mother. A hole the size of a small orange has been punched into the arch of her left foot. 'What's happened to Robin, does anyone know?' she calls. She doesn't think her mother could possibly have survived the maelstrom they've just been through.

She lies on Phillip Street and looks at the stars. Her ears are still ringing and half-deafened from the barrage of the police assault, but beneath that, beneath the sounds of running feet and nearby voices, she seems to be immersed in a deep silence—the silence, she thinks, of a stricken city. Quietly she starts singing to herself the old spiritual anthem *Amazing Grace*.

As she is being helped into an ambulance, she hears a police officer call, 'We've got your mother!'

Louisa can't believe they have both come through this alive. 'Holy hell, how did that happen,' she wonders. 'We were standing either side of that man. The police killed him and not us. It was astounding to me.'

For the ambulance crews on standby since mid-morning of Monday 15 December, it had been a long slow wait. By late afternoon it had become apparent there was going to be no swift resolution of the siege, and paramedic supervisors began making arrangements for relief shifts to take over in the evening.

Among the many called in to bolster the night shift were Daniel Trincado, Oliver Aleman, Chris Ennis and Oliver Ellis. The four, all highly experienced paramedics in their late thirties or early forties, were members of the Special Operations Team (SOT), an elite group of paramedics specially trained to work with tactical police units in high-risk incidents. The SOT crews carried extra kit in addition to their first aid equipment: ballistic helmets and vests. If any of the tactical police were injured, SOT members would treat them as well as any injured hostages.

Two ambulance staging posts had been established close to the café, one just to the north-east near the corner of Macquarie and Hunter Streets, the other to the south near the corner of Martin Place and Elizabeth Street. By 9 p.m. Trincado, Aleman, Ennis and Ellis were in the positions they had been ordered to take up at the southern staging post, stationed alongside the bomb squad. They were briefed by police liaison officers, though it seemed to some of the paramedics that the briefings were more perfunctory than usual. Ennis had been on five jobs with the tactical police in recent weeks. Compared with those jobs, there seemed less information available than he would have liked. Trincado was feeling a similar sense of unease about the information flow.

The hours dragged by. Midnight came and went. Low-key talk dropped away as each man settled into his own thoughts, conserving energy for what they'd been told could be a long wait, even perhaps extending into the next day.

At 2.03 a.m. the enveloping silence was shattered by the first shot from Monis' gun. Moments later the pack of terrified hostages, Jarrod in the lead, came flying down Martin Place in what one of the waiting paramedics would later describe as a 'bullrush' of escapees.

As the group tore around the corner, the paramedics tried to slow their flight. Aleman grabbed for Julie Taylor, who collapsed to the ground, her legs still pumping frantically as she lay there. 'You have to help them—he is going to kill them all,' Julie gasped, chest heaving.

Aleman tried to calm her, and supported her the short distance to the holding area inside the leagues' club. He told the paramedic there not to let Julie go. She was so agitated that he worried she might try to resume her flight, as if she imagined the gunman was still right behind her.

Trincado had managed to corral three of the other escapees. Police wanted them searched for explosives before they were allowed into the hostage reception centre, but there was no way of holding them back. He jogged them towards the back entrance of the leagues' club, before rejoining Aleman and Ellis at the staging post, 45 metres down the slope of Martin Place from the café.

Eight minutes later, at 2.11 a.m., came the sound of Monis' second gunshot. Already on high alert, the waiting paramedics knew the end game must be close. They readied for action.

Three minutes later, at 2.14 a.m., all hell broke loose as the police unleashed their assault on the café. As soon as the barrage ended, there was a brief lull, then came the shouts of 'Ambos! Ambos!'

Grabbing their gear, paramedics at the southern staging post headed towards the stronghold, pausing momentarily when a single loud report put everyone on edge again. It was one of the TOU men, setting off a flashbang that had lost its pin. Then the paramedics set off running up Martin Place, where police directed them towards the café's doors.

Inside lay a scene of devastation. Through the smoke and the darkness, they could make out broken furniture and debris lying strewn around the room as if tossed about by a hurricane. Broken glass crunched underfoot. Acrid smoke hung heavy in the air.

Louisa, Robin, Marcia and Selina had already been rushed out of the café by the tactical officers. Monis' body lay bloodied and broken towards the back of the room, near the waiter's nook where he had spent most of the last hours of the siege.

Another shout directed Ennis towards the back corner. The paramedic could see two officers there, near where Monis' body was lying. As he approached, he could make out a woman, motionless on the ground. To reach her he would have to step over Monis. He pulled the two TOU men out of the way. 'They appeared unable to hear me,' he told investigators later. 'I assumed they were still affected by the noise of the flashbangs.'

He crouched down to assess her. She was unresponsive, her breathing laboured. Trincado joined him.

The pair decided they had to get her out of the café at once: there was too much broken glass around to treat her safely in situ, and there was still the possibility of an explosive device somewhere inside. Carrying her out onto Phillip Street, they could detect no obvious injuries at first. Then they gently rolled her onto her side and saw the wounds to her upper back. The injuries looked like they had been inflicted by shrapnel. Swiftly they unpacked their equipment and got to work.

Twenty-nine-year-old paramedic David Lambert and colleague Michael Thomson were stationed at the northern staging post when they heard the unmistakable sounds of the police storming the café. Lambert was told to get his ambulance immediately across to the southern side, which meant working his way back around the block.

Travelling along Macquarie Street, he saw police tape up ahead strung across the road. This was no time for niceties—he barged straight through.

Arriving at the southern staging post, Lambert and Thomson removed their stretcher from the van. They stood there briefly while supervisors debated whether it was safe for them to go forward. 'There appeared to be some confusion as to whether it was safe to proceed,' Lambert told investigators later. 'We were told to "Go" and "Wait" two or three times before actually proceeding on foot up Martin Place.'

They got the green light and hurried towards the front entrance of the café, where Ennis and Trincado were working on the patient they would later come to know was Katrina Dawson. Lambert got his torch out and held it over the two men to give them more light. Then he heard a 'lot of yelling' from police still inside the café. One of the TOU men shouted a code word, which appeared to the paramedics to be an evacuation order.

They placed Katrina on a stretcher and hurried down Martin Place towards an ambulance equipped for critically ill patients. At 2.25 a.m. it sped towards the Royal Prince Alfred Hospital (RPA), lights flashing and siren blaring, for what at that hour of night, with the roads clear, was a ten-minute journey. In the rear, specialist paramedics worked frantically to try and stabilise their patient, but her condition was deteriorating fast.

Paramedic Fernando Costa arrived in the vicinity of the café as stun grenades were still going off inside. In the back of his mind, he noted some of the paramedics had bullet-proof vests on. He wondered why his team had not been issued them. Once the barrage had subsided, he hurried to the café entrance and saw one of the tactical police performing CPR on a fair-haired man, aged in his thirties, lying to the left of the doors. Costa knelt down to check for a pulse but the patient, clad in dark-coloured clothing, was no longer breathing.

After the evacuation codeword had been shouted, Costa and his colleagues swiftly picked the man up and placed him on a stretcher inside an ambulance. The body of Tori Johnson would remain unidentified in the back of Ambulance 557 for the next hour and a half.

By late Monday evening, forty or more family members and friends had convened at the hurriedly set aside family reception centre in the old Supreme Court building. Rosie, Tori's mother was there, along with Thomas and Tori's father Ken. Senior Lindt staff were also present.

The Dawsons would not arrive until the early hours of the next morning. Despite the fact that an officer had been assigned earlier in the day to liaise with the Dawson family, the police did not tell them of the reception centre. The Dawsons would only learn about this from a TV broadcast in the early hours of the morning as Katrina's parents, Sandy senior and Jane, were preparing to go to bed.

Indeed, earlier in the evening the clan had gathered at Katrina's house for dinner. The news from police was reassuring: don't worry, the guy's a talker, it's likely to fizzle out. 'We felt somewhat relieved by that,' Angus Dawson recalled later. 'The mood was one of cautious optimism based on what we'd heard from the police.'

Among the growing throng at the Supreme Court were Jarrod's mother, Danielle, his father, Mark, their respective partners and several other members of his extended family.

Danielle had asked her partner, Julian, to travel in to the leagues' club (where family members had first gathered) in the late morning but she had kept herself at home, where she began compulsively cleaning and tidying her son's room. It was the best way she could think of to keep her head clear and keep a modicum of calm. At least, she thought, it would give Jarrod an ordered, peaceful place to recover in when he came home, as (she kept telling herself) he would.

She had texted Jarrod briefly that morning: 'Just remain calm, the police are everywhere, you will be OK.' She heard nothing back. With nightfall, she grew increasingly uneasy and made her way into the city to join the others.

Jorge, Harriette's partner, was beginning to sharply question the lack of police action and getting increasingly testy responses. 'Why don't you go in there and shoot him?' Jorge asked. 'This is not the movies and we are not in America,' a senior officer told him brusquely.

For the families there had been little news since 6.30 p.m., when a senior policewoman had given some of them a general rundown on the management of the siege. Time had become a blur, Rosie said later. 'We were demanding information but, way into the night, there was nothing. The attitude was just, "This is the way we do it, and this is the way we will proceed".' At 11 p.m. the senior female officer briefed them again, and then once more just before 1 a.m. But no additional information was forthcoming.

At one of the late briefings, Danielle said she'd heard nothing of her son all day. By contrast, some of the others had made brief contact with their loved ones inside the café. It was getting harder to keep telling herself that everything would be fine. 'What is his name?' the officer asked her. 'Jarrod,' she said. 'We know Jarrod,' the policewoman replied. Danielle allowed herself to feel a small upwelling of relief.

Soon after midnight, forty-four-year-old Detective Sergeant Sheldon Klotz, normally attached to the Organised Crime Squad, was told he and his small team of officers would be placed in charge of the Supreme Court hostage reception area for the rest of the night. Klotz had already put in a long day, having started work at 4 a.m. Now, late at night, he was aware of the restive mood among the waiting groups of family and friends.

Police commanders had decided earlier in the evening not to allow a working television into the reception centre, fearing it would sow more unease among the waiting loved ones. It was a fundamental miscalculation that overlooked the access the families already had to news websites and social media on their smart phones.

Adding to the emotionally fraught atmosphere was the fact that the exclusion zone set up around the café by the police had been narrowed as the evening wore on. Now the Supreme Court lay outside the protection of the police cordon, giving camera crews a chance to set up almost on the waiting families' doorstep. It was one more headache for Klotz and his small team to manage as they tried to reduce the stress on the families.

'It was just a horrible feeling, waiting and waiting,' one parent recalled. 'And knowing that the media was outside—that cameras were trained on the doorway and you couldn't walk out there without your picture being taken—that was horrible too.'

Shortly after 2.03 a.m., the families became aware of the hostage breakout. Jorge got a call from Harriette. 'I'm out, I'm out!' she told him.

Immediately a swarm of relatives and friends of the others clustered around him, hungry for news. 'All these people were around me asking "Who else? Who else? Is such and such out?" I didn't know most of them, and I asked Harriette how many had come out and she said about eight. But nobody was really sure what was happening.'

They had barely had time to absorb this hopeful news when the horrifying sounds of the TOU assault erupted. Thomas would later say it sounded as if everyone in the café was being shot. Joel Herat's father recalled everyone letting out 'an awful sigh, and a wail'. The families had no way of knowing that most of the explosions they were hearing were being set off by the stun grenades that were hurled into the stronghold.

A number of the family members surged down the Supreme Court steps towards the café. Klotz and his team tried to restrain some of them. 'We all started heading up that street,' recalls Jorge. 'The police were trying to stop us, saying "It's just the stun grenades." I turned around, and somehow we all sort of pulled up.'

But now a new sound was cutting through the night, nearly as chilling: the wailing of ambulances converging on the café.

Later the police would concede they should never have kept waiting friends and family at a site so close to the siege. But it was too late to do anything about it now.

Inside the leagues' club, the escaped hostages were still in a state of tumult. Some were crying, telling the police how dangerous Monis was. Julie Taylor sat on the floor with her head in her hands. She had thought Katrina was ahead of her as the group fled through the lobby. Now, learning otherwise, she was consumed with anxiety about what might be happening to her.

'My friend is still in there, please help her, you have to help my friend,' she pleaded. A female police officer knelt beside her, offering comfort. 'The police will be doing all they can to help Katrina,' the officer told her.

Harriette was just as worried about Tori, and concerned that Louisa with her MS, and Robin, being elderly, would not be able to make it out; and Viswa and Puspendu were worried sick about Marcia. Jarrod meanwhile was explaining to the police that they had been left with no choice but to flee: 'He was going to kill us all. If we didn't get out, we were all going to die.' Sitting with Joel, he was momentarily swept up in the euphoria of being free. 'We were like, "Oh my God, I can't believe we're alive,"' Jarrod says.

But where was Tori? Only now were they beginning to realise that he was still at the café.

Jarrod passed the café's basement storage key to police, although he knew it was not going to be of much use. He told them that if they came across strange-looking packages in the sink these were not explosives—they were the bottles Monis had blown cigarette smoke into. He also inquired whether they had ever got the scraps of notes he'd written on business cards and pushed under the fire door. No, an officer replied.

Jarrod does not recall, in the minutes immediately after the escape, anyone asking him about Monis' backpack, or whether he thought there was a bomb in there.

When the sounds of the police assault on the café, just eighty or so paces away, broke out at 2.14 a.m., the hostages at the leagues' club were plunged back into the nightmare they had just freed themselves from. Some screamed, or ducked their heads. The noise was deafening; they could feel the vibrations from the explosions shuddering through their bodies. Viswa looked like he might faint. Harriette buried her head in a police officer's shoulder.

'It's all right, it's us, it's the good guys,' one of the officers assured them.

Fiona Ma unexpectedly appeared in their midst. She was ushered in from the vehicle bay, where she had been when the police assault commenced.

Harriette was relieved to see her, but fretting about Tori. 'Is everyone out?' she asked.

'Yes,' came the reply. 'Everyone is out.'

Harriette felt a small wave of relief wash over her. He must be safe.

Jane and Sandy Dawson were just about to switch out the light to try and grab a few hours' rest when Katrina's husband Paul rang just after 2.00 a.m. and urged them to switch on the TV. An awful conviction came over Jane when she saw the footage. 'Oh, my God, they've killed her,' she exclaimed. But despite the rising dread, she and Sandy knew they had to stay focused on practicalities. They drove to Katrina's house to wait for the regular carer for Katrina and Paul's young children to show up. They then drove into the city to join Paul's medically trained brother Mark and Katrina's brothers at the Supreme Court. The longest and most agonising wait of their lives was just beginning.

For those who'd had no news of their loved ones since the escape, the worst phase of the evening was about to unfold. Klotz made repeated calls to the forward command post yet was getting no updates. He told his superiors someone in authority had to come down straight away. The families 'seemed to know more about what had occurred than we did', he later complained.

Thomas Zinn, Tori's partner, had been frantically checking news websites and found one German newspaper reporting 'Gunmen and Two Hostages Dead'. Zinn pressed an officer for more information, in vain.

At 2.30 a.m. Ken Johnson, Tori's father, was overcome with stress and needed a paramedic.

At 3.00 a.m. two inspectors finally appeared at the Supreme Court. Grimly, they delivered the news that a hostage had been killed, one was in cardiac arrest and several others wounded. Inspector Joel Murchie told the families police were not yet in a position to give any names. This prompted an immediate outcry. 'The response by the families to this information was overwhelming,' Klotz would report later.

Privately some of the police family liaison officers at the Supreme Court were themselves feeling mounting frustration. Klotz would later give a startlingly frank account of his own unhappiness. 'The mood of the families continued to deteriorate, due to the lack of information being supplied to them versus what they were able to see via news feeds,' he said in a statement to investigators. He persisted with calls to the police forward command post: 'Each time I was not given any information that I could convey to the families so as to alleviate their stress and trauma.'

From around 2.45 a.m. Inspector Jennine Kiely from the New South Wales Ambulance Service began updating the Police Operations Centre (POC) and senior commanders with the dismaying news: one hostage dead, one critical and several wounded, including a police tactical officer.

Forward commander Victor's mood was darkening with each addition to the casualty list. 'As commander, standing there, [I'm] listening to that thinking, "Far out". You know, the count was going up. You don't want to hear that,' he would tell investigators later. 'It was a bitter pill for [me] to swallow as the forward commander . . . I'm thinking, "Christ, you know, we've let them down. But what do you do?"' For Victor, time seemed to come to a grinding halt.

But the commanders had no choice now other than to focus on managing the chaotic aftermath. The outcome was what it was.

At three Sydney hospitals, emergency departments were now in full swing caring for the wounded hostages. Robin had been transported west to the Royal Prince Alfred, where heroic efforts were still being made to save Katrina. Julie had also been admitted to RPA as an obstetric patient. Marcia had been taken north across the Harbour Bridge to the Royal North Shore Hospital, with shrapnel wounds to both her lower legs. Harriette was also taken there for observation. Louisa was whisked east, to the Prince of Wales Hospital. Selina, miraculously, had emerged physically unscathed.

At the Prince of Wales, Louisa was frantically trying to recount as much as she could to the two officers at her bedside before being wheeled into surgery. 'I was pouring everything out, talking at a hundred miles an hour. Then my emergency nurse comes towards me with a pair of scissors saying, "I'm going to cut your clothes off now".' Louisa recoiled. The dress was brand new, one of her favourites. Irrationally, she began arguing with the nurse, even appealing to the officers who were now taking their leave. Her protests fell on deaf ears. The nurse carefully cut the dress and pulled it up over Louisa's head. Louisa ran her hands down her body, wondering why they felt wet. Then she held them up and looked at them: they were slick with blood. She'd had no awareness of the pieces of shrapnel that had sprayed into her abdomen. 'I looked at that nurse, she looked at me: we both knew she had been right,' Louisa said.

There was one more casualty to attend to. During the police assault on the café Officer B, the only other police officer to fire at Monis aside from Officer A, had suffered a superficial wound to his upper cheek. He wasn't sure what had caused it: flying glass, or shrapnel, or even Monis' shotgun. He could only recall a sharp stinging sensation.

Ambulance officers assessed him as not badly wounded but obviously shaken. One of the paramedics, Benjamin Gilmour, asked Officer B: 'What happened in there?' The reply stayed with Gilmour for a long time afterwards. 'Man,' said Officer B, 'it was a fuck-up.'

Later, Officer B would say he had no recollection of this conversation. He told the coroner: 'It was a very surreal experience for me', and added that he was 'in shock' when he spoke to the paramedics. 'I may have said "That was fucked up"—not "This is a fuck-up"—because it was a fucked-up situation. No one wanted to go into that café, sir.'

Gilmour gave a statement to the police clearly setting out his recollection of the words Officer B had said to him. The paramedic was never called to give evidence from the witness box.

The State Crisis Centre had become relatively quiet in the run-up to 2 a.m. Premier Mike Baird and Police Minister Stuart Ayres left soon after midnight, checking in to the Sheraton on the Park, an up-market hotel on nearby Hyde Park. Neither man lived close to the city, and both wanted to be nearby as long as the siege remained unresolved.

Baird had left instructions that he was to be phoned if there were developments overnight. Stuart Ayres' ministerial aide, John Redman, says there was a clear feeling among ministers, advisers and senior police that the café was going to remain relatively stable for the night.

'At that point, most people thought it was going to end calmly,' Redman recalls. 'People just thought that, if this guy was going to do anything, he would have done it already. Everyone just thought, "Let him tire out, let him fall asleep. Then we will get them out and, with luck, he will be the only one left in the room." We thought we would wake up in the morning and that the police would have arrested this bloke and it would all have come out fine. No one thought it was going to go down the way it did.'

He does, however, remember one oddly prescient conversation earlier in the evening. 'There were a few of us just sitting there eating pizza and I remember saying to Troy [Deputy Premier Troy Grant], "How is this going to end?" And he said—and I will never forget this—"I don't know how it will go down but it will start to happen at two o'clock. This guy is getting tired—give it till two o'clock." And I took that to mean, you know, the gunman had been going all day, maybe he would start to nod off or quieten down. But I didn't give it too much thought at the time.'

Redman went home soon after Minister Ayres, but couldn't relax. It was all over the TV, and not just in Australia. The US was now waking up and it was the headline story there, too. 'I'm watching the news, watching CNN, FOX—they all had rolling coverage. I had maybe half an hour on the couch when I get the call from Tess Salmon [Troy Grant's media person] saying it had all happened and to get in quick.'

Baird had barely had time for a nap. His head hit the pillow just after 1.00 a.m. Not much more than an hour later the phone rang. It was one of the senior officers—though later he couldn't remember who—breaking the news of the end of the siege to him.

'I just remember the voice,' Baird says. 'He was saying that we've had to go in, and that there were people down. It was as if the world was swallowing me up when I received that phone call. And then I remember hearing the sound of ambulances roaring past on the way to try and save the victims.'

At around 3.15 a.m. the ministers, their senior staffers and the police top brass joined the sombre gathering at the State Crisis Centre for the first full briefing, the group now including Police Commissioner Scipione, who had returned at 3 a.m. Mark Jenkins provided an update.

The atmosphere, recalls Baird, was 'terrible'. 'Everyone, from the junior officers to the senior officers, had had this fierce determination to get everyone out. Knowing that that hadn't happened was devastating, completely and utterly devastating.' Baird described Scipione as shattered, 'utterly . . . almost to the point that [one would think] he'd lost members of his family'.

No one could yet say whether the gravely wounded hostage was the victim of police bullets or Monis' shotgun. Nor was it entirely clear from the briefing whether the group of hostages whose flight had triggered the end of the siege had been released or broken free on their own initiative. The forward command post had still not checked with the snipers about their observations immediately prior to Tori's execution, and rumours were circulating that Monis had been in some kind of scuffle with the hostages before he'd shot one of them.

Sometime before 4 a.m., Baird and his ministers learnt that the critically wounded hostage at RPA had died. Redman says the government team was growing increasingly anxious about getting clear information to pass on to the waiting media, 'We knew we were soon going to have to go out there and drop the news.'

The premier and his advisers began the delicate task of fine-tuning the language he would use for the media briefing, which had been scheduled for a couple of hours' hence. Baird sweated over trying to find the right words. His main goal at this point, he says, was to 'keep the city together, and do what I could for the victims' families'. Over the next few days he would try to make contact with all the hostages. He also attended the TOU operations base to thank the men who had stormed the café for their bravery—the 'elite of the elite', as he called them.

Baird took the events of the siege to heart in ways he would not reveal until a long time afterwards. 'I think my heart was broken,' he told me in late 2017, nearly a year after he had stepped down from the job as premier. 'I've reflected on this with my wife since: something inside me broke that day. I will never be the same again. I found myself in the middle of the situation with senior responsibility and we lost two people. I just felt it very personally . . . two beautiful young lives, just innocently [taken].'

It was nearly three hours before the bereaved families discovered, for sure, that Tori and Katrina had died. As time dragged on with no news, they braced for what was to come.

At 2.45 a.m. Detective Sergeant Jason Pietruszka, who had performed CPR on Tori in the immediate aftermath of the shooting, told his superiors that a male hostage he described as being 'Caucasian in his thirties' had been found dead inside the café and was now in an ambulance outside.

The officer conveyed an accurate description of Tori and his clothes, including his distinctive black shirt. Why this did not lead to his identification soon afterwards was never explained. Ambulance officers were told to leave the hostage's body in the ambulance and hand the matter over to police.

Despite the extraordinary efforts of paramedics and doctors, Katrina was declared dead shortly after 3.12 a.m. Again, none of the authorities yet knew who she was.

An inspector from the Newtown police command was told to document details of her appearance. He took photos of Katrina's distinctive engagement ring and at around 3.30 a.m. showed these to Julie Taylor's husband, Bruce, who was at RPA hospital comforting his wife. Bruce confirmed it was the same ring Katrina wore. The grim implications of this were clear to him immediately, but for now he kept the news to himself.

The police could see that the evidence almost certainly pointed towards Katrina and Tori having died. An entry to this effect was made in the POC log book, but still they hesitated to inform the families.

At 4 a.m. on 16 December, a frustrated Klotz finally rang the forward command post and said, 'How about *I* tell *you* who the deceased are?' He then provided the names of Katrina and Tori and their dates of birth.

Five minutes later he got a call back from an officer at the leagues' club giving him exactly the same information he had just passed on.

At the old Supreme Court building, those who were waiting for officers to finish interviewing the escaped hostages could see that only two families—the Dawsons and the Johnsons—had not yet had word of their loved ones. 'It was such an awful position to put us in—and to put them in,' one of the other parents told me later. Around 4.30 a.m. a chaplain arrived, his silent presence adding to the general discomfort.

At 4.40 a.m. Klotz finally received official confirmation of the names and was told he should break the news to the two waiting families within twenty minutes, because a news conference had been scheduled.

Klotz and two of his team approached the Johnsons first, and took them into a small adjacent room. The family only had to take one look at his face to know what he was about to tell them. Ten to fifteen minutes later, it was the Dawsons' turn.

There was no privacy. Bruce Herat, waiting to be re-united with his son Joel, was in tears himself as he listened to the sounds of anguish from the bereaved families. 'For me, the moment was bittersweet: I was elated that Joel was okay, but absolutely shattered that others were not. It was the saddest thing I had ever heard,' he said.

Grief-stricken, the Dawsons were horrified to be told by police that they would have to travel to the morgue to identify their daughter. It was Katrina's brother-in-law Mark who intervened. He told the police there was no reason why she could not be kept at the hospital for identification, and he arranged for that to happen. Then they embarked on the desperately sad journey to RPA to farewell Katrina—a daughter, a sister, a wife, a mother.

Both the Johnsons and the Dawsons would later protest bitterly about the needlessly prolonged identification process, and the additional agony it put the families through.

Ray Hadley departed the 2GB studio at around 6 p.m. Later that night he found it almost impossible to sleep, tossing and turning and worrying about Katrina, the sister of his barrister friend Sandy Dawson.

Michael McLaren had taken over the early morning shift in the studio. During the late stages of the siege, Hadley kept ringing in to remind the staff: 'Please don't do anything that could put anyone in jeopardy.'

Eventually Hadley decided there was no point in even trying to sleep and headed back to the station. He was still in his car when he heard the news of the police assault on the café.

At 6 a.m., Sandy Dawson rang him to tell him Katrina hadn't made it. 'We were both crying. I just said, "Sorry, mate, I don't know what could have been done."'

At the leagues' club, Jarrod was still unaware of what had happened to Tori. The police had taken his clothing for forensic testing, and the young man was now sitting in a blue forensic jumpsuit undergoing hours of debriefing. It was some time before he asked the way to the nearest bathroom. He was directed through the main room, where TV coverage was on a loop, playing the end of the siege over and over.

On the screen Jarrod saw a body being wheeled away on a stretcher, with just one shoe showing. Unmistakably, it was Tori's: 'I went to the bathroom and came back and sat down. "Tori's dead, isn't he?" The debrief guy said, "Yes". And then he said, "It just sucks". And it was what I needed to hear. I didn't want a hug—I just wanted someone in my own vernacular to acknowledge the sadness of that. "It just sucks" was a summary of the whole day.'

Arriving at the Prince of Wales Hospital desperate to see Harriette, Jorge saw the shoe on television too and instantly knew it had to be Tori. Harriette had begun to fear the worst and had been ringing Tori's phone over and over without success. In desperation, she rang her father and asked him to go online and see what he could find.

A police officer finally came to her to break the news. 'He cried with me,' she told her family later. 'That was comforting . . . I knew Tori wasn't going to run—he wouldn't have left without any of us.'

In the darkened and silent Channel 7 building, Greg Parker and Chris Reason were trying to process the enormity of what they had witnessed. 'From the moment we found out it was Monis, I thought they would talk him out of it. It didn't pan out the way a lot of people thought it would that day,' Reason says. 'The gunshot that killed Tori is a sound that will stay with me for the rest of my life. It was an awful, harrowing thing to go through.'

Parker had been on station for nearly as long as the TOU men: hour after hour, streaming vital intelligence back to the police. 'What he did that day was extraordinary,' Reason says. 'Battling the exhaustion, his endurance, it's extremely difficult to man a camera for that many hours through such gut-wrenching scenes. He produced something not only of enormous news value but critically important for the police operation and the inquest that followed.'

Chris Reason himself did not leave for home until after 6 p.m. on Tuesday 16 December, concerned that he would not be able to re-enter the building if he left earlier. When he walked out, floral tributes were starting to appear on Martin Place. 'I turned and walked the other way. I honestly didn't think I could face it.'

There had been no improvised explosive device in Monis' backpack. When the bomb disposal experts finally emptied it, they found nothing more than a home stereo speaker with some wires trailing from the back, along with a small knife, some sunglasses and a torch. But other mysteries remained. Where had he got the gun? And had Monis intended to die?

Police found a curious thing on his body after his death. In his pockets was a handwritten list, in English and Farsi, of his personal contacts and his lawyers. He'd also included a list of MIN (master index numbers), the numbers used to identify and contact prisoners. If he had ended up in prison after the siege, these numbers would have been useful to him.

Did this mean he might have been anticipating jail? That he hadn't necessarily decided to self-annihilate? That he had believed his plan to get Tony Abbott on air might have come off and that he would then have walked into the arms of police? After the siege, the Dawsons' lawyers speculated that there was an outside possibility that Monis had remained open to releasing hostages in exchange for some deal on his demands. 'He was simply never provided with an opportunity to advance these offers,' the Dawson's legal team argued.

But Manny Conditsis, the lawyer who probably had the most dealings with Monis, doubts the gunman was ever reconciled to a return to jail. He remembers how much Monis hated his few weeks behind bars at the end of 2013 while awaiting his ultimately successful bail hearing on the accessory to murder charge. He had complained to the lawyer about excrement on the cell walls and of 'torture' inside the prison. Conditsis believes Monis was never going to walk out of the café alive. But he would have guessed suicide before murder. 'My view is he may not have had an express intention of killing anyone, but that it was his last stand for the public attention which he so craved, his last opportunity to be seen as a martyr to the cause,' Conditsis told me.

On that judgment, another of Monis' lawyers, Nazir Daawar, vigorously disagrees. Monis, he says, struck him as 'evil'.

In the months after the siege, Conditsis read a book on narcissism, convinced that Monis possessed all the hallmarks of the condition. He was startled to discover how strongly those same traits featured in the makeup of other killers, including the Norwegian mass killer Anders Behring Breivik.

CHAPTER 14

THE INQUEST

Michael Barnes, the New South Wales coroner, surveyed the shattered interior of the Lindt café. It was Wednesday 17 December, less than forty-eight hours after the end of the siege. A former journalist, he knew the value of getting early to the aftermath of an event such as this. Now he stood looking at the Lindt Café much as it had been left by the paramedics and tactical teams the day before: furniture shattered and overturned, glass strewn underfoot, ominous stains on the floor, and pockmarks and scars disfiguring the walls and ceilings of the once-gracious room.

Barnes had been out of Sydney as the siege was unfolding, overseeing another inquest in the country town of Walgett. He'd watched the coverage until around midnight, then went to bed. When the phone shrilled at 2.22 a.m. he knew immediately why it was ringing. On the other end of the line was the head of Homicide, Superintendent Mick Willing, telling him of the siege's bloody finale.

At this early stage, Katrina's survival was still uncertain. The gunman and another as-yet-unidentified hostage were confirmed fatalities. As with any death during a police operation, let alone an event that had paralysed the city for a day and a night, a coronial probe was automatically triggered. Barnes made plans to get back to Sydney immediately.

Soon after calling the coroner, Superintendent Willing rang fifty-four-year-old Detective Inspector Angelo Memmolo, a seasoned veteran of the Homicide Squad, putting him in charge of the critical incident investigation. Memmolo arrived at the shell-shocked Police Operations Centre (POC), where the senior commanders were still gathered, at 3.40 a.m., less than two hours after the siege had ended. At 4.30 a.m. he sat down with the handful of detectives he'd put together as the nucleus of his team, and replayed the media footage of the storming of the café.

Memmolo then drove to the forward command post, where the crestfallen men of the Alpha, Papa, Charlie and Delta teams were waiting in the leagues' club gym. He told them they would be spoken to individually, and that their kits and firearms would be taken for inspection and testing. 'I'm giving you a direction now not to speak to anyone or discuss this matter with anyone,' he said.

He asked each to identify the kit they had used during the emergency entry and who had fired. Officer A told Memmolo, 'You want to speak to me.' It was a statement, not a question.

The only key person missing was Officer B, who'd been taken to hospital for assessment of the glancing wound to his face.

Memmolo's team, dubbed Strike Force Verum, would eventually build to around thirty detectives conducting the largest critical incident investigation in Australia's history. It would not be a job for the faint-hearted. The team would have to comb through the actions and judgments of dozens of colleagues and superiors. The coroner would later acknowledge the courage and 'unstinting commitment to integrity' this required of them.

Michael Barnes had his own reputation for doggedness. In Queensland, where he had been coroner for ten years prior to taking the New South Wales job in January 2014, he'd earned the nickname 'Cold Case Barnes' for drilling down into long-unresolved cases. Nor was he delicate about taking on government, as he'd shown with damning findings after a probe into the deaths of three young Queensland men who'd died while installing 'pink batts' roof insulation—part of a hastily designed government program rolled out in response to the global financial crisis of 2008.

The Lindt inquiry was certain to extend into even more sensitive areas of official activity. There was going to be institutional resistance. Barnes would need someone with a proven track record to help get to the truth.

Senior Counsel Jeremy Gormly and his wife Claudia were moored on a boat a thousand kilometres away in picturesque Wineglass Bay on Tasmania's east coast when Monis commenced his attack. Nothing could have been further from the carnage than this haven in the waters of the Freycinet National Park, with its white sand beach and the pink granite peaks of the Hazards towering in the background.

For the first few hours the couple were blissfully unaware of the drama unfolding in the heart of Australia's most iconic city. Both keen sailors, they were aboard their 48-foot sloop waiting for the weather to clear so they could begin their homeward leg after a five-month break that had taken them up and down the east coast of the continent.

Gormly, sixty-one, had a stellar reputation at the Sydney Bar. As a junior barrister he had assisted in the most complex inquest the country had ever seen—the probe into the 1997 deaths of eighteen Australians whose ski lodge had been engulfed by a landslide at Thredbo, in the Snowy Mountains. Since then he had been lead barrister assisting twenty-five inquests or inquiries, and had appeared for affected parties in scores of others. Few were better equipped to take on the challenge of Lindt.

Gormly still knew nothing of the disaster when he and Claudia rowed ashore on Monday 15 December to hitchhike into the nearest town for a coffee while waiting for the skies to clear. An Adelaide couple who stopped to give them a lift imparted the first snippets of news from Sydney.

Two days later, Gormly received a call from government solicitor Melissa Heris who'd been seconded to work with Barnes. When

Heris asked whether he would accept the lead counsel's role, Gormly didn't hesitate. He and his wife turned their sloop northward and sailed for home.

On 21 December, the couple tied up at the New South Wales south coast fishing port of Ulladulla and Gormly hired a car to drive to Sydney. By the following afternoon, 22 December, he was ensconced in a Sydney office with Barnes and Heris, the three of them furiously mapping out the legal terrain ahead.

Even then he had no idea of just how fraught this inquest was going to become.

A bunch of white roses was the first of the floral tributes to be laid on Martin Place. They were left against the base of a pole a block below the now sealed-off café. Within hours as commuters started returning to the city, hundreds more bouquets had joined that first one, swelling to thousands and then eventually tens of thousands as Sydneysiders formed queues to lay floral tributes and stand in silent contemplation of the horror that had unfurled in the heart of their city.

Notes of sympathy and expressions of heartbreak appeared among the vast sea of blooms. Fiona Ma's sister, Helen, left a note addressed to Tori Johnson: 'Love you for who you are and thank you for looking out for my sister and the others.'

Lindt staff penned a handwritten tribute to Tori, their 'brother and hero'.

Premier Mike Baird gave the Dawson and Johnson families his personal number to call. Baird told Tori's mother, Rosie Connellan, that he would answer them whatever hour of the day or night they called. 'And he did,' she says. 'He said to Thomas, "Look, if it's 11 p.m. at night, ring me. I will pick up the phone to you." Who offers that? He said it was the darkest day of his career, and I imagine he was very genuine about that.'

Away from the public gaze, Baird reached out to the tactical police. The mood at the meeting, recalls one of the observers, was sombre: 'There was a low-key reception at the Sydney Police Centre for the premier and the police minister to meet the TOU [Tactical Operations Unit] guys. Officer B still had the wound to his face. Baird said a few words and so did Scip [Scipione], commending them on their courage. The tone of the speeches was "There are not many who would have done what you did. Thanks for your bravery".'

Tony Abbott also met with the tactical officers in person soon after the siege, and explained later why he felt it had been important to go and thank them. 'They had been in an incredibly stressful position,' Abbott told me. 'I mean, they were not to know that the guy did not have a bomb, and even if he didn't he obviously had a shotgun. And if you are one of the first guys inside the room charging a bloke armed with a shotgun, you might have a Kevlar shield in front of you but I don't know if I would be particularly happy to do that.'

'Whatever observations people might have had in hindsight about how many shots were fired, and whether they should have fired as many shots, whether there was perhaps a degree of overexcitement, I think [those criticisms] were pretty unrealistic given [that] for all of them it was the first time,' he said.

The inquest opened on the morning of 29 January 2015 broadcast live on ABC television and streamed live via YouTube. The reason for the haste was simple: the anxiety remained that Lindt might be just the first of a wave of attacks.

In his opening remarks, Barnes acknowledged the pain the Johnsons and Dawsons would be put through having to relive the events of the siege so soon after Tori and Katrina had perished. But balancing that, he said, was the need to send a message of reassurance to the public at large and to shore up the security of the community.

Gormly spoke of how the siege had 'broken its way into the intimacy of daily Sydney life'. The hostages had lived through 'an experience that most of us would struggle to even imagine'. As they took the stand in the months to come, the survivors would be the 'eyes and ears and memory of what happened during those hours inside the Lindt Café', he promised.

The opening session was packed tight. It took place at the aging Glebe Coroner's Court, in a cramped, windowless room above the morgue. The registrar had to temporarily give up his office to make room for Gormly, the legal team and their mountain of files.

It was obvious that new premises would have to be found, and fast. The police had their own reasons for wanting the inquest moved: their tactical operators and senior counter-terrorism commanders were going to be called to give evidence and the place was a security nightmare—a cluster of low-rise buildings in an exposed position on busy Parramatta Road opposite Sydney University.

Accordingly, by May the inquest had been given a new home in a specially fitted-out courtroom on floor 8 of the John Maddison Tower in the city. The courtroom was equipped with state-of-the-art technology and a purpose-built media room, to which only reporters with special accreditation would be admitted.

To give the grieving families a place of refuge, private rooms were equipped with screens linked directly to the proceedings in the courtroom. But on most days, Tori's and Katrina's parents could be seen sitting in the hearing room itself. 'I had to do that for Tori, I had to be there for him,' Rosie said. Jane and Sandy Dawson felt the same way. 'We were there nearly every day for the whole of the inquest,' Jane said. 'Hard though it was, we deliberately sat in the courtroom so those giving evidence could see the human cost, so that the tragedy didn't become drowned in the endless redactions, objections and obfuscation.'

For Memmolo and his team, the Lindt Café after the emergency entry presented a particularly complex crime scene. Investigators were left with a huge volume of ballistic evidence to sift through. Every shot—not just from Monis' weapon, but from the TOU shotguns used to breach the glass door and from the police M4 carbines—had to be matched up to scattered ammunition casings and the scars and pockmarks inside the café.

The movement of each officer in the moments leading up to, during and after the assault had to be tracked to the second. To help achieve this, 3D scans and specialised computer software were used to create an interactive model of the café, pinpointing precise distances and angles of the shots that had been fired. Ballistics testing was carried out on specially procured chairs identical to those inside the café.

Forensic examiners determined that Monis had died from two gunshot wounds to the head, while other bullets and fragments of ammunition had perforated his bowel and lungs and ruptured his heart. His body carried a total of sixteen entry wounds including one to the right foot.

Officers A and B had collectively fired a total of twenty-two bullets, of which between seven and nine struck the gunman. The rest appeared to have slammed into the barricade made of café furniture that Monis had forced the hostages to construct in the north-west corner of the café.

By the afternoon of Wednesday 17 December, the ballistics unit had established beyond doubt that Katrina had died from wounds inflicted by a police weapon. Memmolo travelled to her family home to deliver the news to her husband Paul, brother Angus and brother-in-law Dr Mark Smith. Lethal bullet fragments had entered her upper back and right shoulder, penetrating her lung, pulmonary artery and heart. Further testing established that in all likelihood those fragments had come from a single bullet fired from a .223 calibre police weapon. One chair in particular had been hit by ten bullets, nine of which seemed to have travelled largely intact through the chair's soft back support but the tenth of which had struck the rear left leg. Testing of the pattern of fragmentation against the leg of an identical chair indicated that it matched the pattern of Katrina's wounds. Whether that shot came from officer A or Officer B's weapon was never established.

Tori had not had a chance. The end of the barrel of Monis' sawn-off shotgun had been less than a metre from his head when the gunman fired.

Two days before Christmas a funeral was held for Tori at St Stephen's Church in the city, just a few hundred metres from where the siege took place. Katrina's memorial service took place in the Great Hall of Sydney University, and was attended by Prime Minister Tony Abbott, Premier Mike Baird, police commissioner Scipione, judges, barristers and many other members of the Sydney legal fraternity. Her father and brothers wore aqua ties and mother Jane a similarly hued jacket, in honour of Katrina's favourite colour. Former governor general Quentin Bryce told the gathering, 'She was not too good to be true—but she was nearly so.'

Tori's white coffin was solemnly carried into church by six pall-bearers, including his grief-stricken partner Thomas, his father Ken and his brother James. Among the mourners were Governor David Hurley, Communications Minister Malcolm Turnbull, Andrew

Scipione and Mike Baird, who arrived alongside several of the still traumatised hostages.

Monis was formally identified by Amirah Droudis, at the Glebe morgue on 20 December. His body was sent for burial at an unknown location.

After the formal one-day opening in late January, public hearings before the state coroner did not start again until May 2015 as investigators got on with their work. Meanwhile, battle lines were being drawn up behind the scenes. The families, the police, individual police officers, the New South Wales Department of Justice and the Commonwealth all began staking out their positions and hiring legal counsel to represent them.

Back-room dramas of a different kind swirled around the surviving hostages, as rival commercial TV stations began bidding for their stories. Channels 7 and 9 were in a race to round up as many of the survivors as they could.

For fifty-two-year-old Louisa, lying in her hospital bed, the unsavoury money politics—the whispers about who was being offered what—were dispiriting and unsettling. Six-figure sums were being bandied around in the press, and the phone calls were incessant. She asked a close friend to handle the media onslaught.

She was shocked when one outlet indicated it could jump her up the queue for a place on a multiple sclerosis stem cell research program in the United States. 'I just thought that was so vulgar,' she says. 'These people had decided this was my point of weakness, and the idea that they would jump me over someone else waiting for that treatment seemed so wrong.' She finally accepted Channel 9's offer of $25,000 for a nurses' charity she had decided to set up.

Channels 7 and 9 went to air head to head with competing prime-time specials on Sunday 8 February. Channel 9 had secured interviews with Louisa, Robin, Fiona, Jarrod, Joel, Selina, Paolo and Harriette for its flagship program *60 Minutes*. Seven's special featured Marcia, John O'Brien, Elly, April, Puspendu and Viswa.

The Dawsons and Johnsons steered well clear of the media fray, as did Julie Taylor and Stefan Balafoutis.

Not everyone was impressed with the rush to bag the first interviews. Former state coroner John Abernethy and former Director of Public Prosecutions Nicholas Cowdery publicly aired concerns that the hostage interviews could taint critical evidence. But Barnes would later slap the critics down, saying Memmolo's team had already interviewed the survivors by the time the interviews went to air. 'Criticism of hostages who chose to participate in media interviews was misplaced, in my view,' he said.

There was one more awkward and emotionally draining hurdle to clear before the inquest got into full swing in May. The first sitting day of the federal parliament, 9 February, had been designated a day for MPs to formally offer their condolences to the victims of the siege.

The hostages and bereaved family members were brought to Canberra for the event only to find it upstaged by an attempted party-room coup against Prime Minister Tony Abbott. He was facing a spill motion against his leadership in the Liberal party room. Abbott survived the morning, as no challenger came forward, but the political drama curdled the atmosphere for the commemoration event that afternoon.

TV crews massed around the parliamentary doors. The hostages traversed the underground entrance via the long passageways below the main building. It was a taxing and dispiriting walk for Marcia, still recovering from shrapnel wounds, for Louisa in her wheelchair and for Robin. Louisa says it was always going to be a challenging occasion: 'It was the first time we had been all together since the siege, so there was some excitement about that, but we were in grief for the families. Julie had lost her best friend; all those young people had lost Tori, who they knew and loved. It was that hard thing, where you are happy that you survived but heartbroken that people died.'

That evening, the emotionally drained hostages and families were in the Qantas lounge at Canberra airport waiting for a flight home when one of the tyres on Louisa's hired wheelchair exploded. It sent palpable shock waves through the group. Some ducked; the plain clothes police detail went for their guns.

It was an unsettling coda to a difficult day.

When the inquest began public hearings in May a number of the key issues it would be considering had already been widely flagged in the media. So many questions were begging for answers. Why was Monis free on bail in the first place, given the gravity of the outstanding charges against him—multiple counts of sexual assault, plus complicity in his ex-wife's murder? Why had the eighteen calls to the national security hotline about his inflammatory Facebook posts in the week before the siege not triggered an immediate alarm? Was Monis mentally ill? Was he even properly classified as a terrorist?

Why had police waited so long to storm the café? Were they waiting for a hostage to die before they went in? Did they really believe Monis had a bomb? Should the army have been called on to do the job? Why were so many bullets discharged inside the café? Were the weapons and the ammunition used by the TOU too high-powered for such a confined space? And why had snipers not been able to take him out?

Rather than wait for Angelo Memmolo's team of detectives on Strike Force Verum to complete every aspect of the investigation before the inquest started, Barnes and Gormly decided to split the public hearings into four segments. In this way each segment could get underway as successive stages of the investigation wrapped up. The first would focus on Monis himself; the second on his bail history and on terrorism and radicalisation more generally; the third (held largely behind closed doors) would probe what ASIO knew; and the last, and most fraught, would examine the management of the siege itself.

Premier Mike Baird had been outraged to learn Monis had been roaming free on bail for serious offences at the time of the siege. 'We wanted every bit of information about how on earth that had happened,' Baird recalls. 'We only had scant details, the full story came later: not just why he was on bail, but how he had come into the country, and the security. Just on and on and on. But the fact that he was out on bail—that left a bitter taste.'

Yet, as the inquest unfolded, it was clear some arms of government were wary of letting the coroner onto their turf. By constitutional convention, the coroner was unable to examine the actions of magistrates who let Monis free on bail, because only the Supreme Court, parliament and the Judicial Commission can investigate judicial actions.

So the inquest turned to the Office of the Director of Public Prosecutions (ODPP), whose government lawyers had failed to block the bail applications made by Monis after he'd been charged with planning the murder of his ex-wife and with sexually assaulting female clients. The Crown Solicitor and ODPP—both government agencies—tried to argue that questions about bail were beyond the proper scope of the inquest.

Barnes overruled those objections but then ran into a second line of defence, with the Director of Public Prosecutions (DPP) now claiming legal professional privilege over the issue. This blocking manoeuvre was partially successful. The coroner would later remark that the privilege claim had prevented the inquest from 'fully examining all relevant aspects of Monis' bail history'. The waters were further muddied as police and the DPP pointed fingers at each other over the sorry saga of how Monis had come to be roaming free at the time of the siege.

Meanwhile, the police wanted a veil drawn over much of its counter-terrorism apparatus and the identities of its key personnel. The coroner granted non-publication orders shielding the identification of all members of the counter-terrorism command: the tactical commander on the night of the siege, the tactical adviser at the POC, the two forward commanders, the officers who had stormed the café, the negotiators and the police psychiatrist. Many more suppression orders covering 'operationally sensitive' aspects of the police response would be issued during the course of the inquest.

ASIO gave evidence entirely in camera, although Jeremy Gormly's opening remarks for that segment were public. Gormly and two other senior lawyers assisting the inquest had to gain high-level security clearances in order to view the agency's documents and could only work on them on special laptops loaned by ASIO and stored in secure containers supplied by the agency.

The Commonwealth was a reluctant party to the inquest, resorting to 'public interest immunity' claims to keep Defence beyond the scope of the inquest as much as possible.

Even the Iranian authorities, who had once so badly wanted to extradite Monis over the missing funds from the Tehran travel agency, did not respond to requests for information.

Nevertheless, by dint of persistence and negotiation, Gormly, Barnes and Memmolo's team managed between them to bring to light a mass of information, though not as much as the bereaved families would have liked.

'We did run into walls,' Gormly told me later. 'Some were more difficult than others. Many were rejected by the coroner and many were accepted. The public interest immunity [PII] issues were a very substantial and frustrating problem, but much of it was legitimate.'

'I hope a better way of dealing with PII emerges from our experience,' he says.

To ready the hostages for the daunting task of entering the witness box Gormly arranged informal 'hostage nights' for them, bringing them into the hearing room for familiarisation before they were due to take the stand.

Several hostages chose not to give evidence at all, and Robin, Louisa's mother, was too sick to testify. 'It was a very emotionally draining inquest,' a senior insider told me later. 'It began so soon afterwards. The families and hostages were not emotionally ready, and the whole thing was charged with fear and distress. It was not just individuals feeling fear, it was institutions—people did not want to be blamed.'

Eventually more than a hundred people would take the stand as the public hearings wound their way through 2015 and into 2016. Among them were two expert teams brought in from the United Kingdom to review the actions of the police negotiators and to review the management of the siege. A number of their findings pointed to significant deficiencies in the New South Wales Police response.

Senior New South Wales police officers each spent several days in the witness box: the tactical commander; the POC commanders Murdoch and Jenkins; the forward commanders Lima and Victor; the negotiations commander Graeme; and the TOU commander, who had served as the tactical adviser to the POC. Barnes presided over it all with an air of inscrutable authority.

Tempers flared only very rarely. Tori's mother, Rosie, was enraged on one occasion to hear the late night forward commander, Victor, justify yet again the delayed storming of the café by observing that Monis 'had the same rights as anyone else'. 'You're an absolute disgrace,' she shouted across the courtroom, before storming out in tears.

Nor was the Bar table immune from tension as the inquest reached its heated, final weeks in late 2016, when the most senior police—Acting Deputy Commissioner Jeff Loy, Police Commissioner Andrew Scipione and Deputy Commissioner Cath Burn—were finally brought to the witness stand. At one point, barristers for the police and the families traded rhetorical blows as Burn was grilled on how closely she had been monitoring events after going home on Scipione's orders at around

10.10 p.m. on the night of the siege. The silk for the police, Ian Freckelton QC, accused the Johnsons' barrister, Gabrielle Bashir SC, of a 'reprehensible' attempt to sully Burn's 'good name' by probing this issue, drawing fire in turn from the Dawson family barrister, Phillip Boulten SC.

This courtroom dust-up was over in a few minutes, but it was an accurate barometer of how high emotions were running behind the scenes.

By the end of it all the families felt exhausted, and in shock. Their legal teams compiled final submissions for the coroner that catalogued, in detail, the failings that had marred the police response.

While 'contain and negotiate' might have been the appropriate initial response to the siege, it was not a sufficient strategy for the entire duration of the siege, the families' legal teams argued. Police negotiators and commanders had mistaken 'inertia for active policy'. Their 'rigid' thinking had fallen back on habits ingrained from decades of responding to the more familiar scenarios of 'domestic' sieges that routinely involved family distress, inebriation, mental illness or drug busts. If there really had been a bomb, police had all the greater reason to go in earlier. 'Throughout the entire siege the [Lindt] stronghold was a dangerous powder keg, with the conditions inside it potentially more volatile as the night wore on,' the Johnson family's legal team argued.

The team of counsel assisting the coroner had some stinging words of their own. The commanders' 'overwhelming enthusiasm' for 'contain and negotiate' had been a 'triumph of hope over experience', Gormly and his team concluded in the summing up.

Reg—the negotiators' coordinator—had attended three counter-terrorism courses in 2001, 2004 and 2008, but he had learnt little that was different to the techniques taught in standard negotiators' courses. New South Wales Police, Gormly said, had been 'trained to approach negotiations with terrorists in much the same way they [did] any negotiation', despite the fact that 'persons holding terrorist sieges are likely to have significantly different motivations and goals to those conducting domestic sieges'.

In addition to the bomb threat, Gormly floated another possible factor behind the commanders' reluctance to approve a deliberate intervention to rescue the hostages. Perhaps, he said, they feared that initiating a deliberate action [DA] plan 'could result in criticism of police by the community'. Scipione vigorously denied this.

Some of the most striking evidence to emerge from senior police commanders was the radical difference of views about the purpose of a DA. Most officers reiterated the generally accepted doctrine that an emergency action [EA] plan would always be a last resort and something forced on police when a crisis erupted. However, Assistant Commissioner Mark Jenkins took a diametrically opposite view: that *a DA was a last resort*. This was significant given that, as POC commander, he had been the sole officer late on the night of the siege with the power to approve a DA and had declined to do so. In evidence, he was pressed on how he'd arrived at that view.

> *Jenkins*. My starting premise would be that a DA should be the last resort full stop.
>
> Q. No matter what form the DA took, covert, team, break-in, it wouldn't matter what form it took, it was [for you] going to be a last resort?
>
> *Jenkins*. Unless someone could come up with a plan that made it an absolute one hundred per cent certainty of everyone getting out of there safely, which I'm not sure a DA plan could ever do, yes.
>
> Q. That's a nil possibility, isn't it?
>
> *Jenkins*. Yes. It is.
>
> Q. That would never happen, would it?
>
> *Jenkins*. I can't imagine it.

Later in the inquest, Acting Deputy Commissioner Jeff Loy said Jenkins told him on the night of the siege that the DA plan carried with it the 'probable' risk of losing two to three lives. But the inquest failed to unearth anyone who gave that advice.

Further confusion emerged over the related, and equally fundamental, question of what the agreed triggers would be for emergency entry into the café. One officer testified he had been told there were no particular triggers.

The morning forward commander, Superintendent Sicard, was advised that the tripwire for storming the café would be 'death or serious injury' to a hostage. However, Assistant Commissioner Mark Murdoch, the afternoon/evening POC commander, told the inquest he would have gone in at 2.03 a.m. when Monis fired towards the escaping hostages.

Victor, the late-night forward commander, put forward a different view again: 'Presented with the same facts that I knew at 2.03 to 2.13 on that day . . . I would do [now] what I did then.'

Overall, the weight of evidence strongly suggested a collective view among the police commanders by the end of the evening that there would be no forced entry of the café unless a hostage died or was seriously injured. Indeed, the only trigger ever formally recorded on the night for the launch of emergency action was 'death or serious injury', the families pointed out.

The senior officers, however, repeatedly denied that this was the only trigger. In the witness box several insisted that *imminence*, or just the threat of severe injury or death of a hostage had always been in their minds as a 'secondary trigger' for an emergency action.

Yet the shadow of the bomb threat appeared to effectively negate any lower threshold for action. The coroner pressed Victor on this point.

> *Barnes*. Does that suggest that, because of the risk of the bomb, you were never going to go in until someone was killed because absent someone being killed, you were faced with making a

subjective assessment as to the risk of someone being killed?

[Victor]. Yes.

Barnes. Absent the definitive objective evidence that someone had been killed, you couldn't balance the risk of the bomb?

[Victor]. That's right, Your Honour, and it does weigh heavily on me.

However, at a later point in his evidence Victor shifted ground on this point.

Counsel. What do you say to the suggestion that you were going to sit back and not initiate an EA unless someone was dead?

[Victor]. No, I reject that in the strongest terms, Your Honour. Absolutely not . . . it just implies that I'm sitting on my hands waiting for that threshold to be reached.

What remained telling was the vivid language Victor used to describe his feelings as he ordered his men into the café: 'It was probably the hardest bloody decision I've had to make in thirty-five years of policing . . . I was sending those police in to die . . . at the time when I gave the command to go, Your Honour, I actually shut my eyes and braced myself, waiting for the explosion to happen that I knew was going to come.'

The families and the hostages had no doubt about what they were hearing. To their ears, the police were never going to force entry into the café until Monis had killed or maimed someone. They sat in the courtroom horrified.

Katrina's brother Angus said later: 'The idea that we had to wait for somebody to be killed or seriously injured before the police would act was staggering.'

Louisa said the evidence left her head 'exploding': 'I can't fully express how shocking that news was to me. Knowing now that one of us had to die or be seriously injured before the police would initiate a rescue of any kind was utterly gut wrenching.'

It became clearer as the inquest went on that the senior commanders had radically underestimated the threat Monis represented. They were lulled into thinking the gunman was incapable of committing violence by his own hand. It was a deeply flawed call based on misreading the cues coming out of the café, and a fatal misunderstanding of his past.

Neither Brian, the police psychiatrist, nor the negotiators had seen the graphic police fact sheets from the sexual assault charges laid against Monis, the inquest heard. Those fact sheets made clear the lack of consent on the part of his victims, and how Monis had threatened them to coerce them into silence. Not having seen those briefs meant Brian and the negotiating team construed Monis' sexual offences as 'acts of seduction' rather than the menacing crimes they were.

His terrorising of the hostages in the café had also been consistently downplayed. As late as 1.35 a.m. on 16 December, less than an hour before the end of the siege, a police note-taker recorded the view among commanders and the psychiatrist that there had been 'no overt signs of violence towards hostages or ramifications for not meeting demands'.

The Dawsons' legal team had a stinging response to this: 'A shotgun pushed into a person's back (even without regard to the professed terrorist motives of that person) represents a greater degree of overt physical violence and risk than a swinging fist, than a blade [or] hands clamped around a throat. Unlike almost all other forms of "overt physical violence" the degree of separation between that state and the certain death of the hostage by catastrophic damage to the heart and lungs is a millisecond of pressure by the trigger finger.'

The families believed police had failed to take Monis at his word when he declared he was acting in the name of Islamic State. Guided by Brian's view that Monis was grandstanding and that his modus operandi did not fit the profile of an IS attack, senior police overlooked the fact that he appeared to be faithfully following instructions for 'lone wolf' attacks as set out by Islamic State in its slick online magazine *Dabiq*. Those instructions emphasised that attackers should remain anonymous and seek glory, not for themselves, but for Islamic State alone—exactly as Monis had done.

'It just seemed like we were in the twilight zone,' Katrina's brother Angus told *Four Corners* later. 'We had the counter terrorism unit in charge and yet we had the psychiatrist declaring that the perpetrator wasn't a terrorist. I mean, what was going on?'

Expert witness on counter-terrorism, Professor Greg Barton, told the program: 'There wasn't enough weighting given to the possibility that this was a serious terror attack in play, a martyrdom attack that would end in lives being lost.'

The Johnsons' submissions also accused the psychiatrist of 'lacking insight into his own missteps and errors of judgment during the siege'. A prime example was Brian's judgment—recorded in police logs at 1.50 a.m.—that the café was 'settling', and that it was 'probably better he [Monis] has a rest'.

It was an assessment that forward commander Victor had shared. He told the inquest he had held a 'genuine belief that we could get to a point where Man Monis would surrender' and that he and the psychiatrist had discussed whether the gunman was just building 'street cred' because he knew he was going to jail.

A negotiations expert from the United Kingdom, Chief Superintendent Kerrin Smith, told the inquest such an assessment had been completely unwarranted: 'This [wasn't] a holiday camp where people just pack up and go to bed. It's a highly charged situation with somebody who is believed to have an IED and a shotgun with those hostages . . . I don't think there was any prospect that he was going to settle down into a corner and get a couple of hours sleep before he started his tirade again the next morning.'

Gormly's final submissions took a similar view: 'There were three potential exits from the café and, by the time night fell, some thirteen hostages [remaining], none of whom were restrained. Negotiators ought to have recognised that Monis was likely to harbour concerns about his ability to control those hostages, particularly as he began to tire . . . There is no evidence that this . . . was subjected to any close assessment by negotiators or for that matter the psychiatrist advising them.'

The negotiators suffered further pummelling in the witness box for their failure to properly record and review demands; for misreading the cues coming from the café; for failing to come up with new ways of trying to engage Monis; and for missing calls from the hostages late at night because the entire negotiation team was engaged in a handover briefing at the time. The latter is something that should never have happened, acknowledged Mick Fuller, who was appointed Police Commissioner as Scipione's successor in March 2017.

'[The negotiators'] failure was comprehensive and unacceptable in multiple, individual respects,' the Dawsons' lawyers argued. 'Each of the numerous individual failures . . . was avoidable and each contributed to the catastrophic resolution of the siege.'

The lack of record-keeping had been particularly grave in relation to Monis' demand to have the Christmas lights switched off—a demand that was allowed to languish for four hours. Gormly went through in forensic detail exactly how that failure had come about. 'The failure of [negotiation team leader] Reg to raise the matter with the Forward Commanders, the failure of Reg to follow up with the POC the decision he understood was pending . . . the failure of . . . [Lima's] team to raise with him the information that had been obtained about the logistics of turning the lights off and the failure . . . to ensure that Assistant Commissioner Jenkins was briefed about the need for a prompt decision, is very difficult to fathom . . . NSW Police failed to take up what was an excellent opportunity to engage with Monis, encourage him into direct communication and explore the release of one or more hostages.'

Gormly's submission concluded that the negotiations coordinator, Reg, had been of 'insufficient rank, experience and exposure to conduct the role into which he had been thrust and appeared overwhelmed by the size and significance of the task imposed on him'.

Reg's superior officer Graeme, the negotiations commander, eventually conceded in the witness box that 'something has gone wrong, yes'.

Many police actions were predicated on the belief that Monis had a bomb in his backpack, but was this belief well founded? The hostages had grown sceptical of this claim the longer they observed Monis in the café. Those who had broken free early from the café communicated this to police.

Officer B believed he had seen wires coming from the bottom of Monis' backpack when he looked briefly through the café window earlier in the day. Officer B would later claim that Paolo had confirmed to him there were wires coming from the backpack, but Paolo flatly denied this. He later told *Four Corners*, 'I never saw any wires . . . It never, never, never came up in any conversation at all, believe me. I never saw any wires at all. Never at any time.'

He was also adamant that he had told police as soon as he came out of the café he did not believe Monis had a bomb in his backpack. At the inquest, lawyers for the police tried to cast doubt over how clearly Paolo had stated this.

The Johnsons' legal team acknowledged that one of the earliest officers on the scene, Senior Constable Paul Withers, thought he had seen wires coming from the backpack. But they argued there was 'no evidence of a concerted effort having been made [by police] to drill down' into the question of whether or not Monis had a bomb.

They were even more damning of the fact that the snipers' 2.07 a.m. message about Tori being on his knees had never got through to commanders—a 'catastrophic' failing, they said. The inquest never fully resolved whether technical or human factors were to blame for this. The snipers testified to their belief that they had transmitted the message over their TOU radio network, but the tactical commander told the inquest: 'I am unsure to this day whether that was [the case] or was not.'

The Johnsons' lawyers found it 'extraordinary' that the coroner would be unable to get to the bottom of this critical question. 'If the information about Tori being on his knees was received the EA should have been initiated,' their legal team said. 'Should the EA have been initiated, it may have saved Tori's life. It would certainly have meant that Tori would not have been left on his knees for seven long minutes under threat of death.'

Tori, the Johnsons' lawyers added, had shown 'exceptional courage' by resuming his kneeling position after the gunman had unleashed a second shot. Tori had died with 'courage and dignity and in protection of the five remaining women and Fiona Ma, whom the evidence establishes he had determined from the outset of the siege not to leave to fend for themselves'.

CHAPTER 15

NAGGING QUESTIONS

For Tori's loved ones, it was harrowing to hear the details of how he had died: on his knees, knowing that no one was coming to his rescue. 'As the evidence unfolded it was just horrific,' his mother Rosie said. 'Every day we thought "This can't get worse", and every day what came out of the inquest did get worse. That will haunt me forever, [learning] that he was on his knees there, knowing that they were just outside and that they were not coming in. I will never get over the fact that they decided they would not go in until someone died. For me to realise that Tori's life was treated as expendable was beyond belief and unforgivable.'

The Dawson family were just as outraged. They wanted heads to roll, and through their legal team sought adverse findings against several senior New South Wales police officers, as well as heavily criticising the psychiatrist and two of the tactical men: the head of Charlie team, and Officer B. Chief in their sights were Mark Jenkins and Victor, the Police Operations Centre (POC) and field commanders respectively when the siege ended. Both had set the threshold for an emergency entry into the café indefensibly high, the family argued.

They also argued that Jenkins and the earlier POC commander, Mark Murdoch, had significantly erred in failing to approve a planned intervention, or deliberate action (DA) plan. This had become particularly crucial late on the night of 15 December when Jenkins was in charge, the Dawsons' legal submissions said. The failure to approve the DA meant that 'when the situation deteriorated, the only option available was to initiate an EA [emergency action] on terms dictated by the terrorist . . . with all its attendant danger to the hostages and to the TOU [Tactical Operations Unit] entry teams trying to save them'. What had been lacking was a 'culture of leadership that emphasises a proactive and decisive approach,' the family said.

In addition, the bereaved families took aim at Brian, the psychiatrist. The Dawsons urged that he never be used by police again as he'd consistently underestimated Monis' capacity for violence throughout, had discounted Monis' stated allegiance to Islamic State and over-estimated his own counter-terrorism expertise. They pointed to the fact that more than a year after the siege Brian had not shifted in his view that Monis had only been 'masquerading' as an Islamic State terrorist: 'The psychiatrist's unwillingness to accept criticism or to have taken any steps to fill the gaps in his knowledge in a professed area of expertise since the siege confirm . . . that he should never be permitted to play such a role in police operations again,' the Dawson family's lawyers argued in their submission.

Not surprisingly, the police legal team rejected the proposition that any officer should be the subject of adverse findings by the coroner. In a general broadside, they said critics had been able to 'scrutinise every component of what took place in the siege with a fine forensic comb over nearly two years since', while 'police were required to resolve the incident against a background of evolving intelligence with no facility for retrospective insight, but high stakes attaching to their every evaluation and their every action'.

Tori had not been executed because of police error or miscalculation, the police lawyers insisted. He had died 'simply [because] the dynamics within the stronghold changed fundamentally at 2.03 a.m. and that resulted in conduct by Monis that was inconsistent with how he had behaved previously'.

Waiting until 2.13 a.m. to storm the café was a 'valid decision made at the correct time', the police lawyers argued, and even if there had been an earlier intervention there may not have been a different outcome. Jenkins' failure to approve a deliberate action plan they categorised as a 'matter of discretion in respect of which reasonable minds can differ'. Further, they argued, a DA could have been approved and authorised in quick succession had Jenkins changed his mind.

They dismissed criticism of the negotiators as 'emotive and generated in hindsight'. To the contrary, they argued: 'the time during the siege when Monis had not shot anybody, not violently assaulted anybody, not ritually humiliated anybody was a success that deserved to be recognised.' As another broad observation, the police lawyers said that if there was to be a 'cultural shift' towards earlier intervention in terrorist sieges then that would require a discussion within the community about preparedness to accept civilian casualties.

Curiously, the police submissions reiterated the view that Monis was 'not an ISIS operative' despite agreeing it was 'feasible' he had been motivated by the call to attack western civilians issued by IS spokesman Abu Muhammad al-Adnani in September 2014. They rehashed the idea that Monis' motives remained unclear, except that 'a significant part of his aspirations was to draw attention to himself and to make it appear that he was a good deal more significant and influential than he was'.

Thus, even two years after the siege, the formal police submission to the inquest was effectively still dismissing Monis as a 'grandstander'. Overall, its tone was defensive and unrepentant.

Barristers for the police psychiatrist likewise vigorously rejected criticisms of their client. Reflecting on Brian's forceful personality and dominant role in the negotiation room, his legal team said the doctor's goal on the night had not been 'to make friends'. 'Some may view (perhaps too sensitively) him as unyielding (or to use the somewhat emotive term of Counsel Assisting, "dogmatic"). It is in fact that quality that assisted him to provide unbiased and unabashed opinion on human behaviour in a high pressure and tense environment.'

———

The coroner had originally set aside a year for the Lindt inquest. But by the middle of 2016 it was clear there were still many months to run. Jeremy Gormly, assisting Barnes, now proposed drastically culling the remaining witness list, restricting it to those he considered 'essential'. Barnes agreed, after the key legal teams had been consulted. But it meant, among other things, that the state technical police (STIB) were never called to the witness box to explain their failures.

The second anniversary of the siege was approaching, and there was still intense skirmishing between legal teams over the shape of the final submissions. The inquest team was working punishing hours, and frequently at weekends. Each of the many barristers involved sought several weeks to dissect the other parties' final submissions, further throwing out Barnes' schedule for producing his by now long-awaited report.

Several important documents suddenly surfaced at the end of 2016, including two internal reports prepared by the Australian Federal Police that had endeavoured to calculate (not very effectively) what sort of blast power a bomb in Monis' backpack might have had. Gormly and the Commonwealth clashed publicly over why these had come before the inquest so late in the piece.

As Christmas of 2016 drew near, Barnes accepted that the report would not see the light of day until the following year.

The date the coroner picked to unveil his findings was 24 May 2017.

It was warm as Louisa drove in through thick morning traffic with her mother and sister, a knot in her stomach. 'We had so many expectations of this report,' she recalls. 'All these days of going in and out to the inquest—I had my own opinions of what to expect.'

The media was massed on the pavement outside the main entrance of the John Maddison Tower, a small army encamped at the base of a fortress. Senior police, their lawyers, the families and the hostages braved the unblinking gaze of the TV cameras one last time.

The coroner and his legal team had combed through an immense amount of material: 1200 witness statements, 200 hours of media footage, 1000 hours of CCTV footage, transcripts of dozens of national security hotline reports and intercepted calls and 10,000 pages of running sheets as well as the police logs recording thousands of decisions made by individual officers. The transcript of public hearings had added more than 8000 pages of evidence.

This had all been distilled into a brick of a report—nearly 500-pages long, culminating in forty-five recommendations covering everything from police procedure, training and doctrine to Australian Defence Force call-out arrangements.

One headline dominated all others as journalists rushed to file their early reports. The coroner had not accepted police excuses for delayed entry to the café. Instead, he said, the police should have gone in on the heels of Monis' first shot at 2.03 a.m., pausing only to quickly gather 'relevant information'. With the firing of that shot, Barnes said, the threat to the remaining hostages had risen to extreme.

The coroner also found that police commanders and snipers had taken an 'unduly restrictive' view of their legal powers to shoot Monis (even though few sniping opportunities had presented themselves on the night). They should have had more regard to 'Monis' possession of a shotgun and suspected IED [improvised explosives device], his threats, his claimed allegiance to Islamic State, his unwillingness to negotiate and his continuing to unlawfully deprive the hostages of their liberty'. Barnes recommended clarifying the special powers police can invoke during a terrorist incident to make crystal clear they had the right to use deadly force.

Barnes also closed down debate about whether Monis had been correctly categorised as a terrorist. Immediately after the siege, some commentators had mounted an argument that the attacker was mentally ill and not a 'true' terrorist at all. Among those espousing that view was the long-time Sydney Lord Mayor Clover Moore, who on the first anniversary of the siege told the ABC: 'It wasn't a terrorist event. I didn't want our multicultural, harmonious society to be divided.' Experts who gave evidence at the inquest were also divided on the issue.

But Barnes' conclusion was unequivocal. Monis, he said, had become progressively radicalised from 2007 onwards and on the day of the siege had acted in a controlled and methodical manner; he had threatened, and finally used, extreme violence with the political aim of influencing government action in the Middle East. 'That clearly brings his crimes within the accepted definition of terrorism,' Barnes said. That his life may have also been in a downward spiral and beset by legal problems did not alter that fact: 'That he may have been driven in part by personal reasons does not mean he was not a terrorist.'

A senior member of one of the legal teams welcomed this finding. 'It was important to knock on the head early this idea that Monis was just a nut job,' the barrister told me. 'He had a personality disorder, not a mental illness.'

The UK's Deputy Chief Constable Simon Chesterman, the leading expert witness, was of the same view: 'It matters not that he was not displaying the sort of . . . traditional IS methodology; the fact that in his mind he felt he was an IS sympathiser, there's every chance he had no expectation of survival and that he fully intended to kill hostages.'

In a stiff rebuke to the police, Barnes also agreed with the families that there had been no justification for the refusal of the two POC commanders, first Murdoch and later Jenkins, to approve a deliberate action rescue plan. That failure had been an 'error of judgment' that deprived the tactical officers of the chance to rehearse a DA and thus be 'as well prepared as they could have been.'

Even though the commanders might ultimately not have authorised the use of the DA, the coroner said, having one in hand would have left their men with more options for resolving the siege. Both the expert team from the United Kingdom and the tactical commander and adviser had 'made it clear that the DA plan entailed a lower level of risk than the EA plan'. But Barnes stopped short of saying the POC commanders should have *enacted* a rescue plan. What let them off the hook, he suggested, was that they had been acting on 'flawed advice'—mainly from the psychiatrist and the negotiators. Nevertheless, he urged the New South Wales Police to overhaul the training provided to commanders in DA planning.

The coroner accepted that police had grossly underestimated Monis' capacity for violence: 'It seems that [police] commanders and negotiation unit leaders, in part because of advice from the psychiatrist advising them, adopted a view that Monis was conducting the siege for personal reasons rather than on behalf of IS,' he said.

While 'contain and negotiate' had been an appropriate response for the first hours of the siege, it should have become apparent to police during the afternoon that the strategy of trying to engage Monis through the hostages was not working. The negotiators had failed to explore other ways of engaging the gunman 'because of a lack of experience in terrorist negotiations, a lack of flexibility in approach and a lack of initiative', Barnes said. In future, it should be recognised that 'contain and negotiate' might be 'counterproductive' in terrorist situations.

He also condemned the fact that the negotiation team had missed several late-night hostage calls from the café after hours had gone by without any contact. That had been a 'significant failure in a basic component of siege management'.

Likewise, he found that the psychiatrist's performance had been 'suboptimal'. The doctor had been allowed to go well beyond his expertise in giving advice about Islamic State and terrorism; he had made 'erroneous and unrealistic assessments' about the mood inside the café, and given 'ambiguous' advice about Monis' behaviour. Barnes recommended that, in future, the police expand their panel of psychological advisers and the range of experts they consulted.

The intelligence resources used during the siege had also suffered from being poorly coordinated, Barnes said. There had been a 'multitude' of different logs and data systems used by different police units (iSurv, Indigo, Eagle-i and Noggin) over the seventeen hours of the crisis, none of which had been accessible to all the relevant officers. Steve and Mick, who had been left alone to monitor the listening device, had been placed in critical roles without sufficient support.

The eighteen complaints made to the national security hotline about Monis' 'Sheikh Haron' Facebook page in the week leading up to the siege had not been reviewed by New South Wales Police intelligence during the crisis, and senior commanders were not made aware of them. This was inexplicable, Barnes said, although he noted police had since overhauled their intelligence coordination systems.

The saga of why Monis was on bail was also put under the microscope. The early decision by the Director of Public Prosecutions (DPP) to invoke the protection of legal professional privilege—against the wishes of the inquest—had thrown down road spikes. Katrina's brother Sandy said, 'It was an unedifying spectacle, one government body trying to prevent by all means possible another government body (the Coroner) from doing its job.' Yet the inquest team was still able to unearth a damning trail of missteps by government lawyers who'd been briefed by police to oppose bail for Monis. These included losing files, failing to fully grasp the relevant law, failing to put all the relevant information before the magistrate and failing to 'diligently or effectively' prepare the arguments in court for denying Monis bail. The officer who had led the investigation into the murder of Monis' wife, Detective Senior Constable Melanie Staples, was so furious about Monis walking free on the accessory to murder charges that she was unable to even speak afterwards to the government lawyer responsible.

In late 2014, the authorities had missed another opportunity to lock Monis up on the sexual assault charges. A senior officer from the Sex Crimes Squad repeatedly urged the government lawyer from the prosecutor's office to apply for revocation of Monis' bail. But the overseas-trained lawyer, who had never before handled a bail application in New South Wales, did not do so. Nor did he seek advice from his more experienced superiors. He had been hired into the DPP's office less than two months before the matter came before the magistrate.

Despite these many shortcomings, the Coroner softened his criticism by observing that none of those involved in the bail fiasco could have foreseen 'how Monis would abuse the liberty he was granted'. Thus, he said, they bore no responsibility for what he'd done.

The Dawsons were not going to let the DPP off so lightly. Katrina's father, Sandy Dawson senior, told *Four Corners*: 'The fact that the DPP didn't oppose bail was extraordinary. But what was even more extraordinary was they tried to have any consideration of bail excluded from the inquest. And so when a lot of the documents came in from the DPP they were very heavily redacted, so we couldn't see them, our legal counsel couldn't see them. You had people from the DPP in the witness box [saying]—"I don't recall", "I don't recall". It was just extraordinary.'

One question that continued to nag at the minds of the families was whether police had done enough to explore a covert entry to the café to disable Monis.

When the deliberate action plan (the one that never got approved) was first drawn up by tactical officer Delta Alpha, he'd tried to locate a secret route into the café. He'd even climbed onto the roof of the building and examined a large air conditioning shaft that ran all the way to the bottom, coming out at a small closed doorway in the stairwell that gave access to the women's toilets.

Delta Alpha decided there was no way a TOU officer could have descended the shaft with all his gear and that, even if he had tried to do it stripped down to a bare minimum of equipment, the noise would have given them away. The coroner accepted this.

But Barnes was less convinced that police had done enough with the information conveyed by Elly and April after they escaped (and later by Tori) that the lobby doors were unlocked. In evidence, the deputy tactical commander was asked if the TOU had tried exploring a possible covert entry through those doors. 'There was no attempts, no,' he replied.

Jeremy Gormly submitted the police should have revisited the possibility of entering via the lobby entrance after they had been alerted to Tori's 7.40 p.m. text stating, 'The lobby door is unlocked. He is sitting in the corner on his own.' The families branded this a glaring missed opportunity.

The police disagreed, claiming the foyer doors had clear glass panels that were 'in the line of sight of where [Monis] was situated for most of the day'. This assertion was patently wrong, as Barnes pointed out. Floor plans made it clear the foyer doors could not be seen from the alcove where Monis spent most of his time from the late afternoon onwards. Despite this, the coroner accepted the police excuse that, without 'eyes' inside the cafe, they could not tell if the doors had been relocked. It's an excuse that would not have withstood scrutiny had STIB managed to fulfil its mandate of providing full surveillance.

'Against what standard does one judge a man demanded to stare down death to save strangers? Who would dare say they could have done better?' These lines, eloquently penned by Barnes on the third page of his report, followed an admission by him that the closer he came to analysing the climax of the siege 'the more difficult it became to remain clinical'.

The sound and fury of the police entry stunned many who saw it live on television. This was a single adversary armed with a sawn-off shotgun—had it really required a barrage lasting well over a half a minute to subdue Monis? Had the entry been as clinical as it might have been? Had there been too many bullets fired, too many stun grenades thrown into the café? Were the M4 assault rifles too high-powered for such a confined space? And was it fair to criticise the police tactical teams, as the families had done, for not achieving simultaneous entry?

Officer A, the primary shooter from Alpha team, was fairly sure he'd unleashed his seventeen bullets within the first few seconds of entering the café. Officer B's memories of firing his weapon were hazier, and changed over time—possibly not helped by his being slightly wounded during the emergency entry.

At the inquest, one of the barristers representing the Dawsons, Michael O'Connell SC, asked Officer A if he could have 'achieved the objective' without firing as many bullets. The burly tactical officer replied: 'Since this incident I've thought about not much else and I've gone over it many, many, many times in my head if I could have—if my actions could have been different in relation to Monis and the engagement. I don't believe that it could have been done any differently.'

The coroner accepted this, saying the pair had not fired 'indiscriminately or excessively'. 'Katrina was taking cover on the floor. The officers could not have seen her and could have done nothing to enhance her safety that was consistent with their primary imperative to incapacitate Monis,' the coroner found.

However, Barnes was more critical of the number of SF9 stun grenades—known to the men as 'stunnies' or 'flashbangs'—thrown as the TOU teams entered the café. The British reviewing team found that, with each of the eleven devices thrown causing nine separate explosions and some of the men not wearing hearing protection (despite being required to do so in training), the effect had been to 'distract and disorient' some of their own team-mates.

An acoustics analysis of the emergency entry identified stun grenades still being hurled up to seventeen seconds *after* officers A and B had finished firing their weapons. 'There was an awful lot of noise in that stronghold . . . and they weren't wearing any hearing protection. That's bound to have affected them,' said Chesterman. The over-use of stun grenades also heightened the risk to the hostages; it was well known the devices could wound if they came into direct contact. Overall, the team from the United Kingdom judged that the use of the devices had been 'poorly controlled'.

Barnes agreed but deflected blame from the TOU, saying it was the fault of the New South Wales Police for not having a policy in place governing the use of flashbangs.

The weapons and ammunition used by the police also came under scrutiny at the inquest, although not as intensely as other aspects of the police entry. It was known to several journalists covering the siege that some former soldiers, especially those with Special Forces experience, privately questioned why tactical police used weapons as high-powered as the M4 carbines in the confined quarters of the café. Their chief criticism was that the .223 rounds fired by the M4s had more than double the velocity and a greater chance of ricochet and fragmentation than the slower 9-millimetre rounds fired, for example, by submachine guns.

The coroner took expert evidence on the issue of police munitions and ultimately decided that the weapons used by the TOU during the siege were 'appropriate'. He did, however, point to the recommendation of the review team from the United Kingdom, that the New South Wales Police should switch to bonded bullets rather than continue with the type of soft-point ammunition they used inside the Lindt Café. This, he said, was because 'tactical bonded rounds carry a reduced risk of fragmentation'.

In military circles beyond the inquest, informal debate continued over whether the police were correctly equipped. 'They were over-armed,' one ex-soldier told me adamantly. 'Going in with the weapons and ammunition calibres they went in with just made no sense.'

The emergency action plan called for the police teams to enter the front and rear of the café at the same time. The thinking behind this was to confuse Monis and improve the chances of the tactical officers overwhelming him before he could harm another hostage. In fact, the combined Charlie/Delta team did not make it through the lobby doors until at least *twelve seconds* after Alpha team had stormed in through the front.

The reasons for the delay showed up starkly in footage from a camera that had been trained on the foyer (a camera that did not, however, have line of sight into the café). It revealed Charlie team officers threw at least two stun grenades that bounced off the closed lobby doors before they even entered the café. This resulted in the stunnies going off next to the men, who appeared to briefly back away in response. Charlie team leader Delta Alpha was then further held up in the lobby while he paused (possibly dazzled) to adjust his older-style night vision goggles. The entire team waited until he had done this before they entered the stronghold, by which time Monis was already dead.

The other expert from the United Kingdom who reviewed the entry for the inquest, Inspector Nigel Kefford, said he would have expected a faster entry by Charlie team: it should not have been necessary for the others to wait and let the team leader enter first. 'I would be disappointed with a twelve-second delay on an entry team,' Kefford told the coroner.

The Dawson family maintained simultaneous entry would have 'markedly' increased the safety of the hostages, giving the TOU a different (they said safer) line of fire to take Monis down.

Barnes deemed this speculative. Louisa, he said, might even have been at greater risk, given she appeared to have been standing between Monis and the lobby door (although Louisa later told me it was Robin standing between the gunman and that doorway). A simultaneous entry might also have meant three officers, rather than two, firing their weapons at once the coroner cautioned. While the outcome might have been different, 'it would not necessarily have been better'.

Jane and Sandy Dawson have not revised their views on this since the inquest. They still believe Katrina would have had a better chance of survival if Charlie team had got into the café at the same time as Alpha team and incapacitated Monis from the position of the lobby doors. They believe this would have meant the angle of fire was not directed towards where their daughter had taken shelter on the floor.

There were other delays that the coroner deemed serious. The first was the failure to begin the search of Monis' flat until around 11 p.m. on the night of the siege. The most pressing reason for conducting that search as soon as possible was to see if it turned up even a shred of evidence to support Monis' claim he had a bomb. It might also have turned up a suicide note, or some other sign of Monis' intentions. Barnes found the police produced no convincing reason for delaying the search, which should have taken place much earlier.

He was also highly critical of the prolonged agony of uncertainty the Johnson and Dawson families were forced to endure as they waited for nearly three hours after the end of the siege to find out that Tori and Katrina had died. This delay, Barnes found, was 'unjustified' and almost indefensible. He recommended that police urgently overhaul their procedures for identifying the victims of any similar incident in the future.

Police Commissioner Andrew Scipione and his deputy Cath Burn were largely relegated to minor mentions in Barnes' report, to the chagrin of the families. Burn and Scipione's lawyers mounted a forceful case against them being called into the witness box at all, saying their appearance would have little 'forensic utility.' The families, however, persisted.

Burn became the second-last witness to appear (from 15 August to the morning of 17 August 2016) and Scipione the last, on 17 August 2016.

The Dawsons would later tell me of the behind-the-scenes battle they felt they had to wage to get this to happen. Jane Dawson described it as 'one of the biggest battles'. 'We felt that the inquest could not possibly be complete without evidence from Scipione and Burn,' the family explained. 'The police legal team resisted very strongly every attempt by us—and the Johnsons—to get them to attend. Eventually, after a lot of pressure and [coverage in] the media, the coroner agreed to call them. But we were very restricted on what topics they could be questioned about.'

Scipione declared from the witness box: 'I was accountable, and will always stand accountable as the Commissioner of Police in this state. I wasn't responsible for the decisions that were made but, in terms of the buck, it stopped with me.' Nevertheless, he and Burn maintained their original position that they had not given any 'orders, directions or provide[d] any guidance or advice in respect of the conduct of the siege on the day'.

Scipione was asked how he reconciled this with an email he sent to Mark Jenkins and Acting Deputy Commissioner Jeff Loy at 11.59 p.m. on the night of the siege, saying the hostage videos shot from inside the café should be removed from YouTube. With a link to one of the videos, the email read: 'Gents, this has just been sent to me. Let's move to have it pulled down from YouTube asap. I will leave it with you.'

Seven minutes later, Jenkins replied, 'On to it'. (As the inquest heard, the mood of desperation in the café was intensifying as the hostages struggled to get their videos out.)

Gormly put to Scipione that his email had been 'as close to a direction as one could get'. The police commissioner vehemently denied this, insisting it was 'an advice' only and that the relevant officers had already moved to take the clips down at their own initiative.

But Barnes did not find for Scipione on this point. Whatever his intention, the coroner said, the language of Scipione's email was 'susceptible to be read as a direction and seems to have been treated as such'. While determining that 'no harm' had come from the communication, the coroner said that it had been 'unwise' for Scipione to make a suggestion on an operational matter without first 'discussing it with relevant officers and informing himself of the consequences of the proposal'.

By the time Scipione heard this he had already left the force, retiring as commissioner the month before the inquest report came down.

Cath Burn had the ultimate line responsibility for counter terrorism at the time of the siege. But when questioned about the multitude of equipment problems that dogged her officers during the siege response, she told the coroner, 'Nothing was brought to my attention.'

The deputy commissioner had an uncomfortable moment when it emerged that she had deleted all her text messages from the day and night of the siege itself. Nor could the phone she'd used that night be found as she'd had several new ones since. Defending the decision to delete texts, Burn said this was something she did routinely if she didn't consider the messages important. Moreover, she had been told as early as the morning after the siege that she was not considered an 'involved person' for the purposes of the subsequent investigation.

In senior law enforcement circles, the revelation she had wiped her texts was greeted with surprise. Barnes accepted her evidence that the deleted texts contained nothing significant. But he remarked that it would have been 'preferable' for her to have kept those records.

Burn's performance in the witness box did not impress a number of the journalists who had gathered in the media room to hear her and Scipione testify. Senior reporter for the *Daily Telegraph* Janet Fife-Yeomans wrote the next day that Burn had said 'can't recall' or that she couldn't remember close to sixty times during her evidence. Stung, Burn would later tell others, 'I went in there and did my absolute best'.

On the day he handed down his report, the coroner spoke from the bench for nearly an hour, setting the stage for his findings. He appeared loathe to heap too much blame on senior hierarchy of the New South Wales Police for the failures the inquest had uncovered. 'Those [police] commanders must live with the outcome of their decisions, the likes of which their critics will never need to make,' he said. Ultimately, he took the view that, even if police had mounted a textbook response at every level, 'there is no certainty the outcome would have been any better—that more of the hostages would have left the café alive.'

There had been no lack of dedication to duty from any officer or lack of commitment to rescuing the hostages, he said. And when the assault teams finally got the order to storm the café, 'they did not hesitate' despite the risks they faced. 'It is tragic that two innocent lives were lost but when critiquing the police response it is important to remember that right from the outset eighteen lives were imperilled. For families other than Katrina's and Tori's the outcome could have been far worse.'

As the coroner left the courtroom and journalists raced to scramble from the media room to file their stories, the families and their lawyers huddled in private to absorb what they had just heard.

Louisa remembers an 'unexpected, peculiar feeling of almost dead nothingness' overwhelming her. Perhaps unrealistically, she had expected some sense of closure. 'I had tried to keep a lid on it all through the inquest and tried not to make disparaging remarks to the press, when there were days I could have. But I wanted to respect the process. Then to hear the coroner talking, so matter-of-factly, in black and white statements about those things that had been so highly emotional for me—it was very bizarre.

'It was that moment when we just sort of went, "Oh, is that all there is?" Mr Barnes made his comments and he formally said, "And these are my findings". Then he stood up, bowed and walked out. And that's it.'

From the inquest, Katrina's family had learnt how she had died—but not why she did not join the other hostages fleeing at 2.03 a.m. 'All that we know for sure is that Katrina's family meant everything to her, and being safely united with her children and her family and ensuring the welfare of others would have been at the forefront of her every thought and action,' her parents told me.

ABC TV's *Four Corners* aired a two-part special on the siege on the Monday before and the Monday after the inquest report came down. With only a few days to reflect on the report, Jane Dawson told reporter Sarah Ferguson that the inquest had been 'worth it in the sense that the truth [about the flawed response] came out, despite the best efforts of people to conceal it'.

Katrina's brother Sandy, however, spoke bitterly of having to watch his parents go through the process of waiting fruitlessly for an apology: '[The family went] through every day almost, waiting for somebody to say: "This went wrong, we could have done this better, we made this mistake and we're sorry." No one was prepared to do that, for the entirety of the inquest. It is demeaning and unfair that our family and the Johnson family were reduced to the cliché of begging for the truth.'

When I met with Katrina's brothers and parents in early 2018, it was clear that the inquest had not brought them any sense of justice having been fully delivered. If anything, their anger had grown in the months since the report was handed down. Amplifying their grief was their sense that the inquest had ended, in Jane Dawson's words, 'not with a bang but a whimper'.

'We felt we had been in an immense struggle to get the truth,' Jane told me. 'It was disappointing. All that effort, all that energy and trust we placed in the inquest to make sure that we could get those involved to tell the truth—in the end it failed to make any of those in charge accountable. I have always emphasised that there are many good and brave police. They do an amazing job. But they were let down during the siege by their superiors.

'This was not just about improving equipment and process. This was about getting people to accept that they weren't aware of their responsibilities, or good enough for the job—having the grace to apologise and resign. That is accountability.'

Katrina's father and brothers felt the same way. 'The counter-terrorism teams were [plainly] under-resourced, and under-prepared,' Katrina's brother Sandy said. 'Our family was staggered that the inquest did not make any adverse finding against those who were responsible for that.'

CHAPTER 16

SCARS AND MEMORIES

Lindt ripped away Sydney's sense that 'it couldn't happen here'. It made Sydneysiders members of a club no city wants to join: a club that Paris, Nice, Brussels, Birmingham, London, Berlin, Istanbul and Baghdad were, or would soon be, members of—hit by Islamic State-inspired attacks on an even more devastating scale.

The loss suffered by the Johnson and Dawson families was profound and incalculable, but many of those who survived the seventeen hours in the café were left with deep scars of their own, whether physical or psychological.

In a victim impact statement prepared for the coroner at the conclusion of the inquest, Louisa Hope tried to convey how fundamentally her life had changed: 'The impact of the siege has not been limited to the seventeen hours we spent as hostages in the café. It extends well beyond that for many of us, each being impacted differently,' she wrote.

Louisa spent three months in hospital being treated for her injuries, her progress set back when she acquired a stubborn infection. Today she still carries small pieces of shrapnel in her abdomen. A hospital doctor told her that the extra weight she carries around her belly may have saved her life. 'All those years I spent thinking about what diet to go on this week—and then the thing that I most cursed, saved me. You have to wonder about that.' Her disfigured and painful foot will never be the same; it impacts her sleep, balance and ability to walk.

Mentally she feels sound enough, but she can no longer tolerate the depiction of gun violence, whether on the news or in movies or on television. 'Having experienced it first hand, I am bewildered as to why we consider such things entertainment,' she says.

Within days of the siege, the Dawsons announced they were setting up a foundation in Katrina's name to assist exceptional young women by way of funded scholarships to The Women's College at Sydney University, where Katrina spent happy years as an undergraduate.

Louisa has also worked hard to extract some good from the tragic events that unfolded at the café, setting up twin charities to fund educational and research projects, designed for nurses by nurses, at two of Sydney's major hospitals, the Prince of Wales and Nepean. Those charities are now supported annually by the New South Wales Police.

Yet even with the completion of the inquest, Louisa's mind still gnaws at some questions she believes were not fully resolved. She does not believe, for instance, that it got to the bottom of whatever it was that the Office of the Director of Public Prosecutions seemed keen to hide. She also wants more done to track the life cycle of guns, all guns, through all the owners. Monis acquired his shotgun on the black market, but how was never established. It was believed to have been originally imported into Australia in 1960.

Louisa remains puzzled by what she saw as the police failure to assiduously probe Monis' claim he had a bomb. 'I was struck by the UK experts saying that, over there, the threat of a bomb makes them go in quicker. Here, it seemed to be the opposite. Once again, this exposed the emptiness of the insistence at the time that we had world's best practice.'

She remains concerned about the role the media played during the siege, in an era of smart phones. 'Anything could have turned our situation deadly as we listened . . . I'm a great believer in the free press, but in these live situations the media is no longer a passive observer, it becomes an active player. They have to seriously consider how their reporting will impact, and whether a story is worth a life.'

The greatest personal cost of the siege, however, has been seeing the impact on her mother, Robin. From being a cheerful and energetic person socially engaged and an active community volunteer, Robin became withdrawn and anxious, showing all the symptoms of post-traumatic stress.

Others have been similarly afflicted. Harriette's life continues to be shadowed by the trauma of the siege and the loss of her friend Tori. She never had the chance to give him the Christmas card she brought in to work that morning, stowing it in her locker so she could hand it to him once she had finished her shift. Harriette had planned to ask Tori to be godfather to her child.

The birth of her and Jorge's daughter, has given the couple a welcome new focus to their lives. But they don't venture out as often as they used to—especially not to the city. 'A lot of things have changed,' says Jorge, simply.

Guilt lingers for some who escaped—repetitive thoughts about whether there was more they could have done, or whether things might have turned out differently if they had stayed. Such questions are impossible what-ifs.

After several hours in hospital on the night of the siege, Paolo went home and switched on the TV to watch horrified as the police launched their assault on the café. Even then, his gut instinct told him that Tori had not made it out: 'I just knew he wasn't gonna leave there. That's the type of person he was—he always put others first.'

In shock, Paolo was unable to sleep for days afterwards. He told *60 Minutes* a few weeks later: 'Part of me wishes I didn't run sometimes . . . As bad as it sounds and as ungrateful as it sounds, I almost wish I got killed in there.'

Two years after the siege he told the inquest he was still trying to make sense of what happened inside the café, questioning why he left and why he put trust in other people: 'I wanted the police to end it on their terms,' he said. 'That way it would have given the people half a chance . . . I pushed for them to go in as quick as they can, not to wait. For it to end like that you know, it kills me.'

Joel Herat sent Tori's mother a touching message in which he remembered how Tori had mentored and encouraged him. Joel too wrestled with guilt, telling reporter Liz Hayes that at times he had worried he'd left his 'dear friend' there to die. But he picked up his studies, and in 2015 he was the only one of the hostages to return to work at the café.

Selina Win Pe told the inquest she was dogged by anxiety and extreme vigilance. 'I have not returned to my previous capacity, nor will I . . . I have had to re-learn at the ages of forty-three and forty-four to re-normalise and re-program, to know that I am no longer in that café. My entire life has changed dramatically.'

Marcia Mikhael moved overseas with her husband and children. She wanted to be somewhere where there would be no reminders, somewhere where she would not be recognised on the street. She tried, unsuccessfully, to return to work but suffered a nervous breakdown, and has been unable, so far, to resume her body building and fitness interests. Marcia tells friends she feels 'robbed of my old self; I am not the person I used to be'.

Julie Taylor moved interstate. Her daughter was born safely after the siege, and she returned to practising law.

Jarrod Morton-Hoffman changed tack and embarked on a law degree, an interest sparked by his contact with the many lawyers he crossed paths with during the inquest. He studied at night while working fulltime at an advertising agency during the day.

Jarrod thinks what may have buffered him against more severe psychological after-effects of the siege was that he never felt completely robbed of agency throughout the ordeal. When small opportunities came along during those seventeen hours he made the most of them: volunteering early to work the phones for Monis; planning stratagems like leaving the cards under the fire door for the police; devising lines to placate Monis when the gunman was at his most volatile; handling Monis like a dangerous toddler. He and Fiona worked together to lull their adversary into thinking he could trust them, so they could retain some ability to move around the cafe. For Jarrod, it was part of trying to shape events in order to stay alive.

The siege altered him, nonetheless. 'I was pretty normal: I played video games with friends, used to jig school occasionally, played a bit of sport. I was on a trajectory of normality—and then I got knocked off that. It would be hubris to suggest that I escaped unscathed—I don't think I had PTSD, but I was in shock for a long time afterwards.' Nearly three years after the siege, he finally felt his brain was 'returning to its state of normalcy'.

Still, he doesn't like Christmas anymore; it's too close to the anniversary of Monis' attack. Nor can he tolerate fireworks. They bring back a pit-of-the-stomach memory of the explosions, which they could hear and feel from within the leagues' club as police stormed the café not more than a hundred paces along the street. There was a red-handled knife in his kitchen drawer at home he couldn't bear to touch, although he finally forced himself to pick it up again. It was similar to the one he'd stuffed down his sock late in the siege, half-thinking he might have a chance to use it against Monis.

Like some of the others he periodically rakes over the way it all ended, wondering whether he should have done something different. 'I hate the word haunt, but the thoughts don't leave—though they get easier. It's always when I'm on the bus. It's questions like, What could I have done more? What could I have done differently? It's not that bad now, but it was for a while.

'I don't regret making the choice, but I regret ever having to be in a position of having to make the choice. Would the situation have played out differently if I hadn't run? Is it my fault that Tori and Katrina died? I don't want to believe that is true and I don't think it is, but you can never truly know. You can only make an assumption based upon the evidence you had at the time, and the evidence available to me at that time was this was the only viable option to save as many lives as possible.'

Once Jarrod's session in the witness box was over, counsel assisting Jeremy Gormly asked whether he wished to tell the court any more about how he was travelling. 'I would prefer not to, to be honest,' Jarrod replied—eight words that spoke volumes.

Some relationships grew stronger after the siege, some frayed. The hostages discovered that shared trauma does not always make for lasting bonds. As Louisa says, there was an irony in the fact that despite the long, desperate hours in each other's company, 'we did not know that much more about each other by the end'.

She and Jarrod have forged one of the more durable friendships to come from the ordeal, despite the three decades' difference in age between them.

Inevitably there was some commentary in the wake of Monis' attack about the decision of the older men to escape on the afternoon of the siege. Outspoken New South Wales Upper House member the Reverend Fred Nile put the accusations most bluntly, suggesting they should have stayed to protect the women and accusing them of 'saving their own skin'.

Nile's statements were widely condemned, with a sharp rejoinder from the head of the New South Wales Bar Association Jane Needham SC. 'Women don't need to be rescued; men don't have to be rescuers; victims shouldn't be blamed,' she tweeted.

Yet, in the privacy of their own homes, many Sydneysiders asked themselves what decisions they would have made under the same circumstances: how would they have balanced the visceral drive to get home to young children or fragile dependents against obligations to those who remained trapped inside.

Jeremy Gormly publicly urged that none of the hostages be judged. 'All of us will have wondered how we would have reacted had we been trapped in the siege and faced the events of those seventeen hours,' the barrister said. 'Only armchair hostages have a confident answer to how they would have reacted, and it is no part of the business of this inquest to form moral judgments about such matters or to engage in philosophical hypotheticals.'

In March 2018, Tori Johnson was honoured with the Star of Courage, the nation's highest bravery award, for displaying 'conspicuous courage' and staying with Robin until the bitter end of the siege. Katrina Dawson was honoured with a bravery award for her actions in seeking to have Stefan Balafoutis leave with her and Julie Taylor when Monis seemed to offer the two women an early release. When that was refused, 'Ms Dawson continued to provide genuine support to other hostages throughout the ordeal', the citation said.

Jarrod, too, was honoured with a bravery award, particularly for the many times he helped defuse threats Monis made against fellow hostages. Mulling over the actions of those inside the cafe months after the inquest closed, Jeremy Gormly told me that all the hostages had conducted themselves with courage. But he singled out Jarrod and Fiona as 'remarkable' given their extreme youth.

'Monis had a large, heavy, intimidating physical presence,' he said. 'Jarrod was only nineteen at the time, tallish but very slim with the build of a very young man. [Yet] he showed a resourcefulness, a leadership and a calm presence of mind in the most trying and threatening of circumstances. He considered trapping, stabbing and otherwise disabling Monis and sensibly decided against it—curiously, for reasons quite similar to some of those of the police who decided against a sniper shot—that is, the risk to others if he failed. He and Fiona provided lines of communication among the other hostages. They made themselves useful to others. They dealt with Monis. Others did this too, but Jarrod was particularly effective . . . The other hostages say that as well. I suspect we have many Jarrods and Fionas in our community—young people who think and act with real courage.'

Jarrod's mother, Danielle, insists her son benefited as much from the actions of others, too. 'It amazes me that, even without clear lines of communication, how well the group worked together,' she told me. 'It wouldn't be surprising in a hostage situation for [there to have been] greater self-interest, but there are numerous examples of the way the group supported and worked together. Jarrod may well owe his life to the quick thinking of some of the other hostages, and for this I am eternally grateful.'

Katrina's husband, Paul Smith, held no doubts about who his wife would have put first had she had another chance to leave the café. He made a point at her funeral of correcting early media speculation that she deliberately sacrificed herself to protect her pregnant friend, Julie Taylor. 'I doubt she laid down her life for Julie,' he said. 'Not because she didn't love Julie—everyone was worried about Julie and her unborn child. But from every report I've had, her focus was a hundred per cent on getting home for [her children] Chloe, Oliver and Sasha. And to me that makes her more of a hero.'

For nearly two and a half years after the siege the New South Wales Police barely conceded any errors at all. The overriding tone of the final submission to the inquest lodged by the police legal team in late 2016 was one of self-justification. While extending condolences to the families on their profound loss, the submission fell back on a somewhat grudging 'acknowledgement' that 'some of its systems could have been better, some of its policies and procedures should be reviewed'.

There was a defiant note to its assertion in the closing legal submissions of 2016 that the 'Commissioner of Police [then still Scipione] leads a team of highly trained, professional and dedicated officers who responded to an unprecedented situation . . . in a swift, coordinated, orderly and comprehensive manner'.

The late-night forward commander, Victor, was eventually prodded into some soul searching before the coroner. Asked by

Gabrielle Bashir SC, the barrister acting for the Johnsons, whether he could think of any steps to improve the forward command response if there should ever be a 'next time', his answer was, effectively, that he could not.

'Every day I think of this,' Victor told the inquest. 'You know, three people lost their lives because of me, my decision. I can't change that. Every day I think about this and wrack through my head—you know, what could I have done differently? What should I have done? But I can never mitigate the risk of a bomb. I could never take that off the table. And I always get back to that, Your Honour . . . when I reflect on this every day, I don't know what I could have changed . . . The right people were with me on the night, the right people were providing me information. Yes, we've identified that there's some information gaps and things that need to be improved on the micro scale . . . What could I change differently? I don't—I turn to the wisdom of this court, Your Honour.'

Some senior police I spoke to after the siege told me they thought the coroner's report was fair. Equally, many were unhappy that the force's entrails had been forensically examined, in such microscopic detail, with the luxury of two years to probe every police decision.

This was reflected in a blistering broadside issued by the powerful Police Association of NSW, the police union, just two days before the coroner's report was due to be handed down in May 2017. The association's acting head, Tony King, said the stress of the inquiry had had a 'devastating effect' on a number of police, and that some had left their jobs because of the 'worry of it all'. In a lengthy article emailed to association members, King said the men of the Tactical Operations Unit had been steeling themselves never to see their families again before they assaulted the café: fourteen of them had 'called their loved ones and said their goodbyes', he wrote.

'For those who stormed the cafe—and the hundreds of officers who supported them that day—there would be no peace once the guns went silent. Instead they have been subjected to a two-year ordeal by a coronial inquest driven by lawyers who were hell-bent on turning the inquiry into a public witch-hunt,' King charged.

King also lambasted the bungling by the Office of the Director of Public Prosecutions (ODPP) on Monis' bail applications. Why, he asked, had the ODPP not been subjected to the same inquisition as the police? 'It's a simple fact [that] if he [Monis] were in jail, there would have been no Lindt,' King thundered.

The families were outraged by the union attack on the inquest. Rosie Connellan, Tori's mother, responded on Facebook with grief and rage to King's description of the inquiry as a witch hunt. 'This gentle soul [Tori] HAD to die before police would enter the Lindt Café to rescue anyone,' she posted. 'It's a national disgrace. To say this is a witch hunt against the police means they have learnt nothing from this tragedy. The tears keep rolling.'

Yet it was true, as King suggested, that some police officers had also paid a high personal price for their presence that night.

In 2015 Detective Superintendent Luke Moore, who had been part of the Strike Force Eagle investigation team during the siege, leapt thirteen storeys while staying in a hotel with his wife and children on a family holiday on Hamilton Island. His life was saved by a laundry skip at the end of his fall. Moore was subsequently diagnosed with PTSD and two years later he went public to encourage other traumatised officers to seek help. He acknowledged that his condition was the product of years of accumulated trauma in the job. But he said the Lindt siege had been a personal tipping point, given all the 'commentary about what should and shouldn't have happened'.

Moore told the *Daily Telegraph* that as he was writing his statement for the inquest he kept asking himself, '"Was there something that I should have done that could have prevented people being killed?" In my rational mind I knew that, No, there was nothing extra, but my brain got so scrambled. And after that, things started to go downhill.'

Officer B, who had fired five of the twenty-two high-powered bullets that ended the siege, told the coroner he didn't want to sound 'callous', but that 'this is as much a traumatic event for me, sir, as it was for everyone else involved. Reliving this event, which I have done for the last eighteen months, has had an impact on me.'

In April 2017, Andrew Scipione retired as Commissioner of Police, following Mike Baird, who had stepped down as premier four months earlier to return to banking. The new premier, Gladys Berejiklian, was left with the job of appointing Scipione's successor. In cabinet circles there was talk of needing a new broom, perhaps a candidate from interstate or from a federal agency, to mark a clean break from the feuding that had dogged the top echelon of the force.

Cath Burn applied for Scipione's job, as did several other senior officers. Nick Kaldas, who had resigned from the New South Wales Police in March 2016 and taken a prestigious policing job with the United Nations, threw his hat in the ring from overseas.

Two months after the Lindt Café siege, the bad blood between Kaldas and Burn had burst into the open. Before a state parliamentary inquiry, Kaldas accused Burn of being responsible for dropping his name into the Operation Mascot investigation. She in turn vehemently denied any suggestion of ill-will. Ultimately, Kaldas received a formal apology from the New South Wales Crime Commission for the bugging scandal.

Neither Burn nor Kaldas succeeded Scipione. Instead a man relatively unknown to the public, Assistant Commissioner Mick Fuller, was picked and leapfrogged into the position over the existing deputies.

Within days of the inquest report being handed down on 24 May 2017, Fuller had markedly changed the police tune on the siege and spoke the words the families had been waiting nearly two and a half years to hear. Yes, he acknowledged, the police should have gone in earlier— certainly before the shot that lead to Tori's death.

But he went further, suggesting police should have gone in on the basis of a deliberate action plan and arguably before the first shot had even been fired by Monis. 'The challenge for me as the commissioner is not about should we have gone in after the first shot [at 2.03 a.m.], but we should have gone in as a deliberate action *before* the first shot, which is a much preferred strategy for any tactical officer,' Fuller told ABC TV's *7.30 Report*.

It was a long way from the previous assertion by Assistant Commissioner Jenkins—the man who'd been in charge of the Police Operations Centre that night—that a deliberate action was not to be embarked upon because it was a 'last resort'. It was also some distance from Fuller's original position at the inquest, [articulated in April 2016] that a decision to send the police assault teams in at 2.03 a.m. would not have 'stood the scrutiny'.

Fuller told me later that he had been 'flying blind' at the time he gave evidence, being the first major police witness before the inquest. 'I never really knew the entire picture from a full evidentiary perspective until after the inquest. By the end of it, reading the coroner's report and piecing it all together, I certainly had a different view.'

Fuller acknowledged the Johnson and Dawson families were entitled to feel 'let down' and implied that it had not been a good look for his predecessor Andrew Scipione to have gone home before midnight on the evening of the siege. 'Where the commissioner sleeps will never have an outcome on the performance of an operation,' Fuller told *Four Corners*. 'But it's clear the community's expectation . . . if you are the leader, [is that] you are there for the long haul.'

He later expanded on this theme. He told me that soon after becoming Commissioner of Police, he'd gone to Premier Gladys Berejiklian and sought what the media dubbed a new 'shoot to kill' law, in line with the coroner's recommendation that police powers to use lethal force in terrorist situations be clarified, and strengthened. Fuller argued for the triggering of those powers to rest in his own hands.

'Post-Lindt, I don't think a commissioner in the future can *not* play an active role in major events,' he told me.

'The Commissioner of the day and Cath [Burn] did play by the rules, they were not shirking their responsibility at the time, but the public were not happy with those rules. At the end of the day we represent the community, and I think the community would expect the next commissioner to come in and play a strong role in these events.'

Fuller defended his officers by noting that the siege would have tested 'any law enforcement agency across the world'. He said that lessons had been learnt from it worldwide and there had been a deep change in the police mindset since the siege: 'If there was a terrorist attack today similar to Lindt Cafe, then we would respond with the same highly trained police. But [with] a different philosophy, based on the fact that terrorism has changed not just New South Wales police, not just police around Australia, but the way the world responds to terrorism. I give everyone this assurance: we won't wait seventeen hours again.'

He added the important qualifier that earlier intervention to save the hostages might not have resulted in fewer lives being lost—just 'different' lives. Lowering the threshold for intervention was not going to be without risks. 'I need to start a conversation with the community that early intervention with terrorist sieges is a world standard now, following the Lindt Café,' Fuller said.

He dropped a strong hint that Brian, the consultant psychiatrist who had been advising police on the night of the siege, would not be working with the force again.

Tori Johnson's family welcomed the admission of errors. It took 'great strength' to do that, Rosie said. Tori's partner, Thomas Zinn, said the inquest had consisted of 'one shocking discovery following the next', but that the family had high regard for the police tactical officers who had 'put their lives at risk after waiting so long for orders to act—we acknowledge the grief and trauma that they have experienced'.

Stuart Ayres, the man who was police minister at the time of the siege, told me: 'I was immensely proud of the efforts of the New South Wales police force over that forty-eight hours. They did all of the things that they thought were the right things to do to save citizens' lives.' But he added: 'No doubt they have learned a lot from the experience. That will mean they're in a much better place for dealing with an incident should it happen again in the future.'

Mike Baird said he understood the desire to 'look for someone or something to blame. I think it's very easy to say, over a long period, looking at every decision in the chess game, you should have moved the pawn there, you should have moved the bishop here, but to me Mick [Fuller] did exactly the right thing, acknowledged the things that were not right. [But] every man and woman involved in that was doing the best they possibly could.'

The Dawson family were unswayed. Katrina's brother Sandy told *Four Corners*: 'The entire management of the siege was a disaster. It cannot happen again that way, ever.'

Buried in the fine print of the New South Wales Police's 400-page final submission to the inquest were admissions of a swathe of changes underway as a result of the siege. These included an overhaul of negotiations capability, a sweeping review of counter-terrorism response arrangements 'benchmarked against international best practice' and a range of equipment upgrades.

The police assault teams would be getting new laser sighting devices, a new radio network, new communications headsets, replacements for their M4 carbines and upgraded ballistics helmets and hearing protection.

A new, more technologically advanced 'rapid deployment kit' was being developed that could be rapidly unpacked to deliver more sophisticated support to forward commanders in future. Snipers were to get better gear for breaching glass, and the police technical unit was being re-equipped with new surveillance devices and other upgraded capabilities for 'high risk deployments'.

Anticipating one of the coroner's key recommendations, a fixated persons unit was set up to try to prevent self-radicalisers like Monis drifting off the radar in future.

Every one of the inquest's forty-five recommendations were accepted by the federal and New South Wales governments.

As one of the oldest and largest police forces in the world, the New South Wales Police has a long and largely proud track record behind it. However, the Lindt Café siege exposed a comprehensive failure of suppleness, doctrine, training and judgement in the face of the twenty-first century threat of jihadi-inspired terrorism.

Over coffee one morning a senior New South Wales police officer said, 'I'll tell you one thing: we will never see another Lindt siege again.' What he meant by that was the police could nail down every lesson from the night, yet the next attack would never be an exact replica, and they could still be caught out 'fighting the last war'.

But if there was one clear lesson to be learnt it was the absolute necessity for federal and state governments to mesh more seamlessly against any future attacks. The Dawsons were right to assert that on the night of the siege the New South Wales Police applied 'too high a bar' in assessing whether they could have used help from Commonwealth agencies.

The inquest never got to the nub of exactly what capabilities the Australian Defence Force might have been able to offer had the police been more willing to reach out for help. Jeremy Gormly declared the Defence issue was 'thorny'. It was 'the most difficult of areas to investigate and examine' in part because of the military's resistance to exposing its counter-terrorism methodologies.

Coroner Michael Barnes, noting his inability to fully assess what assistance the military could have offered short of a complete formal call-out, had asked Defence to make available a senior officer to address the inquiry on this point. But the request had been denied. The formal New South Wales police submission to the inquest seemed to illustrate a boundary-marking mentality as entrenched as ever. 'It is fundamental to the division of responsibilities between the commonwealth and the states/territories that when a crisis is being managed by a state/territory the commonwealth, the ADF [Australian Defence Force] should not *intrude* by way of direct or formal substantive involvement,' it said.

For its part, the Commonwealth told the inquest it took the view 'at all times' that managing the siege was 'well within the capacity' of the New South Wales Police. But this mutual standoffishness was to change too. In July 2017 Malcolm Turnbull, Tony Abbott's successor as prime minister, announced that Canberra would pursue ways to 'enhance' Defence support to counter-terrorism arrangements, even as state police remained primary responders. The army's Special Forces would step up training for state tactical police; the federal government would 'make it easier' for states and territories to seek help; and new legislation would 'clearly enable the ADF to protect life during emergencies', the Defence Department said.

Justice Minister Michael Keenan said, 'The key thing we need is the most flexible possible arrangements—the threat's changed very significantly.' Mick Fuller told me that 'one of the challenges at the time was that you couldn't just request a part of TAG-East. If we said "we are missing this or that technical piece, send this unit to support us", it doesn't work that way. They don't come and work under our command and control, they come under their own command and control. That's one of the complexities. We are still working on how do we better work together.'

But he'd made it a priority to meet with the head of the Commando unit soon after taking over the top police job. The Army has since further opened up its bases for the police tactical units and public order squad to train on. 'I'd like to think we have taken the next step; if there was a perception that New South Wales Police and the ADF didn't have a good tactical relationship, I'm doing my best to dispel that.'

In private, some army officers acknowledged that there had not been effective liaison in closing the capability gaps facing the New South Wales Police on the day and night of the siege. One very senior former officer told me: 'They had Defence liaison people there; they could have asked for anything. All they had to do was ask. So it was a really unfortunate incident. But the positive side is, through this hard lesson, when it happens again I hope it will be handled very differently.'

Even for some of those not directly involved, the siege woke dark demons. The Bar Association brought in counsellors to help lawyers and members of their offices who had been traumatised by the event. One barrister told me how oppressive he found it walking through the sea of flowers every day to work through the holiday period. He believes it helped trigger for the deep depression that followed some weeks later.

Empathy for the suffering of the bereaved families played out in sometimes surprising ways. Dean Smith, the Western Australian Liberal senator whose private members' bill finally delivered same-sex marriage to the nation in late 2017, says he was moved to act in part by the story of Tori and Thomas. Smith had once opposed same-sex marriage. Asked by a reporter what the catalyst had been for his change of heart, he replied: 'I was particularly moved by the story of Tori Johnson in the Lindt Café. I came to the conclusion that had Tori and his partner been wanting to get married, or waiting to get married in the same way [as] so many gay and lesbian Australians and then his life was taken in such a tragic way . . . that moved me and it just reinforced my resolve.'

On the first anniversary of his son's death, Ken Johnson wrote: 'The grieving and coming to terms with losing my son have been extraordinarily painful. The memory of being around the corner in Martin Place as the siege unfolded, unable to help my son as he was held hostage, will stay with me forever.' Ken has since travelled the world erecting small stone cairns in Tori's memory.

On 16 December 2017, the third anniversary of the siege, the families of Katrina Dawson and Tori Johnson came together with most of the surviving hostages for the opening of a memorial to Tori and Katrina in Martin Place. Embedded in the granite, more than two hundred hand-carved flowers encased in mirrored cubes in a work entitled *Reflection* referenced the nearly 100,000 bouquets Sydneysiders laid at the site in the days after the attack.

Prime Minister Malcolm Turnbull and other VIPs were among the guests at the simple ceremony. Premier Gladys Berejiklian paid tribute to the two young Australians, saying their 'bravery and selflessness' would always be remembered and honoured. The memorial, she added, was testimony to the way the city's inhabitants 'supported one another in one of our darkest times'.

The Dawsons grieve still. Katrina had not yet reached her prime: she had three children she adored, a happy marriage and a career that was flourishing and set to soar even further. It is easy to eulogise someone whose life is cut short, her mother Jane acknowledges. Such a person is always 'wonderful', or a 'great human being'. But Katrina, she says, 'really was; we loved her to bits, we all miss her in every fibre of our being and, as time goes on, the hole Katrina's death has made in our lives gets larger.'

Rosie says she still swings between 'anger and complete devastation at how I'm going to cope with losing my beautiful boy'. Late at night, she becomes troubled by imagining her son's last thoughts. 'I'm sure any parent who lost a child in such a violent way would feel the same,' she told me. 'We thought we lived in a country where the safety of human life, especially of innocent citizens, would be of paramount concern. Our trust has been shattered.'

She has inscribed his name and a dedication on a simple bench near the cliffs along Sydney's Eastern Beaches Coastal Walk, a place the two of them loved to go together. It was where she and Tori used to come as they waited for Thomas to finish work and join them for a drink.

She thinks of the life Tori might have led, the houses he might have designed and built, the love he was lucky enough to find with Thomas for those fourteen years leading up to the siege, and the family life he enriched while he was alive. When she visits that bench, she looks out to the misted horizon, and thinks of her son.

POSTSCRIPT

In November 2016, Justice Peter Johnson of the New South Wales Supreme Court found Amirah Droudis guilty of murdering Helen Lee. He found Monis had 'enthralled' Droudis and indoctrinated her into his 'extreme and perverse' view of the world.

Droudis showed no emotion when two months later he sentenced her to forty-four years in jail, with a non-parole period of thirty-three years. She is appealing her conviction.

Of Monis, the judge said simply: 'No one mourns his passing.'

AFTERWORD
A letter from Louisa Hope

Dear friends,

Arriving here, having read Deborah Snow's gripping and detailed analysis of the Lindt Café siege, I'm sure you are as shocked and bewildered by what you've learnt as I was.

It's not lost on me, having spent those seventeen arduous hours in the café with my fellow hostages, and having sat through the resulting inquest, that I am still finding new information about this day that changed all of our lives.

What is even harder to comprehend, however, are the things we don't know. For example, how did the gunman arrive at Martin Place that morning, how did he get the gun, why was a man of such dubious character even allowed into the country and why, considering his chargesheet, was he even out on bail?

By the time we got to the inquest I had come accept that some things were simply unknowable. Other things, perhaps required a tad more effort and transparency on behalf of the agencies that had charge over them on our behalf. Why he was on bail for example, despite the best efforts of counsel assisting the coroner at the inquest, was never fully revealed.

Nothing we can ever do will bring back the beloved people we have lost due to one man's incomprehensible and violent choices. The officers from the Tactical Operations Unit had patiently waited with us all day and in the hot sun, worked diligently on possible direct-action plans to come and rescue us. Tragically that came to naught, but no one can ever deny their bravery on that day.

Now the inquest has given us recommendations for operational changes and improvements, and we can take heart in the knowledge that the New South Wales Police at least have embraced the recommendations given to them by the coroner. If other agencies proceed with the same good will and pro-active effort, then perhaps this will give us a more positive resolution next time something like this happens.

Not within the inquest's brief, however, was any consideration of the psycho-emotional impact of the siege on our national psyche and social cohesion. In the immediate aftermath, several anxious thoughts pressed on my heart, one being that we would be facing race riots in the street after this awful tragedy. The next morning, the news slowly trickled in from friends and family visiting me in hospital of what was actually happening in Martin Place. Our nation was coming together in common grief, but also in hope. The extension of comfort and friendship from one random stranger to another was happening in real time as the morning after became the day after and then the day after that . . .The encouraging and unifying effect, as Sydney brought flowers in response to this tragedy, eased my mind and gave me great comfort, leaving me to focus on the three months of hospital that lay ahead.

In more recent times, however, the siege has been mentioned in the media and used at political rallies to harden the political rhetoric against people of Muslim faith, and that worries me very much. I have no doubt that the fear, anger and hatred coming from certain quarters within our society is all consuming and somewhat emotionally disabling for them. It is obvious too, that Daesh does not want the Muslim diaspora to be happily and successfully integrated into western countries, living peacefully together.

So how do we learn the lessons and respond differently next time? I have in recent times formed the opinion that it does not matter who the 'terrorists' are; what actually matters is who we are instead?

This global threat only really wins when we allow fear to mould us in its image. Of course, we must prepare and defend. That's the role of our government and institutions like the military, police and ASIO. But in the meantime, how we respond as a nation in this age of terror is a test of our maturity and of how much we hold onto those espoused values of inclusion, freedom, and a fair go for all.

We build resilience, as we face the threat and carry on regardless. We progress our society when we move forward in neighbourly generosity, purposeful inclusion and social equity for all. I personally remain committed to encouraging our whole country to hold on to the very best of our glorious multiculturalism because it is this very thing, so loathed by the enemies of humanity, that makes us strong enough to maintain our way of life.

Together with you in good faith,
Louisa Hope
#HopeMatters

ACKNOWLEDGEMENTS

Thanks to Louisa Hope and Jarrod Morton-Hoffman for their tireless patience and help over many months. Thank you to the families of Tori Johnson and Katrina Dawson, who graciously made time to speak with me, despite the terrible loss inflicted on them and the pain of going back over the events of the siege.

Richard Walsh and Rebecca Kaiser of Allen & Unwin were inspirational and meticulous guides and editors. I am grateful also to Lisa Davies, editor of the *Sydney Morning Herald*, for allowing me the time to complete the book.

Thank you to those who agreed to be interviewed, and to contacts and colleagues who chipped in with helpful advice and leads. Particular thanks to Sarah Ferguson and Jenny Cooke. And to JC, Laurie, Isla and Jack—thank you for unstinting love and support.

INDEX